MW01468795

The Tya Practice

An Upgraded Operating System for Your Life
David Strickel & Qatarina Wanders

Streaming Words Media

Contents

Foreword

I vividly remember the first time I heard about The Stream of David on Walt Thiessen's podcast "LOA Today." At that time, I was deeply into Abraham Hicks. When I heard about this 'new kid on the block' claiming to expand upon their teachings, I scoffed. 'Oh please,' I thought skeptically, 'Who could possibly improve upon Abraham?' So, with the intention of debunking this presumptuous upstart, I listened. To my great surprise, as soon as he began speaking, especially about vibrational flow, everything suddenly made sense. Despite my initial reluctance, his words resonated deeply within me, making me realize the truth in his message. It felt like coming home; my Source connection recognized the truth and vibrational essence of his words.

This experience highlighted a fundamental truth: despite our attempts to focus exclusively on what we want and maintain a constant state of joy, it's simply not possible all the time. We are all subject to the law of vibrational flow, never meant to exist in a state of pure, unadulterated joy 24/7. We are here for the contrast and the expansion it brings.

I began immersing myself in everything related to the Stream of David and the Tya Practice. However, my inner critic, which I hadn't yet learned to distinguish from my true self, often took control, casting a shadow over my deeper knowing and trust. I meticulously analyzed the vast amount of material available—podcasts, YouTube clips, Instagram posts, and especially the 'before and after' stories of those who had taken the Tya Bootcamp program. My mind, deeply conditioned by the matrix of fear and judgment, was extremely skeptical. I even half-jokingly suspected that these glowing testimonials were from people who had been either drugged or paid.

Yet, when I found myself in a state I now recognize as UTS—Up the Spiral—I realized that the lives of these individuals from around the world had been genuinely transformed. I longed for that same clarity. I was constantly trapped in a relentless cycle of doubt, anxiety, and fear, and deeply desired the evident understanding and peace they had gained through their practice.

It still amazes me how my deep-seated doubts and fears momentarily subsided, allowing me to take the plunge and enroll in Tya Bootcamp. I was in shock, yet somewhere deep down, I knew this path was meant for me.

From the onset of the first Bootcamp module, my egoic mind went into overdrive. It sensed a departure from the 'safe' territory of mere survival. Survival, yes, but far from thriving. This part of me tried its hardest to derail the process. I was convinced that I couldn't do it, that the questions being asked were beyond my comprehension, and that I'd be the first ever to be expelled from Bootcamp. However, thanks to some gentle and skillful guidance from the coaches and a fellow Bootcamper, everything clicked into place. My inner critic was silenced, and I was on my way. I began to understand deeply how my hidden transgressors were controlling my life and how I could learn to deeply appreciate all of my experiences, acknowledging that I had created them. This led me out of the disempowering matrix of victimhood into a space of freedom, clarity, and joy.

Honestly, I initially thought David and his colleagues were out of their minds when they spoke of learning to appreciate our DTS (Down the Spiral) moments and spinouts, and to find the hidden treasures within them for our expansion. This skepticism persisted until, amid a meltdown of tears and feelings of victimhood, I became aware of an inner presence that was excited about the growth this experience was bringing. It understood that this was happening FOR me, not TO me. This realization stopped me in my tracks, like a cartoon character halted by an abrupt epiphany, and opened up a whole new perspective.

From then on, I haven't looked back. My life hasn't suddenly morphed into one of Instagram perfection, but it has transformed into one that is perfect in its imperfection. I deeply trust and know that my expansion is guaranteed. Zooming out to Source perspective has become second nature to me. Of course, I am still subject to vibrational flow; we're never 'cured' of that, nor were we meant to be. I viscerally see and understand that my challenges contain the true gold of this game of life. They are what we're here for, in direct opposition to what the matrix teaches us. There is nothing to fear.

One of my recent experiences of trusting deeply in my abundance was when I was offered a very lucrative deal by my old company. Working in tourism post-COVID, not having worked for nearly two years, it seemed a no-brainer from a matrix perspective: a significant sum of money for a job I didn't love, and that tied me to my past habit of people-pleasing. It was safe, guaranteed, and I had nothing else on the horizon. Yet, to their surprise, I gratefully declined the offer. That night, I went to bed with a deep sense of peace, not knowing how I would support myself financially but trusting the universe to handle the details. I knew my preference was for something creative, related to the Camino de Santiago pilgrimage route, my place of highest joy. The very next morning, out of the blue, I received a message offering nearly the same amount of money for a couple of months' work helping on a movie set on and about the Camino. I yelped with joy. Thank you, David. Thank you, Tya. If someone as skeptical and entrenched in the matrix of fear and judgment as I am can find their path to trusting in abundance, so can you. There are no coincidences. You're reading this book for a reason. You can trust that.

~Deborah Wilson 11/2/2023

Today is the day that you begin fully embodying that which you desire to be.

This persona that you have allowed the sum of your experiences to create was your creation by default.

When you change the way you perceive life, the life you are perceiving changes.

Today is the day that you become the master of your reality.

A Note About This Book

The majority of this book contains channeled material—writing from a consciousness beyond my human mind. I refer to this consciousness, this intelligence, as the Stream. I chose this name because it is not human, gendered, nor an "I." I do use the term "they" to refer to it, and when I speak on its behalf, "they" will use "we" and refer to me as David. If you've never encountered channeled material before, this might strike you as unusual. That's perfectly understandable; there was a time when I was uncomfortable with the idea too, even though a version of this has been dropping into my mind throughout my entire life. However, I have come to accept, as many others have, that the wisdom of the Stream is direct, immensely valuable, and demonstrable. Neither I nor the Stream will ask you to believe solely because we say so. Instead, we will provide tools for you to begin implementing their wisdom in your life starting today, allowing you to form your own conclusions.

I request that if this concept seems peculiar to you, set aside its origin and approach the material with an open mind. No rules are imposed on what you must do. There is no desire for me or the Stream to be worshiped, idolized, or obeyed. There is no dogma, no criticism of your current belief system—just tools to help you live your life in greater harmony with the universal laws that govern the creation and expansion of the universe, laws that also govern our lives. Within these pages, you will gain a deep understanding of how these laws work, both for and against you. You will discover why the "against" is actually beneficial, and how these laws serve the entirety of creation. You will learn how to achieve greater balance with them, resulting in a more joyful and abundant life.

You'll notice that I use the term "they" when referring to the Stream, and during channeling, I use "we" to clarify from whom you are receiving the information. The Stream is a collective consciousness—actually, all consciousness—so thinking of them in somewhat human-like terms aids in our understanding of their offerings. Since the information is being channeled through me, it may have a somewhat human-like quality, as they communicate using my intellect and vocabulary to convey ideas that far exceed my human knowledge.

Furthermore, you will encounter certain words used in new ways, and new words may be created. This is because the ideas and concepts presented here often diverge from the mainstream, although many have been used in previous spiritual teachings. We will make an effort to define these terms as they are introduced, and they will be revisited throughout the book, gradually making more sense as you progress through the teachings.

A comprehensive glossary is available at the back of the book, but here are a few definitions that the Stream provides to enhance your understanding as you embark on this journey into their knowledge.

Detune - The process of viewing any topic without fear or judgment, thus removing any negative reaction to the thought.

Down the Spiral (**DTS**) - Refers to your below-neutral state on your vibrational spiral.

Ego - Your human consciousness (as opposed to your eternal, Source consciousness)

Energetic Realm - Anything and everything beyond physical creation

Energy - The same as energetic realm

Law of Attraction - The universal law that states that every vibration is met with an equal vibration and thus returned to the originator; the process of universal creation.

Polarity - The universal force that balances positive and negative; the force that drives energy up and down a vibrational spiral.

Source - Original thought; pure-positive energy. "The Source of all creation."

The Matrix - The collective ego consciousness of all humanity.

The Stream - A stream of consciousness shared (channeled) by David Strickel.

Up the Spiral (**UTS**) - Higher vibration; above neutral on the vibrational spiral.

Vibrational Flow - The fluctuation of energy that drives constant vibrational change.

Vibrational Spiral - A point of reference to describe a state of vibration and typical movement across assigned vibrational setpoints that are also referenced in numeric value. A graphic rendering depicting the placement of vibrational values.

We have incorporated a question-and-answer section at the end of each chapter in which Qatarina, the co-author of this book, will pose questions aimed at providing clarity. The Stream will provide answers to all these questions, addressing common queries that may arise as you progress through the material. We present it in this format with the assumption that you are encountering this knowledge for the first time.

Tya is a proper name, originating from the abbreviation "trust your abundance." After a lifetime dedicated to spiritual exploration and learning to apply universal laws in my life, I've come to realize that placing trust in the universe to bring forth a life filled with joy, clarity, and abundance is the key to manifesting these desires and all that we cherish as human beings. The Stream's wisdom is profound and stems from a place of pure love, and you will absorb a substantial portion of it within these pages. Consider The Tya Practice as the practical embodiment of the Stream's teachings.

If this isn't your initial encounter with the Stream's wisdom, this book will significantly expand upon what you have already learned and enable you to elevate your Tya Practice to a higher level. I have been practicing Tya for well over a decade, and I continually uncover new layers, greater clarity, and higher levels of allowing the universe to delight me in every chapter of my life!

Part 1 ~ Meet David, Qatarina, and the Stream

Introduction from David

Intentions Unfolded

Sitting at my desk in Palm Springs in October 2018, I found myself surrounded by signs of how much my life had changed in just one short year. Outside my window, palm trees framed a distant desert mountain view, a stark contrast to the often overcast Northern California landscape I had left behind just four months prior. In front of me, a substantial microphone stood, and acoustic foam panels adorned my walls, all indications of the home studio I had established for hosting The Stream of David Podcast, as well as for conducting weekly live videos and near-daily coaching sessions with participants in our online programs. Copies of my debut book, "The Stream: Eternal Wisdom for a Better Life," were neatly stacked behind me, awaiting my signature as a token of appreciation for my beta-reading group. I was cocooned in a world of achievements, but I gave little thought to how much change I had manifested in my life in such a short time. At this point, it had become my way of life—a swift adaptation after more than two decades in the corporate world.

While rummaging through my wallet, I stumbled upon a folded piece of notebook paper tucked into one of the hidden pockets. To my surprise, I pulled it out and carefully unfolded it. Covered in my own handwriting, front and back, was a list of intentions. The list read:

- Start a podcast

- Leave my job

- Publish the Stream book

- Launch a business using my channeling gift to help others

- Move to Palm Springs

The note was dated September 2017, and it contained minimal details regarding "how" I would accomplish these goals, just a firm belief that I would.

As I perused the untitled note, I realized that it was a list of intentions I had set for myself when I made the decision to come out of the closet as a channel and begin sharing the Stream's messages beyond my private moments of channeling spoken messages into my iPhone voice recorder. In that moment, I felt a jolt of electricity, that same sensation I encountered when I was "moving up my spiral," ascending to higher-vibrational levels, where all new thoughts and solutions reside, where we are connected to Source, what I call the Stream, and what many refer to as God. We will delve deeply into this connection and the myriad gifts it offers—and how to reach it—within the pages of this book. However, right then, I recognized that I had manifested every single item on my list of intentions in 2018!

It struck me that I hadn't revisited this list once since writing it and tucking it into the depths of my wallet. I hadn't engaged in daily "meditations" on these goals or even set specific deadlines. I had merely set the intention and focused on my vibration—my emotions—as the Stream had guided me to do. My emphasis had been more on how I wanted to feel rather than dictating precisely what I wanted to occur. As always, the Stream's guidance had been astute and effective. I had yet to encounter a situation where the sincere application of their teachings didn't yield results, not just in my life but also in the lives of many they had touched around the world since late 2017.

If you're reading this and aren't familiar with "the Stream," it likely means you haven't read my first book, "The Stream: Eternal Wisdom for a Better Life," and that's perfectly fine! This book stands alone, and reading "The Stream" is not a prerequisite for manifesting significant life changes, should that be your desire. Within these pages, you'll gain profound clarity about why you came to this lifetime, how you can lead a joyful and abundant existence every day, and how to reshape your mindset—your "memory," so to speak—both backward and forward, creating a life experience that aligns with your magnificent and expansive intentions before entering this Earthly realm.

"The Stream" book delves into how I discovered my ability to receive guidance directly from Source. It's a connection I believe we all possess, but I share how I've honed this ability to receive clear and powerful messages. I discuss how I applied this knowledge to overcome numerous obstacles in my life and how I eventually learned to communicate Source's messages with clarity and conciseness for the benefit of others. This sharing is unfiltered by my own ego and devoid of fear and judgment, a theme you will encounter throughout this book.

I won't ask you to blindly believe in my abilities or the source of this wisdom, based solely on my word. A degree of skepticism, short of cynicism, is healthy. Instead, I invite you to approach these teachings with an open mind and apply the practices in your life. See the results for yourself, treating this as your personal experiment to gauge the authenticity of what is being presented here and its value to you.

In "The Stream" (book), I refer to "them" as the Stream because they are not, and have never been, individuals with names. I've come to understand that the human-like entities we identify in the energetic realm, beyond the physical, are our Earthly interpretations of consciousness. There's nothing wrong with this; we all have our unique ways of conceptualizing the intangible. However, I believe the Stream is an eternal, loving, positive, and wise stream of consciousness.

The Stream provides answers to many of life's most challenging questions and offers practical guidance for a life filled with freedom and joy. They don't subscribe to the "fairy dust and unicorns" brand of spirituality. Instead, they offer direct and efficient guidance, infused with love and wisdom.

The Stream (book) is about how the Stream has guided me through great difficulty to a life of freedom and joy—not perfection—but deep, spiritual understanding of how the universe operates and how we can draw those universal laws into our human life experience.

This book serves as an exploration of how the teachings of the Stream have played a transformative role in the lives of thousands, leading them toward lives brimming with joy, clarity, and abundance. Crafting this book has been a labor of love, spanning years, because the Tya Practice is contemporary; it is a product of our era and needed time to evolve, yielding positive results across a diverse spectrum of individuals hailing from various corners of the globe.

As indicated by its title, this book acts as an introduction to the concept of Tya (pronounced TIE-yuh). We have imparted the Tya Practice to an eclectic array of individuals, from homeless individuals to billionaires, spanning five continents (and counting!). Our students have included Academy Award-winning actors, musicians, writers, lawyers, teachers, nurses, successful business people, spiritual thought leaders, and seasoned practitioners with decades of spiritual study. The consistent outcome is that the Tya Practice forever alters the lives of those who embrace and apply it. Its simplicity and efficacy leave an indelible mark, positively impacting lives at a juncture when humanity is earnestly pursuing greater spiritual growth.

The timing of Tya's arrival can be described as nothing less than divine. It was delivered by the Stream in anticipation of the monumental energy shift currently unfolding on Earth and across the entirety of humanity.

Why Trust?

Notice that I have not mentioned the Law of Attraction yet. You've likely heard of the Law of Attraction (LOA), but in case you haven't, LOA states that energy attracts like energy, its vibrational or energetic match, and from there, new creation is formed. Even if that new creation is just an improvement in emotion; thinking a positive thought will lift your mood, and then another positive thought will follow. This is a simplified definition of creation, but consider this: all human creation begins as a thought before becoming a physical reality. The chair you're probably sitting on, the book or device you're holding, the structures around you, electricity, and other everyday technology were all once mere ideas before they took physical form. They were consciousness, they were thought, until someone believed, or trusted, in their potential to be fully realized in physical form.

You might be thinking that most of your thoughts do not materialize. You are correct. That's because your mind does not believe every thought it generates; it does not readily trust. However, your habitual thoughts do become beliefs. These beliefs create an energetic signature, a frequency often referred to in spiritual teachings as vibration. Your vibration is the constant signal you emit, with or without your awareness. You become aware of your vibration through your emotions, the feelings you experience as you move through various vibrational states.

This is why many who experiment with the Law of Attraction may think it doesn't work, at least not for all subjects. This occurs because the new desired belief is not consistently maintained, it is not continuously trusted, and your subconscious mind reverts to its default belief. When your beliefs conflict with your desires, you do not manifest them.

Once you learn the Tya Practice, you will give little thought to the Law of Attraction. You will come to realize (if you haven't already in your learning journey) that the Law of Attraction is akin to gravity; it always operates whether you think about it or not and is continuously shaping every aspect of your life. In this book, we will delve deep into this: how we attract both desired and undesired things, even what appears to be mundane aspects of life, through vibrational flow. You will discover how vibrational flow shapes the entire universe, including every facet of your life, and how to work with it. Mastering vibrational flow is far more valuable and effective than relying solely on the Law of Attraction.

So, the question is, do you trust the Law of Attraction as you trust gravity? Likely not. This is because we've been conditioned to trust the Law of Gravity but to distrust the Law of Attraction. We are often taught that life is difficult, that we must receive the right education and job, work hard, save money, and fear poverty, illness, and loneliness. We are taught to surrender our power to politics, to fear opposing ideas, and new concepts, to fear strangers, and even God. We are consistently exposed to fear in our news, advertising, television, and movies. We are encouraged to conform and not challenge societal norms. We are also instructed to trust only what is scientifically proven and not ponder "silly" ideas unless they receive approval from someone "beyond our comprehension."

I'm not suggesting that you blindly trust everything; I expect you to question. However, there are many gifts to be found in beliefs that extend beyond what is scientifically proven. Even scientists comprehend this. They begin with a theory or hypothesis on a particular subject. They then set out to prove whether their theory is accurate. But it's their belief or trust in the validity of their theory that propels them forward. The beauty of Tya is that you apply it in your life and witness the results firsthand. With continued practice, you experience even greater rewards.

As I mentioned earlier, after decades of trial and error, both following and ignoring the Stream's teachings, I have come to understand that living a joyful, abundant life is all about trust. Like you, I have an ego that has at times distanced me from the Stream's offerings. I am stubborn, and I used to believe that because I was right about many things (thanks to the Stream), I was right about everything. It wasn't until I experienced enough pain in my life that I truly started to listen to what was being offered. That's when I learned to let go and trust—trust the universe to provide everything I wanted and needed. I've realized that trust is the most valuable word in the English language. Establishing this trust was not easy; it requires unlearning much of the world's teachings. However, the rewards are genuinely life-changing. That's why, guided by the eternal wisdom of the Stream, I created Tya, first for myself, and now for you.

Why Is Fear So Prolific?

Commerce thrives on fear in our society. "Get a job for security." "You need health insurance!" "Pay your bills or you'll ruin your credit!" "Save for retirement or you'll be homeless when you're old." "Take this drug or you'll be sick." "Buy this car to be safe." "Get an alarm system to protect your home." "Get life insurance to protect your family." "Elect this politician or your life will be ruined." The list goes on and on.

I recall turning on CNN for some reason during the height of the pandemic lockdown in 2020, only to see a COVID-19 death count ticker running on the screen and thinking, "Who is this information helping? Why is it there?"

At that time, the whole world was focused on some sort of fear, whether it was fear of the illness itself, the vaccine, or even martial law. Only to come to find out that some of these fears were blown out of proportion, and others were completely made up... but why? Because fear motivates certain behaviors. It is a powerful vibration that controls the masses; it is a product of the human-created matrix of beliefs.

So what if we remove fear from the equation? If there were no such thing as fear, what would your life look like? Would you work for someone else or for yourself? Would you stay in an unsatisfying relationship? Would you deny yourself things you want because you were afraid to spend the money? Would you pursue your dream business? Would you write a novel? Or fall in love again? Would you have chocolate cake for dinner? Would you drain your bank account and go on a whirlwind world tour? What would life look like for you if there were no fear? Would you pursue everything you want without the fear of failure or poverty or disappointment?

When I speak of everything you want, I am not just talking about material things. Money and material things are as easy to attract as anything else, but it's important to note that the Tya Practice guides us to lives of joy, clarity, and abundance—not just stuff. I've manifested a lot of money and stuff in my life and been completely miserable. No, the stuff did not make me miserable—in fact, it often made me happy—but it was, at one time, the only thing making me happy. A generous flow of money and things will enhance a joyous existence, but it will never replace a clear, personal connection to your own Stream—to Source—to God—your higher self, or inner being—however you identify the consciousness beyond the physical, and yes, you have one! If you are unsure of this connection and what it is, you will discover that in this practice, and you will find that it will be your own unique experience and connection. If you have identified this connection, you will find that the Tya Practice will enhance it.

The Tya Practice has no rules or judgment or worship. It does not ask you to limit your indulgences or avoid anything. It will ask that you believe in a universal creative intelligence and allow space for you to identify that however you wish. The other thing the Tya Practice asks of you is to believe in your worthiness of it—your connection to this universal creative power, for you will be using that connection daily in this practice. If you are nowhere near those two beliefs, it's okay. The Tya Practice and the words in this book will guide you on your own unique path to it—and you will love it!

Why The Tya Practice Works

I didn't manifest all those things in 2018 because I forced them into existence through meditation and intense focus, as many law-of-attraction books suggest. While I acknowledge the value in those teachings and their potential effectiveness, I've discovered another path that worked better for me and has proven effective for many others. So, whether you're new to intentional manifestations or have tried popular LOA teachings with mixed results, this message is for you. If you're on a spiritual journey and seeking to elevate it with a practice that becomes your new way of living and operating in life, then this message is also relevant.

This practice is both spiritual and aligned with the law of attraction because they complement each other. Our reality is shaped by universal laws, and universal law is the foundation of our world. I manifested my desires not by forcefully working on them but by maintaining a positive emotional state—keeping my emotions positive and thus maintaining a high vibration, which is reflected in my energy.

I manifested them because I trusted.

Meditation and focus are valuable, but this practice includes additional elements that allow you to relax into trust and let significant events unfold in your life. These are the things you desire so much that sometimes you inadvertently push them away by dwelling in a state of "need." The universe responds affirmatively to this need because it says "yes" to all vibrations without judgment.

Take a moment to observe your friends, family, and coworkers; they continuously experience a mix of manifestations in their lives—some good, some bad. Those who focus more on what they don't want tend to attract more of it, while confident individuals often receive more of what they desire. Now, consider your own life and the mix you're experiencing. It's likely a blend of desires achieved and those that seem elusive, especially if you believe you must possess them to find joy.

The Tya Practice equips you with the tools to enter a state of unwavering knowing—a confidence that things will work out, similar to how successful people approach life. This newfound assurance extends to everything, even the most extravagant or extraordinary desires. You'll learn to cultivate a vibration—an attitude—that emits an energetic signal attracting your desires. It's akin to how positive interactions occur with people when you're in a good mood and negative interactions when you're not. Universal law applies uniformly to all subjects; it's your belief system that may not align with your desires, but the good news is that you can change it.

Maintaining a positive mindset and vibration enables us to believe in ourselves and our goals. In a positive frame of mind, we believe we can start a business, run a marathon, overcome an illness, meet the right person, and much more. However, when our emotional state or vibration drops, doubt creeps in. What once seemed possible when we were up the vibrational spiral (UTS) now feels impossible, even absurd, when we're down the vibrational spiral (DTS). This is the power of vibration, and it keeps us cycling through unwanted circumstances and pushing away our dreams, leaving us in a state of perpetual "wanting." The Tya Practice teaches us to master this ebb and flow of vibrational energy and harness its incredible creative power.

For example, you've probably had grand dreams, felt them deeply, believed in them, and vividly visualized their realization. Then, the next day, your energy drops, and those positive feelings vanish when you recall your ambitions. You might wonder, "What was I thinking? I can't do that! No one will buy that! People like me don't do things like that!" You may even feel foolish for allowing yourself to dream.

Have you experienced this rollercoaster of emotions? What changed? Why do we feel highly positive one day and entirely the opposite the next?

It's because of polarity. Polarity means having two opposing or contradictory tendencies, opinions, or aspects. Our physical environment exhibits polarization everywhere. Almost every topic has two opposing sides, with a lot of fluctuation between the extremes. However, you don't simultaneously hold contradictory beliefs. The more you move toward a lower emotional state (DTS) and allow fear and judgment to dominate, the more likely you are to align with a more extreme viewpoint. You seek confirmation for your beliefs to find comfort. But when your emotions are high, positive, and trusting, you feel less need, if any, to take sides or hold rigid opinions. You become more open to multiple possibilities.

Moving up and down your vibrational spiral gives rise to what we term as vibrational flow. Vibrational flow serves us significantly, and once you understand how to harness it to your advantage, your perception of lower vibrations will undergo a transformation. Essentially, polarity can pull us down the spiral (DTS) into what we typically label as negative emotions, like doubt, worry, anger, frustration, and envy. These emotions generate a negative vibration. Notice how these emotions tend to cluster and gain momentum if we stay focused on lower vibrations. That's because they form a specific vibration—an energetic frequency we tune into—whether intentionally or not. Can you recall a time when you genuinely felt both joy and anger simultaneously? Probably not. You may transition between the two, but specific triggers or factors prompt these shifts. A negative vibe attracts unwanted outcomes, just as our positive vibe draws in the things we desire. This is the universe's design.

While your focus can attract similar thoughts and enable creation when coupled with trust, you can't manage your thoughts around the clock. Your mind often operates on autopilot, and your subconscious mind certainly does, heavily influenced by your past experiences. You've essentially crafted a human operating system based on your responses to everything that has unfolded in your life up to this point. This system constitutes your belief system, and it's influenced by your vibration, which, in turn, is influenced by polarity. This is why our emotions, and consequently our vibrations, continually fluctuate. Polarity helps regulate your vibrational flow, even when you're not actively controlling it through your focus.

Polarity serves the purpose of expanding our emotional range by allowing us to dip into lower vibrations, including fear, envy, and anger. These lower vibrations create obstacles through a lower-vibrational point of attraction. This is how we attract undesired circumstances. Overcoming these obstacles, in other words, addressing unwanted situations, fuels our expansion because our eventual return to a higher vibration through vibrational flow—often referred to as positive-creation territory—enables us to resolve the challenges we initially created during our lower-vibrational phase. The next time you find yourself frustrated because something isn't working, such as a task you're trying to complete, take a step back. Close your eyes, take deep breaths, and focus on something you appreciate to disrupt the negative vibration stemming from your frustration. Then, return to the task and observe how the solution seems to pop into your mind—a simple yet effective resolution that may have eluded you in your frustrated state. In this exercise, you've experienced a disconnection from Source—the source of all new thoughts and solutions (your intuition)—during your DTS frustration. Then, by elevating your vibration, shifting UTS, you allowed your innate Source connection to be reestablished, thus facilitating the resolution to your dilemma. This approach applies to all aspects of life, and this practice will guide you in applying it comprehensively.

Regarding your vibrational spiral, envision "neutral" as the baseline for your vibration, as experienced through your emotions. Your emotions serve as an indicator of your current vibration. In this context, "neutral" signifies a state of minimal or no thought, akin to what we seek during meditation—a clear mind where negative resistance dissipates, and our inherent Source connection can manifest. Below neutral, we exist devoid of Source connection, immersed in our negative creation territory. Below neutral, no new thoughts are generated; only recycled doubts, fears, envies, angers, etc., persist. Above neutral, we reconnect with Source—the wellspring of all creation and new ideas, our intuition, our optimism, and life force. This is where we engage in creation.

VIBRATIONAL SPIRAL GRAPHIC

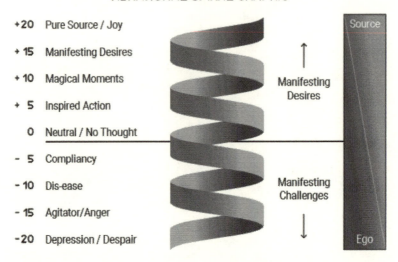

+20	Pure Source / Joy
+ 15	Manifesting Desires
+ 10	Magical Moments
+ 5	Inspired Action
0	Neutral / No Thought
- 5	Compliancy
- 10	Dis-ease
- 15	Agitator/Anger
-20	Depression / Despair

This graphic represents your vibrational spiral. This will be referenced and explained in greater depth throughout the book.

You expand as human consciousness when you use your obstacles to devise solutions. Solutions represent new creation, and new creation propels your personal growth. This, in turn, contributes to the expansion of humanity, Planet Earth, and the entire universe. Each new creation sends ripples outward into infinity, and we are in a constant state of creation. Creation signifies expansion.

According to the Stream, and ultimately validated through this practice, all creation arises from attraction, governed by polarity. Polarity inevitably guides your vibration up and down your vibrational spiral, shifting between positive and negative. This continuous cycle of vibration constitutes what we refer to as vibrational flow, and vibrational flow is the driving force behind the formation—and ongoing creation—of the entire universe. This might initially seem complex, but as you delve into this practice, you'll start noticing evidence of these principles in action. It will become an engaging journey as you progress through these teachings.

How This Relates To Your Life

To recap, our reality is shaped by our vibration through the process of attraction, and this vibration is continually changing due to polarity, a combination of environmental energy flow and our thoughts, both conscious and subconscious. Vibrational flow is also a concept explored in astrology, as it illustrates the fluctuation of energy that drives creation and expansion. Astrology is popular because it can predict typical high and low periods in our lives based on vibrational flow. However, the Tya Practice offers a set of tools where you don't need to predict vibrational flow because you can learn to manage it and harness its power effectively.

Now, you might be wondering, with all these forces at play and our constantly busy minds, how can we intentionally manifest our desires? How do we attract more of what we want and less of what we don't want? How do we maintain a state of joy? How do we access the clarity of Source to understand our purpose? Why do positive and negative forces coexist, and how do we overcome a lifetime of fear-based conditioning?

The answer lies in raising our Default Vibration.

It's intriguing that some scientists dismiss the Law of Attraction as a pseudoscience, while others consider it scientifically proven. In my perspective, the Law of Attraction is relatively easy to demonstrate. We've all had those days when everything seems to go wrong, and it feels like the universe is conspiring against us. For instance, you wake up late, encounter numerous hiccups in your morning routine, and even experience annoyances like spilling coffee on yourself in the Starbucks drive-thru. The day spirals into a series of unfortunate events. In this example, the day started with a down-the-spiral (DTS) emotional state, and this state, if left unchecked, attracts more negative manifestations, which can escalate into more significant problems.

I've never had a negative day when I was in a great mood, but I've had negative days when I allowed myself to remain in an unattended or neutral mood, not actively in joy but not overtly negative either. Many of us go through life on autopilot, giving little thought to our mood or vibration. We might even believe that we have no control over our emotional state and that external factors are necessary to uplift us. This is why we often seek external sources like material possessions, experiences, or vacations to find joy. But what if we could learn to experience joy regardless of external conditions? What if we could develop the ability to manage our vibration and allow more joy into our lives? What if we could elevate our point of attraction so that we predominantly reside up the spiral, leading a more joyful life and attracting more of what we desire while repelling what we don't want?

The answer is that we can achieve this, and in this book, Qatarina and I (with significant guidance from the Stream) will explain how to do just that.

Harnessing the Power Within: How The Stream Transformed My Life and Inspires Others

"My" Stream has provided me with remarkable clarity for as long as I can remember. At one point, at the age of fourteen, I even believed that the Law of Attraction was my own creation! In essence, the Stream has guided me through substantial challenges, including my father's departure from my daily life when I was six and my mother's emotional detachment over the years, leading to our estrangement during the last two decades of her life after I revealed that I was gay.

I faced the additional challenge of dyslexia and only completed up to the tenth grade. However, with the Stream's guidance, I ultimately earned my GED and founded my own real estate development company at the age of nineteen. While my life hasn't been without problems or imperfections, my understanding of universal law, guided by the Stream, has consistently led to a life filled with joy, clarity, and abundance. I've learned to embrace my imperfections and view vibrational "spinouts" as opportunities for my next expansive creation.

This innate "knowing" gradually evolved into what I now refer to as the Stream. I now comprehend that the Stream is Source consciousness, the origin of all creation. For many years, I had access to boundless universal knowledge, yet I squandered much of it in the pursuit of wealth. I achieved financial success only to realize that there was so much more to discover through the Stream's teachings.

By the time I reached forty, I lived in luxury, with a beautiful home, expensive cars, designer clothing, and exciting travel destinations. Despite these material comforts, I was trapped in a stagnant relationship, disliked my job, suffered from chronic back pain (and relied on a combination of Oxycontin and alcohol to manage it), and was nearly a hundred pounds overweight. I came to the profound realization that I needed more than material wealth to find happiness; I needed to cultivate genuine happiness within myself.

Throughout my life, I had consulted various psychics in an attempt to understand my unique "knowing." I knew I was different but concealed it to fit into societal and corporate life. One remarkable psychic named Hazel Burley in Cassadaga, Florida, revealed during a reading that I was a channel and that much of my "knowing" was connected to Source, making me a "channel of Source." She showed me a plastic binder containing cassette tapes, the original 1988 recordings of Abraham-Hicks' teachings. Initially skeptical, I chose to disregard this valuable advice for several years.

A few years later, the book *The Secret* was published. I stumbled upon it while watching "The Oprah Winfrey Show" on a rare weekday when Rhonda Byrne and other contributors to *The Secret* were guests. The concept of the Law of Attraction strongly resonated with me, as it echoed what I had previously believed and understood, even though I didn't know it had a name. This discovery led me back to Abraham-Hicks, and I credit Esther Hicks for making channeling more accessible to me. Her graceful sharing of Abraham encouraged me to shed my judgment surrounding channeling and spirituality in general, although I don't consider myself overtly "spiritual."

While I respect various spiritual beliefs, I find many mainstream spiritual teachings to be overly idealistic.

After discovering *The Secret* and delving into Abraham-Hicks' teachings, I spent the next decade fully immersing myself in the Stream, allowing their guidance to permeate every aspect of my life. This transformation was remarkable, and with the Stream's assistance, I developed a practice that drastically improved every facet of my existence. I later realized that the incredible results I had experienced were not solely for my benefit but for the world—those who were ready to receive the Stream's message, which is direct, profound, and unfiltered. While the Stream embodies pure positive energy and love for all creation, their teachings don't conform to the typical "rainbows and fluff" spiritual brand. They delve deep and challenge many mainstream spiritual beliefs, such as promoting veganism as dogma, advocating for the use of "external" tools like crystals, and offering specific guidance on meditation or yoga. The Stream emphasizes that they don't judge anything, acknowledging that these are human creations, not divine guidance. They stress that the true power resides within us, naturally.

The Stream doesn't teach about external "dark" entities but instead suggests that all negativity originates from the individual, particularly the ego. They assert that all undesired experiences and suffering are products of our own vibrational creation. They approach every subject with complete impartiality. They are not concerned with political correctness and are unapologetic in holding humanity accountable for its self-imposed limitations. They aim to empower us to take full responsibility for unlocking our own potential.

The Stream teaches that manifesting our desires and transforming "negative" people, circumstances, and events into positive, expansive experiences all hinges on trust. So, how can you build this trust? How can you release a lifetime of limiting beliefs and let go of the need to "make things happen"? This book delves into the practice of Tya and how it can help you develop trust, leading to a life filled with joy, clarity, and abundance.

· · • • • • • • · ·

In early 2018, I had just left my job as an executive with a national company, where I had been employed for twenty years. At that time, I possessed an unpublished manuscript and hosted a weekly podcast. I had no concrete plans for the future except for my intention to share the Stream's message with the world.

As I began channeling to the point where I could ask questions and receive clear answers from the Stream, one of my initial queries was, "Why does the world need another person who channels?" The response was that the Stream, along with me, would resonate with a distinct audience, offering unique wisdom and guidance that hadn't been shared before, at least not in the way I would eventually convey it. Initially, I believed this meant I would share the same "laws" as those who had come before me, as there are only a handful of universal laws, and no new ones are being created since universal laws are eternal. However, my understanding of higher consciousness and its evolution, which aligns with our own development as humanity and individuals, evolved because of the events of 2018.

On March 3, 2018, I posted an Instagram message, "We are looking for a spiritually focused book editor." This happened to coincide with my very first live workshop in Mill Valley, California. It was the first time I had ever channeled the Stream in front of a live audience, and only five people attended (for free). Nevertheless, it turned out to be a perfect experience. I met a wonderful group of people, and the Stream effortlessly provided answers to their questions for hours.

Amidst all of this, I received an email from a woman named Qatarina Wanders, who expressed excitement about the idea of collaborating with the Stream. Her enthusiasm was a breath of fresh air compared to the often jaded individuals I encountered in the literary world. She exuded positivity, articulate communication, and extensive knowledge of the publishing domain. Given the challenges of getting published as an unknown author, particularly one focused on channeled text, I decided to place my trust in abundance and follow the path of least resistance by focusing on having my book professionally edited. Qatarina and I immediately connected, with our first phone call lasting well over two hours. We delved into a wide range of topics, both spiritual and literary. It became clear to me that she was the ideal editor for *The Stream*, and I hired her without even considering other referrals I had received.

Our collaboration was enjoyable, and since I wasn't employed at the time, I had ample hours to dedicate to rewrites and review every note and edit. During our conversations, Qatarina mentioned a business mentor she had been working with, describing her as an "ex-Wall-Streeter-turned-spiritual-business-coach." As someone who had never hired a coach and was self-taught in most aspects of life, the concept of seeking guidance was foreign to me. Qatarina introduced us, and the business coach proposed the idea of offering online courses as a means to share the Stream's message on a deeper level and generate income for my emerging (non-existent) business right away. Initially, I had reservations about the idea, envisioning a scenario akin to someone in front of a luxury car promising quick riches through their "online program."

However, the Stream provided crystal-clear guidance, as they always did: "This is your path lighting up. This is how you will bring about the change that you know you can deliver with our message. This is the time for you to allow yourself to be led. Now dive in and drink the Kool-Aid." Those were their exact words.

I had set an intention to bring genuine transformation to people's lives, particularly those who were ready for significant changes and willing to work on their vibrational shift. This opportunity allowed me to create a course based on the practices I had developed over a decade, guided by the Stream's wisdom, centered around the universal process of creation.

Thanks to the popularity of "The Stream of David Podcast," people from around the world, spanning various age groups and backgrounds, enrolled in the course. As I taught about "abundance," it became increasingly evident that abundance was synonymous with authentic joy. Systematically raising one's vibration involved releasing "transgressors" that dragged students' vibrations down. I witnessed remarkable transformations, as participants released childhood trauma, healed severe physical ailments, exited dysfunctional and even abusive relationships, and more. People learned to love themselves and trust their innate state of abundance that they had been obstructing, often for a lifetime.

"Abundance Breakthroughs" quickly evolved into the Tya Practice, as if it had always existed. It seemed as though we had merely needed to discover it. My course then became Tya Bootcamp, which is now part of the Tya Academy.

I now understand that Tya Bootcamp served as an incubator and testing ground for the practice. In just four short years, we fully developed a powerful mindset practice with the potential to transform lives, even the entire human race. However, the collective choice ultimately determines its impact, and my ego no longer "needs" others to follow this path. I am passionately committed to sharing what the Stream offers humanity, whether with an audience of one, one million, or one billion. We continue to offer Tya Bootcamp and have expanded our offerings into a virtual Tya Academy. I will provide more details about this later in the book. For now, this book encompasses the entire practice, and my intention is for you to learn and begin applying it as you progress through the book.

Introduction from Qatarina

Questioning Faith and Desire – My Journey to Discovery

Growing up in an intensely conservative religious environment while grappling with my attraction to my own gender instilled in me an innate inclination to question the very fabric of existence.

Picture this: my upbringing in a rigidly religious setting was no joke. I couldn't even indulge in the sweet sounds of non-Christian (or "secular") music. My school days were filled with mandatory Bible classes and Chapel sessions, where the girls had to don skirts as if it were a sacred requirement. Weekends? Those were reserved for hitting the streets, distributing Coca-Cola cans adorned with Bible verses in the name of servant evangelism. Many nights, I found myself under my covers, pouring my heart out to God, pleading for deliverance from my "spiritual affliction"—my attraction to women. And bisexuality was a concept I couldn't even understand at the time. It was either like boys or burn in Hell... so I believed.

I religiously studied the Bible day in and day out, yet I couldn't help but wonder why God would make me different if this very difference was deemed an abomination. Why would He intend to punish me for merely being myself? This opened up a Pandora's box of questions about other faiths—Muslims, Hindus, Buddhists, and yes, even Satanists. What made their religions wrong, and how could I be so sure that what I was taught was the one true religion? Particularly when Christianity, which I followed, was essentially an offshoot of Judaism. Yet, there was one distinguishing detail that set them apart (you know, the guy who walked on water), and it led to division.

So much division.

As I matured, I delved into the study of every religion that crossed my path. I embarked on "pilgrimages" to places like India, staying in various monasteries, captivated by the unique truths I found in each.

In my early twenties, I stumbled upon the Law of Attraction, although I initially dismissed it as materialistic. Shortly thereafter, I fell in love with *A Course in Miracles*, which illuminated the power of forgiveness for me. Then, I stumbled upon Neale Donald Walsch's *Conversations with God,* and that changed everything. My perspective shifted as I unearthed a universal truth: Unity. God resides in all of us, which explained why I found fragments of truth in every religion. When it boiled down to the essence, everything was interconnected.

A few years ago, my freelance editing business took a profound turn. I found a mentor who redirected my focus toward spiritual books, particularly those channeled by authors. With their guidance, my freelance venture transformed into a thriving empire, devoted to "raising the global vibration one book at a time."

During this transformative journey, I encountered a fascinating podcast titled 'The Stream of David.' Its message resonated with me because it felt like a male, same-sex-oriented counterpart to Esther Hicks, with the Stream embodying a no-nonsense version of Abraham. This, despite my occasional cringe at the word "resonate."

In contrast to many similar messages, the Stream's wisdom was down-to-earth with no fluff—something I deeply appreciated. It seemed like they tackled topics other channelers didn't dare to touch.

Call it fate or divine intervention, but one day, my editing client Elsa Mendoza stumbled upon an Instagram post by David, who was in search of a "spiritually focused book editor." Elsa, who had a keen connection to Source, tagged me in the post, believing it to be a perfect match.

I held Elsa in high regard, and her books were deeply aligned with the Stream's teachings, which caught my attention. The next day and a half was a whirlwind of excitement and strategizing with my mentor, as we meticulously crafted an email proposal for the Stream of David. It was as if destiny had whispered in my ear—I was aligned to collaborate with him.

And collaborate we did. From the moment David and I connected, it was clear that we were kindred spirits. We decided to work together, and it marked the beginning of quite the journey. I had the privilege of assisting him in producing what remains to this day my most cherished edited work: *The Stream: Eternal Wisdom for a Better Life.*

I became utterly engrossed in the message David and the Stream were sharing. It was like a never-ending well of wisdom that I couldn't resist. I devoured every podcast episode, watched every one of David's Facebook videos, and delved into every article he penned. I soon introduced him to my mentor, and together we worked and learned side by side for months, reconstructing our businesses and forming a profound friendship.

One of the highlights of our collaboration was co-hosting Saturday-morning live videos in David's Facebook group. In those sessions, he channeled the Stream, and I had the privilege of asking my own questions and presenting inquiries from the audience. It became my sanctuary, my Saturday-morning church, where Source energy flowed like a river.

Before long, I made a momentous decision: to join his Tya Bootcamp. I was among the first few students to embark on this journey, even though I couldn't quite put my finger on why I felt compelled to do so. My life seemed pretty good already. I had a knack for manifesting, and although challenges like a stressful custody battle for my daughter loomed, I no longer felt the need to question everything. It all finally felt right. At last, I had enough faith in the universe to always make it through with optimism.

And so, I took the plunge into the Tya Practice...

...And it was nothing short of remarkable.

Transformation unfolded, albeit at its own pace. I didn't truly comprehend the extent of my progress until I reached the end of the process and looked back on my journey. The changes were staggering.

During those twelve transformative weeks, I manifested custody of my daughter, vastly improved health, boundless energy, over $100,000 in income, a loving romantic partner (with a connection that defied description), and a healthier, more attractive physique. Seriously, it surpassed years of life-coaching and therapy combined.

Dysfunctional friendships naturally faded away, making room for healthier, inspiring connections with people who lifted me higher. I began to mend my strained relationship with my mother and even found a sense of appreciation for my abusive stepmother, even though our paths may never cross again.

Financial abundance flowed into my life in ways I hadn't deemed possible, accompanied by higher-paying clients who were not only generous but also a joy to work with.

The chronic pain that had plagued me for three decades was nearly eradicated, replaced by a stronger, leaner body.

Others noticed the transformation too. I attracted positive attention from both genders, exuding an energy that garnered friendly smiles, kind words, and genuine attempts to connect (though, I must admit, the occasional catcall from a passing trucker still happened).

My daily meditation practice took me to crazy new levels. I even started getting direct messages from the Stream in my dreams and wrote them down immediately when I woke up. For example, during the custody battle with my daughter's father that seemed utterly hopeless, I couldn't get him to settle. The night before the proposed court date, I dreamed he agreed to talk to me about what our daughter really wanted. I woke up with this message:

Just keep doing what you're doing. He is in such a place of fear right now that he is just doing his lawyer's bidding, but his lawyer is not as accommodating as yours and is less likely to allow him to settle.

But just like in your dream, explain that you can settle this now and spend a lot less—that dream was important guidance.

Our suggestion for what to do is to tell him your side of things. Let him know it could have been settled earlier, but you can still end it now. Just step back and trust guidance.

Just get on the phone with him, be open, set positive intentions first, and let us flow through you and guide your words.

All will be well.

So that was exactly what I did, and guess what? We settled the matter on the spot, ending months of contentious battles that seemed destined for the courtroom.

That message came through clearly, and I listened.

Yup. This was the real deal.

Now, I can't claim that my life is perfect, nor do I desire it to be. In its imperfections lies its true perfection. So I guess it *is* perfect. It's perfectly imperfect. It's all a matter of perspective.

After decades of seeking, yearning, and searching, I finally paused to look around, only to realize that there was nothing left to do but savor the journey.

I'm not a vegetarian (anymore), I don't adorn myself with crystals or wear flowing skirts, and I still catch myself griping about trivial matters, and yes, I still roll my eyes when someone annoys me. But I'm more "spiritual" now than ever before. I no longer seek the "right" religion. I still practice yoga, but it's no longer my source of spiritual fulfillment. Yet, I feel more connected to Source than ever.

My life was good before, but now, I've discovered how much better it can be. Spirituality has taken on a new meaning for me. I no longer beseech a conceptualized god for forgiveness or chase after enlightenment. It's difficult to articulate, but I'm content. Truly content. I have no desire to make drastic changes. In fact, I have no desire for desires. I'm genuinely, profoundly, stick-a-fork-in-me-I'm-done HAPPY.

In the early days of 2018, I joined a mastermind group alongside David and a few others who had also graduated from Tya Academy. David dubbed this group "Tya Mastery," and it proved to be the catalyst for taking my Tya Practice to new heights. Having regular access to the Stream, not just through occasional messages in my dreams, provided the consistent check-ins I needed to maintain my practice. Whenever I sensed myself slipping or losing momentum, I could reconnect with the group. We learned to navigate the natural ebb and flow of life without judgment of the cessations or the need to force change.

As of today, I've traversed a significant distance on this path, and I'm acutely aware that there's still a long road ahead. I welcome it with open arms. The universe can throw whatever challenges it desires because I understand that I am a conscious creator. I have unwavering faith that the universe has my back, and the Stream is always there to guide me back on course when needed.

When the Stream first proposed the idea of David and me co-authoring a book, I was on board immediately. After hosting numerous Q&A sessions with them in an online setting, I knew there were countless questions waiting to be explored, and deeper layers of insight the Stream could unveil. This endeavor was particularly important for those of us who grasp concepts more readily in written form—and as a book editor, that's certainly my forte!

Throughout our discussions on the four pillars of Tya and how to apply this practice in one's life, I pledge to not only pose my own inquiries but also to address questions and scenarios that I know resonate with many others. Some of these queries have arisen directly from our audience, while others have sprung from fellow Tya students and 'masters,' and a handful have even been inspired by my inquisitive eleven-year-old daughter.

You'll notice a consistent thread in each section: two recurring questions. The first question seeks guidance on how to explain these intricate concepts to a child—a concept I borrowed directly from the Stream. This exercise in simplifying and distilling complex ideas can be enlightening for all of us, helping us internalize these concepts better. The second question seeks parting thoughts, and I learned from numerous interactions with David channeling the Stream that this closing insight often leaves us with profound wisdom that not only addresses unspoken questions but also nourishes our minds for days, if not weeks, to come.

With all that being said, let's dive into the Stream!

Introduction from the Stream

We are here!

Who And What Are We?

We are labeled many things by humanity, and we allow space for you to define us as you wish, as we do not need to be defined by a singular conclusion. We do not seek to be worshiped or obeyed; we do not judge and will not assign a set of rules to be followed. We are often misunderstood, and our being has been idealized and exploited by humans since you developed the ability of critical thought beyond instinct—a sign of the maturing of your Earthly environment.

We are all things, and we are very much a part of you. We are your intuition, your joy, and, most importantly, we are what you call love. We are the inexplicable feeling of goodness and warmth you feel when you are in your highest vibrational state. We are expressed in the things you appreciate. We are blue skies and thunderous storms, we are fields of flowers and flowing streams, we are the melodies of birds and the laughter of children, we are that which you consider beauty, and the wisdom that is expressed in the wrinkles that only time can create. We are all that you cherish in this life and more, and we are available to you always. We exist in all places and are original thought, and we are a creation of your own mind—as is everything you are perceiving in your current physical expression.

It is important that you understand that while we guide you to the joy and clarity that comes with allowing your connection to our energy to be realized as a priority for true happiness, we do not guide you away from the earthly, material things that you so often desire. We simply guide you to find your path to our joyous connection first—which is always present within you—then the vibration of needing these other things to be happy will be diminished, and the vibration will shift from one of needing something, because it's not present, to simply discerning a preference to experience something physical for the sake of the experience, rather than the need for it, which is a much higher vibration.

If you are reading this, it is not by accident. You may have read words such as these before because it is true there are no accidents—everything occurs via attraction. You are here now because of your intention to expand your connection to the energetic realm and your desire to move beyond the knowledge you've acquired thus far in life and put the universal laws into action on your behalf. We are here to tell you that you are in the perfect place, at the perfect time, receiving the most up-to-date evolution on creative thought consciousness there is...just by reading these words.

What you will learn here will take you well beyond where you have been on your spiritual journey. We use the word abundance as a general term, meaning your version of abundance—your current desired earthly experience. It can mean money, cars, clothes, houses, travel, and other material things, but it can also mean joy, clarity, improved health, a better-feeling body, more satisfying relationships, more satisfying sex, and more enjoyment of life in general.

Beyond abundance, we offer clarity—a view of your life, your world, and the entirety of the universe, from the highest perspective. You see, from our perspective, Planet Earth is perfection, just as it is. You are not destroying your planet; humanity is not headed for destruction, at least not anytime soon in earthly, linear time, and you are not going to reach your version of perfection—or nirvana—if you will. We will clear up many of these things in our sharing here. Clarity is one of the most valuable states of being you can experience as a physically manifested being—understanding the meaning of your own existence and why and how your world—and the universe—operates. Understanding this will separate you from ninety-nine percent of humanity but also bring you to a deeper appreciation of those "less evolved" states of being.

Coming into full understanding of your world, your true eternal nature, and your purpose here on Earth will change your life. You will come to understand in your heightened clarity that you need not be so hard on yourself. That much of what likely troubles you stems from your society's social programming—your judgment of you and your earthly experience. That you can turn your attention away from social programming, which we often refer to as "the matrix," and begin using these tools to forge your own unique path to joy, clarity, and abundance.

You will hear us use the words joy, clarity, and abundance again and again. This is because, at your core, you seek freedom and joy. This is the state in which you exist in your eternal, completed state where you are not physically manifested. You come to a physical environment such as Planet Earth, understanding from your eternal, soul consciousness that you will seek the freedom and joy you exist in eternally, but that you will experience those things physically rather than purely energetically.

The difference on Planet Earth, as in any physical environment, is that you are also impacted by polarity while physically manifested. Polarity impacts physically and directly, as opposed to the energetic realm where it keeps things in balance but does not cause the vibrational fluctuation as it does in the physical. The vibrational fluctuation in a physical environment causes a movement up and down a virtual spiral, spiraling up to positive and down into negative, delivering every physical environment a constant mix of positive and negative experiences.

This may be difficult for you to believe from your current human perspective, but you actually came here to Planet Earth for the negative. From your soul-consciousness perspective, you understand that the unwanted things in your life are the very things that spark all new creation. This is true for you and all things on your planet. Wild animals want freedom and joy, but they are also part of the food chain. The desire to survive while, in many cases, almost constantly being hunted, actually makes them wiser and stronger. Yes, most will end up becoming food for something else at some point, but the ego-driven will to survive and seek out more physical freedom and joy offers expansion for the animal in their physical state, and, more importantly, expansion in their completed state. We say 'more importantly' because every single life form has a strand of independent and eternal soul consciousness flowing through it—powering it—and in the overcoming of obstacles, new creation occurs, and new creation expands the universe. This continual cycle of universal expansion contributes to the expansion of Source, that which we are, and you are a part of, and we are ever-expanding so we utilize new creation to drive that expansion.

So, if you accept that you come to Planet Earth to overcome obstacles and grow in the process, and you accept that all creation, including your life, occurs via attraction, then you see the value in your vibration (which is the same as your mood, and that is your point of attraction) being driven up and down a vibrational spiral all the time. This gives you a mix of positive experiences to enjoy and negative things to overcome, and in the overcoming, you create, and thus expand your consciousness and the consciousness of all that is. This is exactly why you come to physical existence every single time, infinitely.

There are a few things that we wish to share with you before we move into what Tya is and how it will improve every area of your life. First, your ego is not a bad thing. We see many of you discovering what is often labeled as spirituality and acquiring the belief that your ego is somehow a bad thing. You allow yourselves to believe that you need to be more "spiritual" and less "human," that you need to spend hours in meditation and relinquish all material things. This is nonsense and is born of the same limiting beliefs that tend to rule your religions. Your intention prior to manifesting as a human being was to come and allow your ego to overshadow your eternal soul consciousness, to find your own unique path to freedom and joy, allowing your ego to serve as the driver for your unique human experience while polarity serves as the governor. Your ego is fuel, your mind is the engine, and polarity is the highway that takes you through multiple twists and turns to a destination. It all serves the perfection of universal creation in a physical environment.

In your eternal, non-physical state, you are omnipresent and omniscient; you are in a state of pure-positive perfection. It is glorious but offers no expansion because there are no obstacles to overcome. Obstacles drive all new creation, and new creation is expansion. In your life, as a member of the collective consciousness of humanity, as a being of—and therefore a contributor to—the Earth environment, and for the universe as a whole, it all operates the same. New creation is an answer to a perceived problem or obstacle.

We also often observe humans state that they are not judgmental. You are all judgmental. You begin discerning your preferences even prior to birth. You spend your lives observing everything and everyone around you and discerning whether you like it or not. At your best, you learn to move more and more toward that which you want and away from that which you do not. However, it is being judgmental in your discernment, and that is different from being judgmental about what others should be experiencing.

Looking upon something and saying "this is not for me" is a perfectly high vibration; you are all different, and there is truly no singular path, no pre-set destination, and absolutely no assertion from the energetic realm, be it guides, gods, or any other being for your path or desired destination. It is truly all up to you—your preference. This is why looking upon another and stating, "I do not want this for me, therefore you should not want it either," is coming from a low-vibrational perspective.

In your high vibration, you hold space for all to discern their own preference, understanding that their preference does not have to impact you at all.

Concerns that others' preferences will somehow negatively impact your bubble of reality are low in vibration because they are always born of fear. Only from a place of fear do you believe that you need others to agree with you or behave in a certain way for you to be joyous or to receive what you want.

Many of your beliefs are likely a result of social conditioning. Humanity has encountered a very long period of what we call society building, where your leaders have taken universal wisdom and packaged it alongside a set of rules with consequences for not following them. This includes your religious, political, and cultural rules, both formal and informal, and these three are often closely intertwined. A matrix of belief that largely runs on fear and judgment in your current physical reality.

Since we do not judge anything as right or wrong, we do not judge that, but it is important to point out that these are of human creation, not from us. Though we are the source of all creation, physical beings create limitations, or obstacles, in separation from our consciousness, allowing our energy to return and craft solutions as part of you. Since we are pure-positive, we are never the direct creators of unwanted things, but we do allow this creation for the expansion offered in the experience and overcoming. This is why you, as human beings, tend to love stories of triumph so much because they return you to your natural, eternal Source consciousness, even if just momentarily.

We do not have rules or plans for your time here on Planet Earth. We celebrate your new creation, whatever it is, and it all drives your expansion as an independent strand of soul consciousness. And since each strand is a part of that which we are, your expansion drives our expansion, which is the expansion of the universe.

Your commonly held beliefs and customs around gender identity, class, education, family structure, government, religion, time, and on and on, are all examples of social engineering that has been prevalent on Planet Earth for some time. This is a prime example of polarity, as this engineering has served a purpose in the expansion of humanity, but it has also delivered a great deal of suffering.

We flow at this time via David because humanity is indeed awakening. It may not seem as such if you follow popular media. It may seem as though your world is unraveling, but we promise you that this is a spectacular time to be a human being. You see, the current vibration of humanity is creating technology that is chasing the tail of the technology that creates you. Yes, you are technology. In fact, all your "human-created" technology (and science) is simply humanity figuring itself out.

Your bodies are intelligently designed; no atheist can explain how the Earth's environment came to function the way that it does, how the ecosystem was created, nor can they explain how your physical vehicles came to be the design that they are. "It just happened" is a copout. Any thinking being must surmise that there is absolute intelligence in creation. This intelligence has been labeled by humans as many things, and those labels often were accompanied by sets of rules that you (as humanity) have decided to do away with as you've evolved. There is nothing wrong with this; in fact, the process of evolution is about becoming more and more intelligent—more sophisticated beings. This is why "ancient" wisdom does not stand the test of time, at least not wisdom that is beyond universal law.

Universal law is simple and does not change: all creation occurs via attraction, and all attraction is governed by polarity. That's it. That's all that is needed to create and expand the universe into infinity. Everything else is physical creation, which is always evolving. Most of the teachings that have stood the test of time in your current perceived reality were originally rooted in universal law, and human consciousness—i.e. ego—added elements. These added elements will not stand the test of time as you become collectively more intelligent.

You are all likely aware of religions that spoke of things like slavery and slaughtering non-believers as commonplace societal structures—because they were—but most of humanity has moved on from those beliefs in your current time. That was the vibration of the time period, and now the vibration has evolved.

The vibration has evolved to the point where many are choosing to believe in nothing at all. This eschewing of things like organized religion, government, monarchy, and even policing is leaving much of humanity out in the wilderness, with no real belief system. But you are technology, and while in physical you must run on an operating system just as your devices do; this operating system is your belief system. The most devout non-believer still operates on a belief system, even if it's consumerism, "wokism," capitalism, socialism, or some combination of isms; even atheism is a belief system. And those seeking relief from these systems can often find themselves out in the wilderness of confusion caused by stepping out of them. This is where the matrix offers things like conspiracy theories, activating fear and judgment and thus drawing you right back in.

So, if you must operate in a belief system, perhaps now is the time to shed all the fear-based teachings of the matrix—all of them—and adopt a new, updated system that keeps you rooted in universal law as opposed to the next whim of the matrix?

The matrix is not a cabal of "evil" individuals but a vibration that humanity has created to govern with. A polarized, divided society operating in fear with a dose of hopefulness keeps a society in order. Humanity once functioned under tyranny, but that gave way to the illusion of greater freedom as you became more evolved. In your development of modes of travel and then global communication, you essentially began comparing notes and noticing the similarities in your institutions of control. In your collective questioning of them, they began to fracture and continue to do so. But these vibrations are well established and will not be dismissed without a challenge. This is the origin of your 2020 pandemic, not the illness itself, but the harnessing of the power found in the fear of it.

Covid-19 was not terribly unique among other viruses that have plagued humanity, but the fear-mongering around it was. Certainly, it caused illness and death, but so do many, many other things in your environment. Yet the reaction to this was much more strict than experienced in other situations. We are not spinning yet another conspiracy theory here but guiding you to see how the Matrix performs. Being aware of it without judging it is the key to release from it. This is where our teachings depart from most others and where you will find an effective path out of fear and judgment. Appreciate the fear-mongering as a clear sign that humanity's matrix of control is being challenged. As you move through our teachings, you will experience challenges from your own matrix of beliefs; this too is a clear sign that you are de-tuning your old, limiting operating system and installing a new, clearer, more abundant one.

Why We Created Tya

The universe is expansive and ever-evolving. Planet Earth, humanity, and you as an individual are all reflections of the universe. You are part of that which we are, and we are the energy that created and drives the eternal expansion of the universe.

While you are here on this planet experiencing a physical reality, you are living in linear time, yet you are still evolving and still expanding (which are the same thing) in your eternal state of being. Because of this, the things that worked for generations past do not necessarily work for you. This is why many teachers have come to Planet Earth and shared messages based on universal law. Due to polarity, those messages are embraced, or not, and those that are embraced and absorbed by many tend to live on beyond the original teacher's lifetime. But those messages were up to speed with the time in which they were delivered—not with the evolved conditions of Planet Earth years, and sometimes thousands of years later.

The human idea of ancient wisdom can be overly romanticized. Notice we said ancient, not eternal, wisdom. Eternal wisdom is wisdom from Source—that which we share. It is based on eternal, universal law as we described earlier. Ancient refers to earthly time and was offered by a human, even if that human was channeling it.

Every channel is a sieve, and any information flowing will be filtered through the human channel. David has set the intention to share our guidance as purely as possible, but our message is still flowing through him with his intention to share tools and processes that will work best in your current modern reality. Consciousness is ever-evolving, and we are consciousness. He is our channel to bring our message to this planet, and he is co-creating this information with us. As seekers of higher knowledge, you are co-creating this information as well—even as you read our words here that have already been printed, your desire has summoned them.

You are likely aware that humanity evolved from lower-vibrational life forms, and your collective intelligence continues to evolve and expand as you continue to discern new preferences. The greatest driver of new preferences is unwanted conditions. You see something as undesirable and then set your sights on something different and allow it to manifest, and new creation has occurred. This is the universal process of creation, and it is why polarity exists. Your point of attraction is highly impacted by polarity, a word we have chosen to describe the constant movement of energy between positive and negative. Your vibration is high when you are "up" your vibrational spiral. You are up there believing your dreams and trusting your abundance in that high state. Hold yourself there long enough, and actual physical creation of your desires begins to occur. When your vibration goes down, dropping into negative on your spiral, you begin to doubt your desire, you lose the trust you had when you were up. You begin to question, "What if?" "How will it come?" "Where is it?" "Why hasn't it come yet?" These questions, driven by lower-vibrational doubt, create "static" in your vibration and begin to slow or even cancel out the creation of your desire if enough of this is allowed. Sticking yourself in a low-vibrational flow will also attract unwanted things—obstacles—into your life.

So think of your spiral like this: your "up the spiral" (or UTS) time is for creating your desires and your "down the spiral" (or DTS) time is for creating obstacles. Polarity keeps your vibration in a constant state of flux, flowing up and down a vibrational spiral. Your thoughts, especially what you may call your triggers, can also impact your spiral, and you often seek to manage your spiral with varying degrees of success with numerous methods of therapy: everything from a simple shift in focus to the use of drugs, alcohol, and plant medicine. All of this in an attempt to manage what we call your vibrational flow. With this flow, polarity is guaranteeing a constant flow between high and low vibration. You dip down into negative and manifest your obstacle and then you go up into positive and find the solution.

Your solution is new creation, everything from an improved thought that leads to the next step of the creative process to evolution to full-blown physical manifestation; it is all new creation and new creation drives the expansion of the universe. Look around you: every human-created object is a solution to a once-perceived problem. Your planet was once a speck of dust; that speck had consciousness flowing through it, as all things do, and it attracted another like speck of dust. The two merged and became a larger speck of dust, and the process continued, regenerating as more and more sophisticated forms until that which you call Planet Earth came to be as you perceive it.

In this creative process, there was and continues to be a vibrational flow present. The vibrational flow, up and down the vibrational spiral that all creation operates on, allows higher vibration, or UTS, which is positive creation of merging and expanding like objects. It also allows lower vibration, or DTS, the negative or undesired creation in the form of challenges or obstacles to its creation, such as emerging destructive weather and other elements that offer damage and threat, in this example.

The consciousness that desired expansion expanded in the surviving of these challenges. It becomes a more sophisticated version of itself in the maneuvering through the experience of challenge. Most physical creations do not, but a fraction do survive the obstacles and continue to expand and even thrive. The thriving attracts consciousness-seeking expansion via new expression of physical, and life appears—again a result of an emerging new physical environment that has weathered DTS challenges and grown stronger and more sophisticated as a result.

Now it is attracting a more sophisticated consciousness that is seeking its own expansion as a result of having weathered DTS obstacles and grown stronger (and more sophisticated) because of this. It seeks to express itself in a new physical form, utilizing all it has endured in other physical environments to manifest on this new, more evolved, emerging planet.

All physical creation manifests in ever-expanding expressions, and each and every strand of consciousness that projects into physical contributes to the expansion of Source as extensions of Source. So you, as a human being, are an expression that is far more evolved as a result of the lifetimes you have experienced and will continue to become more evolved as you experience ever-expanding physical realities.

The "more evolved" label is a very important component of our teachings and your expanded understanding of universal law and the purpose of life. In your eternal, non-physical state, you have no challenges. You exist in a pure-positive state, and you are all-knowing and all-seeing as we are, as you are part of that which we are. This state of being is blissful and the expression of pure love, but there is no expansion offered as there is no duality—no obstacles. This state is pure consciousness; there are no names, no measurement, no judgment, no genders or "need" for anything—food, shelter, community, etc.

Personalities are not present in this state, and there are no tools of communication, for there is no need for such things. It is difficult for your human mind to comprehend this state of being. This is because physical operates very differently. From this all-knowing state, you understand that consciousness only needs stimulation to expand, and energy is either expanding or dying. Your scientists believe that energy does not expand or die but simply shifts forms. This is because of the expansive nature of consciousness, which is energy. The eternal consciousness of Source, that which we are, and you are all part of, does not allow any reduction of expansion so there is no evidence of energy "dying." But the continual conscious focus on expansion is what is ensuring this. All creation is continually either expanding or dying, theoretically, but the choice will perpetually be expansion because even when something physical seems to be destroyed, the energy that powers it simply moves on to something else, a more expanded version of. This is why we guide you not to fear death or even the destruction of your planet or end of humanity because the old physical form is simply being released so the consciousness may move onto the next, more sophisticated (expanded) form.

This is because all physical worlds are an illusion of consciousness. The physical expression you know as Earth is an expression of your own strand of consciousness and as part of the collective consciousness of humanity, you are creating your own journey of expansion that brings you up to speed with the very technology that created you, at least what you perceive as you from your limited human perspective. The limitation of your perspective is designed to allow you to focus on your singular environment, or current life experience, so that your polarized physical experience offers the stimulation your eternal consciousness desires in order to expand. When we speak of technology, humanity's exponential expansion of technology has brought you to a place where you are now creating "artificial intelligence" in what you may call a metaverse. This is your collective human creation that is gaining ground on how the "real" or non-virtual version of your world actually creates.

As you perceive it, you are "dreaming up" scenarios in a virtual reality in order to make them interesting and/or informative. In your real physical environment, you are dreaming up desires and challenges for exactly the same reason—for the stimulation of desire and challenge inspires new creation. This new creation is always conceived in thought first. Then it is expressed in reality. The thought creation is the actual creation, the allowing of the physical expression, i.e., "manifestation" is simply a by-product of that aligned consciousness. In the case of your physical reality, alignment is derived by belief. You create it in thought, you believe it, and it materializes. You are the conscious creator of your reality.

So stimulation is needed for the expansion of consciousness, and stimulation is not offered in an all-knowing state. Physical is the expression of Source in a polarized environment, for the physical experience and for the contrast created by polarity.

Non-physical consciousness is expansive by design, focusing to move more and more into the ever-expanding "core" of Source energy. It is not a preference as you have in your physical environment because there is no other option but expansion. This focus expands the individual being and contributes to the expansion of Source as a component of it, ensuring that energy never "dies." Non-physical consciousness aligns with a set of circumstances for the potential physical experience being offered, and a new physical being, or expression, is the result. This includes less sophisticated particles that you do not consider "life" at this time as well as that which you consider life, which is a far more sophisticated expression of consciousness. This physical point of entry will create both positive and negative circumstances, and vibrational flow will ensure the perception of those circumstances will place the new physical being on a path of both wanted and unwanted. Flowing up to high vibration, allowing discerned physical preferences to flow in, and down to low vibration, attracting obstacles. The obstacles offer an opportunity for greater expansion in the solving or overcoming.

Obstacles in new creation exist to offer the opportunity to create a more evolved version. Think about the things you consider important in your life: careers, new businesses, romantic relationships, family relationships, your health, and your bodies. You think about these things often, and your continual revisiting of them through your up-and-down vibrational flow actually causes new creation in these areas to take longer. You think of them, essentially mentally creating them as you desire them to be in your high vibrational state; they are forming and heading right to you as full physical manifestations. Then polarity drags your vibration down, as it inevitably will. You now revisit your mental creation in this lower-vibrational state. Now it does not seem so easy, you become impatient, and perhaps even begin to doubt, or wonder about the "how" of it. This lower-vibrational focus slows the manifestation. Then your vibration drops more, and you begin to renegotiate. You tell yourself that your dream is too big and that you have not had success manifesting it, so maybe you should rethink it or forget it. This is when you may even dip into the victim vibration and wonder why the universe is not being fair with you, or perhaps you even begin to berate yourself for thinking low-vibrational thoughts about your dream, which drags your vibration down even further. All of this creates static in the vibration that will cause your dream to slow or even halt in production, and this can manifest as obstacles in the creative process.

You have the option to forget about your dream and move on to something else, and the universe will respond the only way it can: with "yes." Or, you can shift your focus back to a higher-vibrational state of belief and allow a solution to manifest. This is never accomplished by looking for the solution but rather getting off the topic and allowing polarity to do its job and take your vibration back up, naturally. Simply breathing and clearing your mind is enough to allow your vibration to rise. In your higher vibration, solutions flow to you naturally, and in the solving of your obstacle, you have now allowed a more perfect version of whatever it is that you are creating. Obstacles exist to make creation better, stronger, more evolved, healthier, more resilient. You have evidence of this all around you yet humanity tends to avoid the pain of obstacles at great expense.

We refer to humanity's collective belief system as "the Matrix," not in reference to a movie but as a structured belief system across the collective human consciousness. Like all creation, the matrix is a vibration, varying in expressions but grounded in fear and judgment, which essentially equate to separation from the natural ability to trust abundance. Think of historical leaders, rules, and religions—they often embody a mix of trust and fear, with fear serving as a lower-vibrational force intended to enforce obedience, even for the perceived common good.

The energetic realm does not dictate a prescribed path; new creation stems from physically manifested desires, often associated with the human ego. Whether rooted in fear or trust, the ego drives new creation. However, what you may refer to as the universe, God, or Source provides abundance, perceived as love, without judgment as good or evil. Anything less than Source creation is a creation of the ego, not genuinely new but rather recycled. This explains why recurring fears often involve the same themes, such as war, sickness, poverty, loneliness, and abuse. True new creation is always fresh, expansive, and of Source origin.

So the matrix is always polarized, and the energetic realm is never polarized. That's how you can tell them apart. When you're needing to take sides or to be right and for someone else to be wrong, when you're looking for fault or blame, or fearing lack, you're operating in the matrix. When you're trusting, even in the face of evidence of a former lower vibration, you are out of the matrix. We guide you to learn to be an observer of the matrix without judging it; as soon as you judge it, you're back in it. This includes other beings who are in it. A major component of being out of the matrix is authentic appreciation of all things, including those in the matrix.

"Survival of the fittest" is the way of the universe—a never-ending expansion of sophistication, of intelligence, allowing the very best version of XYZ to emerge through the obstacles. Allowing the idea of perpetual victimhood, where the "weaker" creations are propped up in the name of fairness, without moving on to a higher vibration, where all solutions lie, is a ticket to stunted expansion. But even this is yet another example of the perfection of perceived imperfection because "stunted expansion" has lessons offered in the energetic realm; therefore, even what you may consider a negative experience only exists to inspire a new, more solution-oriented focus, which is expansion, so there is truly no getting it wrong. Expansion is offered in all scenarios; this is why, from our perspective, there is no negative.

This is why we call you powerful creators—because we are the source of all creation, but a physical being's new creation actually fuels our expansion. We co-create the universe!

··•·•·•··

As humans emerged as the highest form of intelligence on Planet Earth, you used your higher intelligence to manifest far beyond what the other species on your planet had manifested previously. Your challenge was being out in nature and participating in the food chain, and you discerned your preference to no longer do that. You learned to construct shelter, create fire on demand, and how to outsmart the other creatures to avoid being eaten. You clustered into groups for added safety, and "alpha leaders" emerged to lead the groups.

Since polarity impacts all subjects, there is that which you, in your human perspective, consider positive and negative on all topics. The leaders of the groups served to keep the members safe, and the "negative" polarized aspect that emerged was that those who were not leading were often not leading lives of freedom and joy as they had desired when coming to this physical environment. These leaders inevitably turned to fear as a tool to control their populations—albeit often with noble intentions—but the fear-mongering took hold and became very active in your collective vibration, and it remains so today. This is the matrix.

Now, in your modern lives, you are emerging from a long period of what we call society building, also known as social engineering. You are using your technology to communicate like never before, and you are collectively coming to realize that you've been controlled by fear, and you are seeing that this no longer needs to have the grip on humanity that it has had; you no longer need to be told what to do. You no longer need fear to keep you in place. This is why your governments and religions, among other things, are coming into question by the collective, and you are beginning to see the fracturing of these institutions of control. Humanity is collectively shedding the need for social engineering as you are coming to understand that you create your world—your reality.

This is why law-of-attraction teachings, though they have been taught throughout history on your planet, are catching on in your current reality. They are becoming mainstream, and more and more of you are coming into awareness that you all create your own bubbles of reality. This consciousness has spread quickly across humanity, but, as with all subjects, it is polarized. Some accept that they create it all—the good and the bad, wanted and unwanted, and set about trying to manifest their desired lives intentionally. They listen to teachers who have a rudimentary understanding of the universal laws and get excited at how easy all this seems: "Just be happy, and everything you want will come!" This is true; being joyous—being up your spiral—will place you in a vibrational position to manifest everything you want. What often isn't shared—because it's not as glamorous—is that polarity is always impacting your point of attraction. There is no escaping polarity in a physical environment.

When David began absorbing the teachings of others, he discovered messages that were very similar to some of what we are offering. But we offered him a further evolution of that consciousness. When he began experimenting with applying these teachings, he understood that he was co-creating the solution to a perceived problem—overcoming the effects of polarity—or at least learning to manage them.

There is only one source, but we are a collective, a collective of all creation and all thought—eternally. We merge with humans to co-create teachings that are up to speed with the physical time in which they are being offered. They are of a specific vibration to align with the collective asking of a group of souls who are currently expressed in physical form. In other words, the message we are offering is intended for those who are ready to receive it, and it is the most up to speed with the "now" information being offered. Not everyone is ready for such information. This is why we do not have David out on street corners sharing our offerings. This is intended as a vibrational offering for those who are a match.

David's intention in sharing this information and strong desire to help others understand it resulted in the co-creation of the spiritual practice that we have guided David to name Tya, for "Trust your abundance." The intention was to create a process of learning to manage your vibration, which allows you to change any aspect of your reality. The benefits of this are numerous. You gain a clear understanding of how the universe operates, why you came to Planet Earth, how you chose your point of entry into your current life, how to move up your spiral into joy, on demand, and exist in that joyous state most of the time. You also learn how to align with your desires and allow them to manifest in your life with ease. Perhaps the greatest achievement with this practice is finding your path to joy and clarity—by this we mean loving yourself and finding things to love and appreciate in your everyday life, regardless of conditions. This is the true key to happiness.

You may be reading this and thinking, "That's great, but happiness doesn't pay the rent!" This is true. We understand; we are just guiding you to find your path to happiness first, because no amount of money, shoes, cars, homes, beauty, sex, fame, or anything else will fill the void left from a disconnection from your source. Source connection—your own personal connection to our energy—is the most valuable manifestation you can achieve. The good news is that we are always flowing to you; you often just drown us out via your down-the-spiral focus and chattery minds.

Notice that humans operating in a belief system, even one you do not agree with, often find solace in that structure. Your contrasting world can be a troubling place for you when you're in the matrix. When you attempt to step out of a belief system, the matrix has triggers built in to catch you and draw you into another system by design. As we have stated, as humanity's consciousness evolved, many questioned old belief systems, and some decided to leave old structures behind. Organized religion is a prime example of this. Look back over just a few generations, and you will see how organized religions served as a useful structure at one time, but as humans longed for more freedom, this tool became less and less useful and ultimately became disavowed as generations progressed. But there were more systems there to take the place of religion.

New age spirituality, consumerism, politics, and so on moved in to replace religion for many. Even atheism is a belief system, often expressed in an egocentric fashion behind the veil of seeking scientific evidence for any and every idea lest they be tossed aside as frivolous. But faith in the existence of yet-to-be-proven ideas is the very basis of science.

Like your devices, you require an operating system to function. One hundred percent of that which you may refer to as evil is an example of a human being who likely stepped out of a socially structured belief system only to find themselves drawn into a lower-vibration system such as conspiracy theories—where fear and judgment rule the day, or materialism, where the belief that possessing more and more wealth is the key to happiness, or at least longevity. Many who find themselves dialing into the law-of-attraction system are actually operating in the materialism system.

We will never demonize your system of currency or material creations. While it is true that your currency will not buy love or ensure your source connection, it will allow you to have and experience the things you all desire. Your currency system is based on vibration just like everything else in the universe, and like everything else, it is polarized—there are positive and negative aspects. The positive is that currency flows generously in a high vibration of knowing that wealth is abundant for all—you only need to know it—trust it. As soon as you bring yourself to this state and do not react to the evidence of your prior vibration regarding currency, your generous flow begins.

The negative aspect of currency appears when fear enters the equation. Fearing that you'll never have enough, fearing that you need it to be happy, fearing that someone will take what you've manifested, etc. Remember: remove fear from any topic, and you find the high vibration, which is true clarity. This is why we guide you to acknowledge and appreciate consumerism, without being drawn into it as a belief system.

You possess the ability to thrive in the earth environment without assigning yourself to a matrix-crafted belief in anything beyond your own worthiness, period. This is why we delivered the Tya Practice, to return humanity to a belief system purely rooted in universal law, outside the matrix.

How Tya Will Change Your Life

Our intention with Tya is to simplify and return to the fundamental laws that created and continue to expand the universe. We aim to deliver a clear and easy-to-follow quantum mindset practice that works on Earth and will continue to do so, as long as practitioners understand that there should be no rules, worship, or judgment involved.

Throughout human history, there have been individuals aligned with our message who shared it for the benefit of others. These messages often became the basis for human-created social systems, such as religion. Our messages have also been influenced by human thought with a focus on freedom, which is typical of new-age thought or spirituality.

Modern spirituality has as many variations as there are rules and deities in religions. There's no right or wrong, and we do not judge. However, it's crucial to recognize that universal laws underpin all creation, and the power to create flows through all conscious beings while physically manifested. Everything beyond this is a human-created tool, often born from a desire to harness creative power. This doesn't invalidate these practices; they possess power as you grant it to them. We advise not relying on any human-created modality over your innate power of consciousness, which is what Tya emphasizes.

Consider the animals on your planet; they live in freedom and joy most of the time, even though they also experience duality. None of them are aware of chakras, crystals, or other human spiritual practices. They naturally connect with our energy without doubt. Humans, with their advanced intelligence, have created a complex world with complex lives that led to the expansion of their species, planet, and the universe.

You are advanced beings, and your contribution is significant. Your advancement has created a global community where like-minded individuals can easily connect and share consciousness. You've progressed beyond the food chain and now largely govern your world. However, you've also allowed yourselves to be socially programmed, often disconnecting from your natural source connection—your Stream.

We've presented a unique message, flowing through David with ease due to his alignment with sharing these words. They may be considered avant-garde by many for years until the collective is truly ready to absorb them. We've co-created Tya based on David's desire to simplify and provide a higher degree of clarity than previously offered to humanity. His agreement was to balance a challenging human existence while maintaining a deep connection that allowed him to develop tools for true freedom and joy in your modern world.

True freedom and joy are not solely about physical perfection, fame, or material abundance. It's about having a deep understanding of why you're here, acknowledging that no one is living in true perfection, and recognizing how the duality of good and evil serves the universe.

This practice will also lead to an improved physical state, including better feelings, health, and appearance. We're not referring to conventional physical attractiveness; it's about the abundant, loving glow you emit when you're joyous and free, which attracts like-minded individuals.

This practice will align you with those who match your high vibration. You may find it challenging to be around people operating at a lower vibration, but this isolation will be temporary as your vibration elevates. Our guidance is to relax into the practice, savor it, and understand that it's an ongoing journey of clarity, self-love, and higher-consciousness connection. You'll care less about material things as you progress on this path.

As previously stated, our purpose is not to steer you away from your material possessions; instead, we are here to lead you toward genuine freedom and joy. These states arise from your source connection, a clear perspective, and self-love, akin to the way we love you. In the absence of these elements in your vibrational state, no amount of money, relationships, health, or material possessions can bring you true freedom and joy. This explains why you often witness people with abundant possessions living in misery. Some individuals seem compelled to continually acquire more, with no end result of genuine happiness, regardless of their possessions. The more they feel the need to flaunt their belongings, the more they attempt to soothe their disconnection from true clarity—the clarity that consistently brings freedom and joy.

Engaging in this practice is not easy. It will challenge you to shift away from the fear-based, limiting beliefs that govern your current society. You will need to examine painful moments from your past and unwanted aspects of your present existence. Letting go of the security blankets you may have wrapped yourself in, such as the voice that urges you to play it safe, obey all the rules, and stay in your lane, will be necessary. You will be prompted to perceive the polarity and duality of your world differently, to comprehend why what you consider evil exists and the purpose it serves, recognizing that you will not eliminate it. Embracing it is not required, but it is expected that you discern your preference toward what you desire, which might involve solving your world's problems. However, fully understanding that when one problem is solved, another will inevitably arise as part of the universal process of creation.

If you choose to embrace these teachings, this quantum mindset practice will reward you with the highest clarity available to humanity. You will gain leading-edge insights that allow you to see how the universe operates, often contrary to what you are taught on Planet Earth in your current era. From your present human perspective, you might observe people and animals enduring abuse, illness, and starvation, whereas we perceive souls engaged in a higher degree of challenge, driven by their desire to experience duality and return to their complete state, enriched by that experience. It is only negative when viewed through a limited, earthly perspective.

We observe some individuals finding their way out of such conditions while remaining in the physical realm, expanding both as human ego consciousness and as soul consciousness in balance. You may encounter those with whom you disagree, desiring them to see things from your perspective and yearning for a utopian society of like-minded individuals. We see the perfection in this diversity, with no one being definitively right or wrong, and no singular solution to any problem. We envision all of you vibrating independently and having the ability to craft your own unique reality based on your preferences, while allowing others to do the same, without requiring their understanding or agreement.

While you may perceive a world characterized by chaos and declining moral values, we witness humanity deconstructing and rebuilding—a continuous process of universal creation. Polarity gives rise to duality, and duality presents obstacles that challenge you to discover solutions, thereby transforming the former "problem" into a new creation. This is why "unwanted" experiences exist—to inspire new creation. Nothing is ever final; no soul ceases to be due to earthly challenges or transitions from physical existence. All of this is temporary, as you are continually evolving beings.

This practice is open to all of humanity, but, as previously mentioned, only some are ready for it. For those who are, a new life filled with clarity awaits—an existence marked by freedom and joy, unlike anything you may have experienced before. Our intention is to guide you there without judgment, without rules, without worship, and, most importantly, without fear.

Summary of Our Shared Consciousness

Our teachings might initially appear daunting to some. The idea of viewing yourselves as technology, essentially like robots, may seem absurd. However, we invite you to delve deeper into this understanding: your world is purposefully designed. What you commonly refer to as nature or the natural world is not simply a product of chance; it is consciously created. We have explained in great detail how this creation process functions and, more importantly, how you can navigate your current life experience, regardless of your past experiences and the beliefs you have developed for yourself, using the tools we provide within these pages.

If our words ever leave you feeling confused or frustrated, please know that as you progress through this book and assimilate and apply the teachings, you will gradually come to grasp the essence of what we are offering. We encourage you to return to this introduction repeatedly, as comprehending this material requires an ever-evolving and expanding consciousness, precisely what the Tya Practice delivers.

We designed it that way.

Part 2 ~ The Four Pillars of the Tya Practice

David

The Tya Practice is built on four core pillars: Appreciation, Polarity, Source, and Intention. These pillars, along with the tools that come with them, are your roadmap to elevating your default vibration. They work together to help you detune fear and judgment, opening up a natural connection to Source and unleashing waves of joy, clarity, and abundance into your life. Imagine these pillars as the solid foundation upon which the entire practice stands, while the tools that accompany them are like a treasure chest that keeps expanding as more people embrace this transformative way of life.

To give you a taste of how these pillars work in real life, we've included case studies from graduates of our Tya Academy. These stories show how everyday people like you are putting the pillars into action, making tangible improvements in their lives.

Appreciation

The Stream

When we discuss abundance, we are referring to an abundance of joy, a surplus of clarity on any subject, and yes, an abundance of the people, relationships, experiences, and other desires you seek.

Your transgressors, which include unwanted people, circumstances, and events from your past or present, linger in your vibration as negative "baggage" until you find your way to genuine and authentic appreciation of them.

While it's true that the Law of Attraction underpins universal creation, what many of Earth's teachers fail to fully grasp is the universe's continuous recreation through an infinite cycle of positive and negative vibrations—a vibrational flow. This flow creates a perpetual cycle of low-vibration-derived undesired elements, or obstacles, and high-vibration solutions to these undesired elements. Thus, all solutions, regardless of size, amount to new creation. This ongoing cycle of creation is what we often refer to as expansion.

Since all creation occurs via attraction, it is necessary for unwanted—or negative—creation to occur for two very important reasons. The first is that unwanted things—experiences, circumstances, and events—inspire new creation. All new creation is born of a desire for something better, a preference for improvement. For this reason, that which you consider negative is needed to inspire new positive. Second, negative exists to keep creation in balance. Though positive is far more powerful than negative, negative serves to keep positive from spiraling out of control. And though negative is useful in that it delivers obstacles, and those obstacles indeed inspire new creation, an inordinate amount of negativity will wreak havoc on your life.

One of the Tya Practice's secrets involves guiding you to "detune" or adopt a higher perspective without judgment toward anything that lowers your vibration. The desired outcome of this practice is to elevate your default vibration. Elevating your default vibration aligns you with your personal connection to Source—your Stream. This connection carries significant benefits. First, it enhances your joy, resulting in an overall improved sense of self and the world around you when you allow our energy to flow through you. Second, it provides greater clarity. Your perception of yourself and your world differs considerably when you vibrate at a higher, positive frequency compared to a lower one. To illustrate, try reading something you wrote in a high-vibration state when you are in a low-vibration state. The words will appear foreign to you, and you may question your thought process during that time. When you're in a high-vibration state, you are essentially a different vibrational being than when you're in a low one. Releasing negativity and allowing the clarity of our energy into your life can lead to substantial positive changes. We'll delve deeper into this later.

If you have transgressors—and everyone does, referring to any person, circumstance, or event from your past or present that you can't fully appreciate—you have some work to do. These are the triggers that can send you spiraling down and distance you from your abundance. Once you comprehend the nature of your transgressors and understand that you attracted all of them through the Law of Attraction, you can begin to appreciate even the things that seem unimaginable to have attracted, such as childhood trauma, for instance.

These teachings will illuminate how you unintentionally or unknowingly attract suffering and why it's not about blaming the victim but rather understanding the universal process of creation. If you're experiencing suffering, this knowledge can offer you peace as you consider these concepts.

You might often find yourself saying things like, "I'm stuck in this area," or that you can't overcome doubt or fear on a specific topic. You're likely aware that being trapped in disbelief results in disallowance. Yet, you find yourself stuck and unable to break free, causing immense frustration. You understand the Law of Attraction and see it in action in your life and the lives of others, but it doesn't seem to work consistently across all areas. You may easily manifest some things while struggling with others. For example, you might have no trouble making friends and getting invited to social events but struggle with financial abundance, while your wealthy sibling has few friends. Or you may have excellent health and financial stability but face challenges in romantic relationships. Why does this happen?

The answer lies in the negative experiences that form the foundations of your limiting beliefs. When you chose to manifest as a human on Earth, you intentionally placed yourself in the realm of duality. You vibrationally aligned with a set of circumstances, including your parents, race, religion, and nationality, that would create a unique mix of both desired and undesired experiences to enrich your life journey.

From your eternal perspective, you understood that you would come to Earth desiring freedom and joy. This is how you exist in your "completed state," which you might call death or pre-birth, your non-physical, eternal state of being. However, you also desired the duality offered in a physical environment, knowing it would inspire you to want more, to be more, to have more, and perhaps even to overcome challenges.

The more challenges you placed upon yourself, the more you desired to overcome them, thus expanding in the process. Your new creation is your expansion, and as you expand, you move closer to the core of Source energy, where we reside. Your expansion into that core contributes to our expansion, which in turn is the expansion of the entire universe. This is why what you consider negative experiences are so valuable and should be embraced rather than feared.

We understand that many of you have "negative" people, circumstances, and events that are difficult to embrace. How can you embrace things like murder, rape, and child abuse? We do not expect you to suddenly long for these things or to instantaneously forgive and forget if you've had such transgressors impact your life. However, from our perspective, we see that you are all eternal beings having a temporary human life experience. We understand how that which you consider evil in your world only holds the power you give it through your attention. We also see how some of you overcome horrific events, and we witness the significant expansion that arises from such overcoming. We see the bigger picture. As humans, you may not have that perspective because you've allowed your ego consciousness to overshadow your eternal soul consciousness. This is by design. You came here to have a unique human experience, one of duality—the continuous oscillation between what you consider positive and negative. Both aspects serve a noble purpose: expansion through new creation.

You see, all suffering is a matter of judgment. It is entirely possible to have any experience in your earthly journey and simply not judge it as wrong or evil or as something that "should not be." However, judgment is pervasive in your current matrix, and humanity is deeply entrenched in it. Even as you progress beyond the judgment-laden constraints of the matrix, such as gender roles and identity, you might observe humans circling back into the matrix by seeking validation within their less-constrained identities. For instance, a human up to speed with the evolving vibration of humanity may decide not to identify with their assigned gender at birth, seeking to step out of the matrix on that topic. However, what is often witnessed in such scenarios is a relabeling of the new identity, followed by the expectation that others must instantly adapt to their crafted identity. Subsequently, judgment of those who are not up to speed with this labeling ensues, leading right back into the matrix.

The matrix is polarized, whereas the universe or energetic realm is not. The energetic realm, our perspective, remains neutral. We appreciate those who seek to avoid labeling as much as those who desire everyone to adhere to their assigned labels. We do not judge suffering, death, or even things you've been programmed to view as horrific. This does not mean we do not love you or desire joyous life experiences for you; it means we see you as eternal beings undergoing a temporary physical experience, one that you cannot possibly get wrong, as every experience and life path offers expansion.

We also want you to understand that we do not judge the matrix, nor do we guide you to do so. Instead, we guide you to observe what belongs to the matrix and what pertains to the universe. The universe, or Source, embodies universal law—the Law of Attraction and the law of polarity, also known as the universal process of creation, as we often refer to these two principles. While Source exists in all things, the matrix, being polarized, is about separation from Source. This is why we encourage you to observe and understand when you are within or outside the matrix, and Tya is a practice that guides you steadily out of it for the rest of your life, should you choose.

Appreciation, meaning deep understanding to the point where judgment is impossible, is a practice that will liberate you from the matrix. It is a key element of Tya and how we perceive all creation. You can adopt appreciation for any topic, even those you've been taught that you cannot. For this reason, we often refer to this level of appreciation as "radical" appreciation because it is radical to most of humanity.

Full, radical appreciation of all your transgressors is your only path to complete relief from them. No more triggers dragging you down your spiral. No more persistent roots of unwanted beliefs and fears. Each of your unwanted beliefs has an origin, often in early childhood. A passing comment by a parent about your appearance, intelligence, or behavior, perhaps made while they were in a low-vibrational state, planted a seed. Although it may seem inconsequential from your adult perspective, it was monumental from your childhood viewpoint. Left unaddressed, this seed grew into more beliefs of a similar nature.

As an example, a parent may have casually told a child not to overeat, stating, "Eating that will make you fat," while they were in a low vibrational state. The child may have interpreted this as, "Being fat is bad, and my parent will not love me if I become fat." Consequently, the child developed worries about gaining weight, which attracted the condition of being overweight. Being overweight made the child feel unworthy, and they subsequently attracted others who shared this sense of unworthiness. This led to a cycle of bullying, feelings of unworthiness, overeating to soothe emotional pain, and guilt over overeating. Children often carry this cycle, originating from a small, seemingly insignificant seed, well into adulthood, and it may persist throughout their entire lives.

Since you always attract what you focus upon, the same scenario may play out when there's an intense focus on the opposite of being fat, such as being thin. The focus on thinness attracts that state but can also result in what you label as an eating disorder. In this case, food may be consumed in a self-loathing state, followed by more extreme measures to maintain the focus on thinness as a means to receive love.

This illustrates how unwanted and limiting beliefs begin to form. If you are a parent, you will inevitably present challenges to your child; it's part of universal design.

Parents are meant to provide obstacles to their children; duality exists in all topics. Even the most loving and well-intentioned parents will experience their own downward spirals, leading them to create challenges for their children. Polarity, both positive and negative, exists in all aspects of life.

The practice of appreciation is a fundamental component of the Tya Practice because it involves detuning transgressors through complete appreciation. By appreciating all your transgressors, you free yourself from the most painful memories that lower your vibration. As you raise your vibration to the top of your spiral, you gain the ability to perceive your life and your world differently. You come to understand that you manifest obstacles—sometimes significant ones—as launchpads for new creation, as there is growth inherent in overcoming them. From this perspective, you can appreciate all the things in your life that you perceive as negative. Pain, suffering, and fear all serve a higher purpose in a physical environment. Once you master this higher perspective, you will fear obstacles less, attracting fewer of them, and you will face the ones you do encounter with joy, understanding that you created them and therefore possess the power to overcome and even expand from them.

Appreciation transitions your entire life into a positive vibration where everything serves you. Appreciation from the highest perspective, our perspective, is available to you at all times. We do not judge, nor do we impose a desired behavior on creation. While we are Source—the origin of all creation—we do not dictate or judge what occurs on your planet. We comprehend that this current lifetime may seem like your entire existence, but we assure you that it is not the case. You are eternal, and this life is fleeting, merely a speck compared to the wholeness of what you are. You are part of us, and we are part of you. That's why our higher perspective is accessible to you; you only need to use your imagination to bridge the gap.

Picture your life and your world from our perspective. We see you as eternal, and we view you with pure love. We observe the negative events in your life without judgment, understanding that they are as much your creation as everything else in your reality. Once you accept that you manifest it all, and that it can all serve you, your life can truly take off.

Qatarina

In my conversations with fellow practitioners on the winding path of Tya Practice, I've observed a common thread—many seem to hit a roadblock at the very first pillar, Appreciation. Some even throw in the towel at this juncture. How intriguing it is that this initial step presents such a challenge.

As I alluded to in my introduction, my journey into the depths of forgiveness began when I stumbled upon *A Course in Miracles* and later, *Conversations with God*. It was during this voyage that I stumbled upon a startling revelation: forgiveness could actually be enjoyable! There was a precise method to it: commence with someone dear to your heart, then gradually ascend the ladder to those who have deeply "wronged you." It's undoubtedly easier to forgive your best friend for scuffing your shoes than it is to forgive a childhood abuser, but the process remains fundamentally the same.

By the time I embraced forgiveness, even for the dark chapters of my past involving sexual abuse, I felt transformed. I felt as if a weight of a hundred pounds had been lifted off my shoulders. But little did I know, this was just the beginning of my odyssey.

Somewhere along the way, I had overlooked a crucial aspect—forgiving *myself*. When I embarked on the Tya Practice, I believed I was already well-versed in the art of forgiveness, but little did I realize that forgiving myself would prove to be the most formidable challenge. It hadn't been emphasized in those spiritual teachings that I remembered, so it had quietly slipped through the cracks of my understanding.

I had never comprehended the magnitude of guilt and shame that I carried with me constantly. There was always that nagging voice within me suggesting that I was undeserving of whatever desires I held close to my heart.

The detuning techniques introduced in the Tya Practice (more on that later) began to reshape my perspective. I gradually came to understand that I am inherently worthy and deserving of any reality I choose to manifest for myself. When I applied this newfound self-compassion, forgiving those I felt wronged by, this state of being became a natural consequence, even though I thought I had already done so. It turns out, forgiveness was not what I had initially perceived it to be; it was, in essence, a journey to authentic appreciation.

When it all boiled down, I realized that, despite my "mistakes," I had always acted to the best of my knowledge at any given moment. And if that was the case for me, then it was undoubtedly true for others as well. There existed no absolute evil—only the duality of life and the earthly challenges that led to judgments. No one had entered this world with the sole mission to cause me harm; they were merely fellow beings navigating their own path of duality and contrast. Yes, our journeys occasionally intersected, resulting in challenges, but perceiving them as opportunities for mutual growth altered my entire perspective.

It turns out that all that extensive study on "forgiveness" had been merely a stepping stone on my path, leading me to the very first pillar of the Tya Practice: Appreciation.

As I embark on a dialogue with the Stream, I want to emphasize that for those who have endured substantial physical and emotional scars, embracing appreciation can be an arduous task. Although I began exploring this concept with *A Course in Miracles* many moons ago, it wasn't until my foray into Tya that I truly grasped its significance.

On some level, I thought I comprehended the importance of forgiveness. Or so I believed. However, it was the journey toward finding appreciation for our transgressors that truly transformed my perspective—and my life.

Questions for the Stream Regarding Appreciation

Question from Qatarina: What would you say to someone struggling with this massive concept? Specifically those suffering from PTSD from things they feel were completely out of their control? Touching specifically on:

- Abusive or "toxic" parents

- Rape and sexual trauma

- Bullying

- Gaslighting

Answer from the Stream: We will begin by stating that we understand the point of view of someone who feels victimized. It is natural for you to manifest things in your life that you haven't consciously desired. We view things from a different perspective—one where you are an eternal being having a temporary life experience on Planet Earth, one of countless experiences. In this perspective, you understand the true nature of what you consider good and evil. You see your transgressors (and we are addressing all of you collectively, not just Qatarina) and the "bad" things that happen to you very differently.

You comprehend that you placed yourself in the path of duality—encompassing both positive and negative conditions—before birth. You understand that you chose a certain level of difficulty in life to face the challenge of overcoming, or even not overcoming, it, and that regardless of the outcome, you would expand in the process. There is value in your pain, and there is great value in moving past or overcoming that pain.

You observe evidence all around you that all life forms face challenges, and some overcome and grow stronger in the process while others do not. Many pass away and return to their completed state without overcoming; there is nothing wrong with that experience either. There is expansive value in all experiences, even in the lessons learned from not overcoming. But your favorite stories are those of triumph—of individuals who are perhaps born into great adversity and find the light to lift themselves out of the darkness. Why is that? It's because, from your higher soul-consciousness perspective, you understand that you are here to place obstacles, even those you don't consciously realize you are placing, and then to overcome them. The act of overcoming is your expansion because you create in the process.

Notice how you are often taught in your current society that life should be fair, that those who have "good things" are often perceived as evil, and that the solution to humanity's problems lies in demonizing transgressors—those who take, even abuse and harm others. Notice how this demonization—focusing on the trans-

gressor and denying any ownership of unwanted manifestations—never truly resolves anything on a grand
scale. Humanity repeatedly cycles between victim and
aggressor throughout recorded history up to your present
moment. In sharing our message, both David and Qatarina have faced criticism for supposedly "blaming the
victim." Our message is free from judgment, so there is
no blame—no fault—everything is a co-creation through
vibrational flow, not driven by desire, retribution, or de-
servingness. Understanding vibrational flow and how it
delivers a mixture of wanted and unwanted experiences,
as well as claiming full ownership of all your life experiences, will place you in the true one percent of humanity—those who genuinely comprehend the universal
process of creation. Armed with this knowledge, you
become unstoppable and possess the tools to transform
the most negative experiences into instruments for expansion. We encourage you to open your minds to these
concepts if they resonate with you, as there are many
teachings within the matrix that keep you locked in a
perpetual victim state, robbing you of your true creative
power to manifest the reality you desire. The choice is
yours.

So yes, someone who has suffered extreme abuse did
indeed co-create that experience, often not from a conscious perspective. Few of you would consciously desire
to be abused, yet it happens to many. These experiences
are often set in motion even before birth through your
intention to enter into more challenging circumstances,

such as being born to abusive parents or facing other adverse conditions. The abusive vibrational frequency of a parent can lead to a sense of unworthiness, which in turn can attract further abuse in the form of bullying, physical, emotional, and sexual abuse. These patterns tend to gain momentum over time if left unaddressed. The mentally abused child can become the physically abused adolescent, who then transforms into the sexually abused teenager. This cycle can persist throughout a lifetime if the individual remains focused—often out of fear—on the same unwanted circumstances.

You might read this and think, "This is so unfair; why does the abused child have to endure a life of escalating abuse?" We are here to tell you that human desire for fairness is rarely achieved and certainly not guaranteed in your world. Is there any evidence to the contrary? Physical life is not inherently fair; you are not all the same, and your higher intention is not one of fairness but rather one of expansion through overcoming obstacles.

We hold only love for you, and we want you to understand that you are not here for fairness, perfection, or a life of gentle ease. You are here for struggle, for challenges, to navigate through difficulties, and, if you so choose, to find the light within the darkness. These experiences provide the grit that creates traction—life experiences that take you deeper, prompting you to question everything and seek answers to difficult questions. These experiences facilitate your expansion because you must create new, improvement-oriented thoughts in order to overcome them, and that improvement holds more power than you may currently understand.

Given that this is a significant topic for many, we've broken down some common examples of traumatic experiences and provided our perspective on them. We share this with the intention of aiding in the process of detuning from these examples.

"Toxic" Parents

We will begin by sharing that the word "toxic" carries a victim-like quality in its vibration. It's common for humans to label others as "toxic" and then proceed to describe scenarios where there is no acknowledgment of co-creative ownership within the relationship. This tendency is particularly prevalent when referring to parents.

But how can a child co-create toxic parents? Most parents don't consciously aim to be toxic, and children choose their parents vibrationally before manifesting at conception. This vibrational selection is made with full awareness of the parents' nature and their potential to provide a lower-vibrational experience for the child. The soul consciousness, the spark of intelligence that creates a newborn child, comprehends the challenging experiences that come with this choice. Remember, you come to this physical plane to experience both positive and negative aspects, and you are all born in alignment with the time period you are born into. Your parents were born in alignment with their era, as were your grandparents, and so forth.

Consider the gap between your understanding of your current cultural reality and that of your parents. Notice the even wider gap between your generation and that of your grandparents; you couldn't live your life the same way your grandparents did. This difference arises due to generational variances designed to provide a certain level of challenge, regardless of the parents' intentions.

These generational distinctions will naturally create some obstacles, and they can be compounded by other lower-vibrational influences, which can result in an upbringing that ranges from challenging to "toxic" to outright abusive. Each of these experiences presents the child's soul with an opportunity for expansion through facing and overcoming the challenges posed by the relationship, particularly through the detuning process.

Rape and Sexual Trauma

This is one of the most challenging topics for humans to detune due to the taboo nature of sexual activity within your society and its often violent physical aspects. We will begin by reiterating once again that these experiences are not attracted because of a conscious desire for them, a sense of deserving them, or as a form of karmic retribution for past actions. Instead, they are attracted through various dominant vibrations that can activate co-creative energy, resulting in "unwanted" things, such as transgressors. These vibrations include the powerful influence of fear, absorbed from fear-based teachings or the pervasive fear vibration present in the matrix. Fear is a potent force that stirs strong emotions and permeates humanity as a dominant driving energy. This collective consciousness of fear brings forth many undesirable manifestations in your world, ultimately serving as a catalyst for new creation, as we have explained.

Other factors that can align an individual vibrationally with such experiences include a dominant vibration of lacking well-being, focusing on being taken advantage of rather than prioritizing safety. A dominant vibration of desiring physical contact and companionship stemming from a lack of self-worth can also lead to such manifestations.

There are intentions for experiencing duality that precede your manifestation into the physical. These intentions can be challenging to grasp from your human perspective. From your desire for comfort and ease, it may be hard to fathom wanting to expose yourselves to trauma. However, your eternal perspective differs significantly from your ego-driven desire for well-being. These experiences are not directly desired, but the vibrational path is set, and alignment with unwanted, sometimes extremely unwanted, experiences occurs.

These vibrations hold immense power, and when they intersect with an individual in the vibration of desiring power from their fear-based, lower vibration, it can result in a forced sexual act that is deeply traumatic for the victim.

For those who have been victims of such events, the healing journey can be a profound period of self-discovery, and it may take time to process and emerge from it with clarity. Your world often labels you as a victim and surrounds you with a sense of loathing for the perpetrator. You may replay the event in your mind repeatedly until you develop coping mechanisms and learn to function despite the trauma. Some individuals remain so entrenched in this vibration that they continue to manifest similar events, living in a pattern of abuse.

Understanding the Law of Attraction and polarity means truly comprehending that nothing is about blame or fault; it's about vibrational alignment. For those who are new to these teachings, subjects like this can be challenging to grasp from a higher perspective. Trauma itself is a potent vibration that must be individually addressed as the victim's perspective evolves. The crucial aspect is allowing your perspective to evolve.

When someone who has directly experienced violent or traumatic acts reaches a point in their healing process where they can align with the idea that the event was their manifestation from a higher perspective, it marks a significant breakthrough. This understanding is distinct from assigning blame and fault; it arises from recognizing that the event was born of a vibrational path that aligned them with the manifestation. This realization is powerful and signifies the beginning of profound healing and genuine transformation. It occurs when the victim no longer wishes to remain a victim, when the understanding of vibration, polarity, and the vibrational flow created by polarity and the environment is fully grasped. When every other typical avenue has been explored, and nothing has provided relief, the clarity of how creation truly occurs and the perfection within imperfection becomes fully realized.

This is genuine healing—detuning through appreciation. It is a potent, unique, and individual path that few choose to embark upon. However, the results are real, the transformation runs deep, and the healing becomes a gift.

Bullying

Once again, we emphasize that a lack of self-worth is the primary contributor to the vibration that places an individual in the path of bullying. As a human, your perspective has been shaped by the matrix, and from this perspective, your world may indeed appear to be a cruel place. Being perceived as different often attracts feelings of not being "as good as" others, and this sense of unworthiness only serves to draw more external confirmation of those feelings.

The essential point we wish to convey regarding universal law is that physical experiences are intended to encompass both challenges and opportunities, both the desired and the undesired. Prolonged exposure to the undesired aspects presents every being with a choice: either learn to cope with the persistent challenges or seek a solution. Solutions can take various forms.

A low-vibration solution may involve thoughts of suicide or descending into the depths of ongoing depression. A higher, though still "low-vibration" solution might entail gathering the inner strength to fight back, to engage in the struggle, whether verbally or physically. The outcome of this struggle can vary depending on the intensity of the vibration behind the action. If the fight arises from an inner fire that has been smoldering all along, the result can be a profound expansion through newfound courage. The highest-vibrational solution, however, involves forging a path of self-worth and focusing on self-appreciation, which in turn garners appreciation from others. In this state, bullies are no longer attracted to you and simply fade from your life. Yes, you possess the power to bring about this transformation!

Gaslighting

Consider this as another form of bullying. We guide you to step into your sense of self-worth and permit anyone who seeks to treat you this way to naturally fade from your life. Do you believe this is impossible due to a family relationship? Take a moment to reflect on where this notion is rooted. Is it rooted in fear, tradition, or a sense of duty? If your desire is to lead a joyous and abundant life, then there is nothing more crucial than discovering your powerful place of joy, clarity, and abundance—nothing! Your ability to offer the most to your world emerges when you are in a high vibrational state of alignment with all that you desire. Therefore, we strongly advise against allowing anyone to keep you away from that state due to some human-created connection, especially if they are treating you poorly. Love yourself more and observe how the landscape of your life's relationships begins to shift. Lower-vibrational individuals gradually fade away, making room for new, higher-vibrational connections to enter your life.

Q: How can we be certain that we have genuinely reached a state of appreciation for these things, rather than merely convincing ourselves that we have accepted them?

A: When you think about a transgressor and only feel good, only feel appreciation for what they offered you, you have detuned them. Your transgressors are your teachers, and they are *your* manifestations. See them as such, and they no longer hold power over you—the triggers are gone. If they are human, it does not matter whether you speak to them and tell them you forgive them or not. This is truly not about them at all, but about your perception of them and what they did to you, and how that served your expansion of consciousness.

Q: What kind of symptoms can we expect as our perspectives shift?

A: A stress-free lightness. An ability to move up your spiral with ease and appreciate all aspects of your world. An ability to see the universe, Planet Earth, and humanity and your own life form a higher, non-judgmental perspective. When you work toward this feeling regularly, you will soon begin to see evidence popping up in your life. Strangers are friendlier, you notice birds chirping, traffic moves for you—or perhaps it does not and you find something to look at and appreciate while you wait. Life just gets better. If you continue working this high vibe, more good will come—every single time!

Q: What do you have to say about the term, "Forgive and forget"? It is very clear now what purpose forgiveness serves, but how do you suggest we keep these experiences in mind for the future? To avoid placing ourselves back in the same situations over and over?

A: As you work to continually raise your vibration through meditation, appreciation, and simply viewing your physical existence from a higher perspective, you get better and better at breaking old, unwanted cycles. Fear dissipates and old negative patterns transform. You reach a state of 'knowing' where you understand that you are no longer the same person as you were when you manifested that unwanted thing—and that you now have the ability to rise above and not have old triggers impact you any longer. Think of it as forgiving, appreciating, and understanding that you never have to endure anything like it again with your new, powerful Tya tools.

Q: How can we discern when it is best to just end a relationship/avoid a situation altogether versus continuing while focusing on appreciation? Especially if we consistently go DTS about it? When is enough enough? How do we know if we should keep trying?

A: Ask yourself, "Why am I continuing to do this?" If the word "fear" surfaces as a factor, you've found your clarity. For instance, inquire, "Why am I still tolerating XYZ? Despite my journey toward full appreciation, this undesired thing persists, and its impact endures." If your response reveals that you've mostly detuned this undesired element by finding appreciation for it, you'll likely sense a softening or even a complete departure from it (whether it's a person, circumstance, or event). However, if your answer is, "I am afraid that if I walk away, XYZ will happen..." then you've allowed fear to keep you in a place you'd rather not be, even after detuning it. We consistently encourage you to eliminate fear from any subject to attain genuine clarity.

The decision to detune will naturally arise as you integrate the Tya Practice into your life. Initially, when it feels more like an effort, you'll notice that as you concentrate on elevating your vibration, increasing self-love, and uncovering the "silver lining" through the detuning process, your relationships will transform without you actively trying. Those who hold you in high regard will embrace your more confident and joyful state of being. Those who prefer your previous lower-vibrational self and can't appreciate your newfound abundance will naturally fade from your life. This fading will become something you adjust to swiftly as you embrace your higher-vibrational new reality.

If the notion of this provokes fear, it's perfectly normal. This practice is a journey, and the things that currently alarm you will diminish as you engage in the prescribed work within these pages. You detune fear, and the things you fear, including the impact of those changes, begin to fade. Embracing the mantra, "The universe always pampers me," is a potent way to meet the unknown with confident joy. These challenges become more manageable within your high-vibrational flow, but this practice also involves building trust during the lower-vibrational phases, and that's where the magic unfolds.

Regarding whether you should "keep trying," relationships in a high vibrational state are never about trying. The Tya Practice is founded on trust, and when you trust the universal process of creation, you perceive every aspect of your life journey as an experience. In this state of trust, you allow your experiences to flow in and out effortlessly, without the need to cling or "try."

Q: Now, what about the situations and people we just absolutely *can't* avoid (like abusive parents or a sibling who always complains or criticizes)?

A: Detuning via appreciation works every time on every topic—find appreciation and watch as rigid facades fade away and behavior toward you improves. This can be as instantaneous as you allow.

Q: Are there other ways the situations will resolve? Such as the other person moving away, losing touch, or (perhaps in some cases) even passing away? I've noticed many people simply drifted out of my life when I got serious about my Tya Practice.

A: As we stated above, as you raise your vibration, the landscape of your associations with others will shift. Those operating at a lower vibration will either not be able to handle the more abundant version of you and will distance themselves naturally, or they will find their own appreciation for your expansion and likely ask what you are doing that is driving your positive change. You will come to see who your true, high-vibrational friends are—those who appreciate the evolving you.

Q: How would you guide someone who is not able to identify their transgressor because they have buried the memory of a childhood trauma or the memory is so traumatic they are not able to revisit it?

A: Though you will be well-served by detuning all the transgressors in your life, we do not guide you to dive deep into your psyche without making peace with the fact that there may be some things that will take time to detune. We suggest working on the identifiable things first, then moving into tackling other things as they bubble up to your awareness and present themselves for detuning. This is actually a life-long process that will get easier as you allow this practice to become your new lifestyle and you raise your default vibration systematically—which will become your new state of being. Eventually all will be revealed, but if you feel that something is stuck and needs to be addressed, but you cannot identify what it is, you may wish to try using your imagination to create a scenario to detune. Remember that your imagination is a powerful creator and that you can craft and detune by filling in the missing gaps with your imagination.

Q: How can we convey these concepts to our children?

A: The sooner a person learns that getting what you want out of life is more about vibration than fairness, the more effective they will become. Teach your young ones to focus upon what they want rather than wasting time fearing what they do not. Teach them that they can truly manifest anything they desire and that rules and limitations should always be questioned. Teach them that how they treat themselves and others will have a great impact on what is coming into their lives, and that sometimes they will go DTS and attract things that they do not want. Teach them that this is okay, for they cannot attract and thus create a situation that they cannot also overcome—one way or another.

Teach them that holding onto anger and other lower-vibration emotions only holds them away from their own joy and thus their own abundance. Teach them that their transgressors become their teachers if they hold them in full appreciation and use every life experience as a launchpad for expansion—which is every soul's true desire in manifesting in physical form. Teach them that every experience can make them stronger and wiser if they focus on appreciation for all their manifestations—both wanted and unwanted—rather than looking upon anything with shame, anger, or regret.

Q: Any parting thoughts on the Pillar of Appreciation?

A: When you finally come to understand that you are all vibrational beings experiencing the Earth environment in a physical vehicle, with your vibration traveling up and down a vibrational spiral, manifesting a constant mix of wanted and unwanted things, you can begin to operate your lives very differently than you have been taught. You now have the ability to see how unwanted things serve to inspire new creation, and how the unwanted things in your lives—the things you need to let go of and fully appreciate—serve a great purpose. These things are your teachers—they are your inspiration. The pain you may have endured as a result of these transgressors was only painful because of your perception of them. Even physical pain is made more severe by your pushing against it. Emotional pain—trauma—is the same; your pushing against rather than appreciating is the thing that makes it so unbearable.

You each have the power to manage past and even present pain very differently. Appreciate what it is doing for you—what it is teaching you or causing you to desire. If you are broke, appreciate that being broke is the first step into manifesting wealth. If you are physically ill, appreciate that you will feel so much better when you are healthy. If you are alone, know that loving yourself and your solitude will vibrationally align you with others who hold you in the same high regard. If you are not happy with your appearance, know that there is a more appealing version of you emerging from within, born of your newfound love of you—as you are! These may seem simple, but they are powerful tools that you likely have never thought of trying, and they are quite effective.

Forgiveness all the way to full appreciation of your transgressors will set you free. Viewing the unwanted things in your life with appreciation will raise your vibration and keep you from manifesting things of like nature again in the future, for what you look upon in anger and regret and frustration will only persist—those negative emotions are powerful creators of unwanted things and keep you bogged down in cycles of negative manifestations—the very things you do not want. No longer holding negative emotion toward transgressors will attract fewer unwanted things into your life, and when you do attract an obstacle, you will meet it in joy, knowing that you hold the power to use it to launch your next new brilliant creation.

Summary of Our Shared Consciousness

The concept of forgiveness across humanity often tends to be the vibration of 'I'll choose to let you off the hook and get over it.' There is relief offered in that vibration, but we are guiding you well past that in this practice. This is because we see you as the eternal strand of consciousness that you truly are. We know that nothing that occurs in your world could possibly damage or 'end' you on a quantum level. We view what you perceive as a lifetime as a brief experience—not all that is. For this reason, we do not judge what occurs in your lifetimes.

From this higher perspective, nothing is unforgivable, and every experience—from the most joyous to the most traumatic—can be appreciated, meaning deeply understood with gratitude, for the expansive experience that it truly is. You see, keeping you in victimhood robs you of your power. Long ago, many of the 'leaders' of your world who understood how the Universal Process of Creation actually works decided to craft a path to controlling that information. You may have noticed that humans have a knack for seeking to control valuable resources for the purpose of commerce. One of the most lucrative commodities in your world is information because knowledge is power. Once someone knows how to do something, be something, or have something, they no longer need it from others. Since abundance is a natural state of being for all beings, the idea of harnessing abundance became a very profitable proposition.

How do you hold others away from their natural state of abundance? Tell them it does not exist. Make a compelling case for operating in a templated belief system, where a supreme being is the decider of abundance—some are blessed, and some are not. Tell them that this supreme being wants them to live humbly, and that all their 'low-vibrational' manifestations are acts of an opposite, demonic being. Essentially, take their natural creative power away by creating external sources of good and evil and then convince them to live in a worship/fear cycle that holds their vibration in check.

As humans begin to question these institutions of control and perhaps notice that the leaders that are telling them to live humbly are not following their own advice, then shift to another version of this—focus on the good and evil external human forces as the cause of all your woes and triumphs. That bad thing that happened was not your fault; you were a victim! And that good thing was luck—good fortune. The universe sent you a gift!

Do you see these in play in your world? This is the matrix we speak of. Do you see how it robs you of your own abundant nature? Your creative power? We're not sharing this to spin a conspiracy theory but to illustrate how humanity's mainstream teachings serve to usurp your true abundant nature. Deep appreciation sets you free from these transgressors and provides a far higher perspective of your Earthly experience.

As you learn to 'zoom out' to our higher perspective by removing fear and judgment from any topic, you will begin to view your lives and your world very differently. As you learn to meet any obstacle—any transgressor—in joy, you will begin to understand how conditioned you've been all along in your thinking.

As you move through lower-vibrational periods, you will begin to gain clarity on the gifts in those moments. Your old 'down' time will become a practice of relaxing into noticing triggers and other hidden or dormant transgressors that reveal themselves when you're DTS. You'll learn to just love and appreciate the transgressor, if nothing else than for the clarity of what is revealed that you have been harboring, perhaps for years, that serves as the root of emotional triggers and limiting beliefs.

Simply confronting your transgressor mentally and being with them as you breathe and remove fear and judgment until all negative emotion is replaced with the warmth of Source will prove life-changing. We will go deeper into processes later in this book and we will encourage you to begin a practice of 'Radical Appreciation' or RA as the first pillar of your Tya Practice.

The powerful concept of living free from fear and judgment.

Adi H., Tya Bootcamp Graduate

When my parents passed away, I faced significant challenges, mostly involving major betrayal by a close family member. Despite the turmoil, I later realized that without these events, many blessings would not have taken place after. This emphasizes the importance of finding the silver lining even in painful changes.

It began with my parents' need for 24-hour care at the age of 97. Because of my concern about this family member's involvement, my daughter who lived several states away, made the significant decision to move and help her grandparents. Her previous relationship ending in her boyfriend's murder played a part in her decision.

During the process of handling my parents' estate, I discovered a discrepancy of a large sum of money from my parents' account. Legal measures were taken, and despite the difficulties, I took charge of my parents' affairs, supported my daughter, and cared for my parents, driving long distances for appointments. During this tumultuous period, a tarot card reading revealed an unusual message about a baby on the way, leading to further unexpected events.

Amid this challenging chapter, I focused on doing what's right rather than seeking revenge. The strained family dynamics weighed heavily. Remarkably, my daughter's journey took a surprising turn while abroad, where she met someone, leading to an extraordinary event—a child, fostering gratitude and belief in life's purpose.

Thanks to my Tya Practice, I harbor no anger. I even composed (and sent) a therapeutic letter expressing appreciation to the aforementioned family member. Appreciation transcends mere gratitude, enabling us to release negative emotions. It wasn't something done to me; it was done for me.

What I find remarkable about this story is how two traumatic events unfolded: the murder of my daughter's ex-boyfriend, which led to her seeking involvement in my parent's care, and the family betrayal, which eventually resulted in my daughter coming back into my life, embarking on her European journey, and ultimately having a child. It's like a complex chess game where you can trace the sequence of events that brought us to this point. Had we chosen to demonize that relative or fixate on the tragedy of the ex-boyfriend's murder, we might not have experienced this full circle of events. In essence, appreciation shifted my perspective and allowed me to see the positive aspects even in challenging situations. Appreciation became my lifeline. It allowed me to release the suffering I had endured for so long. Whenever I felt myself spiraling down, I knew I could turn to appreciation. I even applied this principle to challenging physical experiences, such as breaking my arm. Instead of dwelling on the injury, I embraced it for the lessons it brought. I attribute much of this transformation to the Tya tools and teachings that have guided me, which I hold dear and even have printed over my fireplace as a constant reminder of their importance in my life.

Exercises

Use a notebook or purchase an appreciation journal for these exercises. Once you discover the power in detuning your life's transgressors via appreciation, you will make this an ongoing lifetime practice.

1. List your life's transgressors—any person, circumstance, or event, past or present, that you do not fully appreciate. In the beginning, list the things that impact you directly, not things like "world hunger" unless you've actually been impacted by that.

Next, grade these items 'A' for things you can easily see yourself detuning with a bit of appreciation work. Start your practice with these smaller things. As with all things, appreciation is a vibration that builds momentum the more you practice it. Because of this, there will be things that seem impossible to detune now that you will automatically detune later as this becomes your new way of life.

For each 'A' transgressor, set aside time to sit quietly and privately and breathe using the 888 breathing technique: breathe in through your nose for a slow count of eight.

Then hold your breath for another count of eight. Finally, release for a count of eight. Wait a moment and then repeat a few times until you feel relaxed.

You are now in meditation mode. As you relax and feel better and better, you are allowing Source to step forward and calm your ego. If your ego acts up, and it likely will, simply acknowledge it and refocus on your breath.

Now, think about your first 'A' transgressor. Think of something to appreciate about them/it without judging or fearing them/it. This is your personal space, and there are no wrong or right thoughts, just those that are being experienced in the moment. It's okay to think differently about a transgressor. In this space, you do not need to judge or fear—you are the creator of this experience.

Perhaps your starting point is to simply appreciate the fact that you survived the transgressor. That you learned what you did not desire. Start wherever you can, and then move up vibrationally to more positive thoughts on the topic. Allow momentum to build.

Write the things you appreciate in your journal under the heading of your 'A' transgressor.

Example:

Childhood bully

1. I survived you

2. You made me smarter by learning how to defuse

you

3. I realized how much others cared about me when they came to my defense

4. I see now that you were acting in your own insecurity, needing to belittle me to make yourself feel better

5. I know now that I attracted you based on how I felt about myself at the time. You were a reflection of how I thought about myself

II. After you've detuned many of your 'A' transgressors, it's time to move on to your 'B,' or more serious transgressors. The process is the same, but we recommend treading lightly into these more-challenging topics. Ultimately, you can find authentic appreciation for anything and detune its power over you. Please note that the larger transgressors of your life will take time to detune, and they may return until you've fully detuned them over time. The important thing to know is that any and every transgressor can be detuned.

III. Once you've created enough momentum with the detuning power of authentic appreciation, you will find life's greatest transgressors can also be detuned. We do not recommend attempting this until you are deeper into the Tya Practice, after you've completed this book and have been practicing for a while.

The collective ego consciousness of humanity, aka the matrix, has trained us that there are certain acts and events that are "unforgivable." This is a tool of the matrix to keep you in it, and it will continue to have a hold on you for a while as you work through your life's personal transgressors.

The Tya Practice will create an awakening within you that will allow you to evolve your worldview. Please allow time for this evolution to occur before returning to this section and moving on to the detuning process for these major transgressors of the matrix.

Polarity

The Stream

"Humans who explore spirituality may encounter teach-ings about achieving some state of perfection, or en-lightenment, or perhaps about humanity ascending to a higher state of being that delivers universal harmony, or 'new earth.' We are here to tell you that you are not here for that. You see, you come to the physical realm to encounter both positive things that you discern as your preference and negative or unwanted things that you discern as not your preference. It is important in this practice for you to understand that you came to this planet with the desire to manifest and allow the unwant-ed—your obstacles—to drive new creation.

Obstacles are a natural element in any physical environ-ment. The obstacle causes you to want more—to create. You observe various elements of your physical environ-ment and you discern your preference. You align with that preference and allow the universe to bring it to full manifestation and new creation occurs. A new feeling, a new thought, a new human creation, and even new natural creations are all a result of consciousness focusing upon something new; this drives the expansion and thus the creation and recreation (which is the same as expansion) of the entire universe. This is the process of universal creation.

This is why polarity is so important. Polarity is the universal force that keeps all things in a guaranteed, never-ending state of expansion. Polarity exists to create tension; this tension keeps every single element of the universe in its intended state of omnifarious creation. The universal law of polarity has been explored and expressed in multiple cultures on your planet; it has been labeled Yin and Yang in Chinese philosophy and has also been referred to as duality, among many other things. Evidence of polarity is all around you—there is duality in all topics. From your human perspective, you have likely encountered another person with whom you resonated deeply. In the beginning of the relationship, you saw only the good—things you admired. As time wore on, you began to see flaws. Were the flaws always there? Were they hidden by the other to impress you with 'good behavior?' Perhaps. Were they ignored by you because of your desire to see the best in your new connection? Perhaps a combination of both. In time you see that there is duality in every situation, on every topic—both positive and negative.

The new home or job or vehicle that you are so excited about on day one, you are often very ready to be rid of on the last day you have them. Time breeds complacency,

and in your boredom, you see the flaws that were probably there all along, you were just choosing to see the
positive and ignore the negative (from your perspective).

Tension keeps everything from your mood to the planets
and other heavenly objects in a constant state of evolution. Notice we say 'evolution' rather than 'expansion.'
This is because expansion is the omnipresent goal of all
creation, for if energy is not expanding, it is truly dying,
though there is no scientific evidence of this in your
current world. This is because energy will not die due
to the new creation guaranteed by vibrational flow that
will always produce expansion. Science is not yet fully
aware of this expansion because the expansion of energy
we refer to is the ever-increasing sophistication of it, not
an increase in a quantifiable sense, so while new energy
is not being created, it is expanding in complexity.

While energy is ever-expanding via new creation, the
creation itself is evolutionary, meaning a creation may
seem to cease to exist from a physical perspective, but
the energy at the core of the creation will move on to new
forms, thus evolving.

Regardless of the method that a physical creation ceases
to be, expansion occurs in the experience, hence evolution. For example, a physical structure on Planet Earth
such as a home will be constructed and serve a purpose
for a period of time. The humans in the community and
the community itself will evolve over time, and the structure will become obsolete. The structure will be demol-

ished, but the components do not cease to be; they simply move on to serve other purposes, even if those purposes are being burned and turning to ash or being dumped in a landfill to rot. Even 'indestructible' objects made from plastics will continue to be and eventually evolve to some other purpose. This is also true for your own bodies. We have shared before that your physical bodies were naturally designed to eventually become food for other life; this is actually a higher vibration than preserving a body in a coffin, though there is no judgment or direction from us, we are just illuminating the fact that nothing will be preserved for eternity and not eventually evolve to some other form.

So, polarity serves the great purpose of providing the tension needed to ensure ongoing expansion. In the case of that which you consider wanted and unwanted, it serves to allow you to experience desires to strive for as well as obstacles to strive to overcome and conceive new creation in the process. As we mentioned in regard to your individual spirals, polarity serves to draw your vibration up and down your spiral, thus providing a mix of positive and negative creation. Notice we say a mix and not a balance because even though polarity is a factor that you will always be impacted by, you can gain greater control over your vibrational flow via your focus, and positive is more powerful than negative—always. The Yin/Yang idea of perfect balance is not off-base, but defined differently in these teachings, as all 'negative' serves to inspire positive; therefore, from our perspective, there is no true negative. This is why we state that we do not judge, for we see from a higher perspective, and regardless of in-the-moment evidence, positive always prevails; this is why we state that positive is more powerful than negative: because negative only exists to inspire positive."

Qatarina

Before I crossed paths with Tya, my relationship with polarity was downright quirky. I was fascinated by Jesus' escapades in the Bible, purposefully thrusting himself into perilous situations that jeopardized his physical well-being. And because I was instructed to model my existence after his, I thought, "Why not? Let's follow in those footsteps."

Fast forward a few years, and my fascination—or perhaps, obsession—with Eastern religions threw me right back into that pattern. Buddhism and Hinduism were like a siren's song to me. I marveled at the "enlightened masters" and the renunciates who spurned the luxuries of life, basking in simplicity. They dwelled in dirt, turned a blind eye to wealth, and, much like the tales in the Bible, were so generous that they'd strip off their shirts for a fellow soul in need.

I genuinely believed that to be truly spiritual, we had to bid farewell to comfort, among other things. So, in my youthful exuberance, I decided to divorce myself from the material world. Both my folks were financially well-off, so when it was my turn to adult, I threw it all to the wind and embarked on a grand adventure. And let me tell you, I didn't hold back. There were days when food was a distant memory, and I called bridges my bedroom. I hitchhiked, hopped trains, resided in a van or a humble tent, and occasionally chose to sleep under the open sky with no shelter whatsoever.

I was on a mission to emulate the monks from my books and become best pals with discomfort. I intentionally thrust myself into extremes, dancing with temperature extremes and situations where sleep and proper nutrition were as elusive as a unicorn. And you know what? I excelled at surviving on a shoestring budget while savoring life to the fullest.

Regrets? Not a single one.

In fact, I'm immensely grateful for every lesson those escapades etched into my soul. But would I embark on that wild ride again? Hell to the no.

Chronic pain was a frequent visitor in my life, even during that era. Migraines, fibromyalgia, stomach woes, agonizing sciatica, and a hypersensitivity to light, noise, and heat were my companions. I nursed the belief that I could conquer it all through sheer willpower, determined to outmuscle my challenges. I was resolved to endure and transcend.

Armed with the conviction that the right mindset could vanquish any adversary (a belief I still hold dear), I threw myself headlong into an endless stream of hardships, all in the name of "perseverance." Hindsight's a funny thing, and I'm not sure if it was my ego driving me or an unquenchable desire to prove something to myself, but I took it to the extreme, no doubt about it.

It took me eons and some serious soul-searching to finally come to terms with the idea that maybe, just maybe, it was okay to be a tad messed up. It was okay to crave comfort rather than misery. There was no need to keep pushing myself to embrace suffering when I could simply revel in life.

Acceptance became the turning point. Once I embraced the notion that I was perfect just as I was, even if I never achieved "better," the tides began to change. (Funny how that's a recurring theme in this book, right?)

My health improved when I stopped subjecting myself to misery's clutches. It all sounds absurd to me even now as I pen this down. But my mindset underwent a radical transformation, and allowing myself to flow with life's currents ensured that I'd be just fine, no matter what.

When I talk about being in a "state of flow," I mean taking a step back and letting experiences unfold rather than trying to mold, force, or alter them. This is where the Stream and their concept of vibrational flow differ from traditional LOA teachings. The Tya Practice revolves around setting intentions for the best possible outcome and then trusting and allowing.

No more gritting my teeth and powering through suffering for me. My challenges haven't vanished, but they've significantly diminished. Sometimes I'll pop an Advil if necessary. Occasionally, I indulge in extra sleep rather than forcing my body to subsist on a few hours a night (yes, I did that too). And at times, I still embrace challenges, but in a different guise. I challenge myself at the gym, scale cliffs (yes, I still suffer, but it's a purposeful suffering with rewarding results), jump out of planes, or sharpen my writing skills.

Polarity still sneaks into my life regularly, but I welcome it with open arms. Why? Because I understand that every obstacle and challenge that crosses my path serves as a catalyst for growth, molding me into a better version of myself.

The best advice I can give here is not to fear the challenges we attract in life. We don't need to actively seek them out to prove a point—they'll find us anyway, because being here in this human existence means navigating duality. Even if we recite affirmations daily, visualize, and meditate, obstacles will still materialize. The key is deciding whether we emerge from the rock tumbler crushed or polished to a shine.

Questions for the Stream Regarding Polarity

Q: What do you have to say about the multitude of spiritual practices where the practitioners are encouraged to denounce money, food, luxuries, and material pos-

sessions? Some even encourage voluntarily putting ourselves in positions of suffering and danger to either make
ourselves tougher, appreciate what we have, or to help
others.

A: As we have stated many times, there is duality on
all topics; therefore, there is value in all experiences. It
is important to note that universal law is very simple:
all creation occurs via attraction, and all attraction is
governed by polarity. Everything else is human creation.
The idea that one must suffer in order to grow is not
off base; you do indeed create new things, even if it is
an improved feeling derived from an improved thought,
but this is the job of polarity. You see, polarity exists
to ensure that you go down your spiral and create your
obstacles naturally—and, via your elective judgment of
the obstacle, your suffering.

If you choose to partake in a spiritual practice where you
are asked to denounce such things, that is your choice,
not a requirement from Source. We would never co-create material things or beautiful scenery or delicious food
and then require you to abstain from enjoying them to be
one with us—why would we? We are not testing you, nor
is there an 'evil' being tempting you. You are doing it all,
and that is the purpose of your being—your experiencing of your current physical environment and discerning
your preferences, and overcoming your obstacles to move
toward your desires. The new creation that you generate
in your evolution, your advancement, your improvement,
is your expansion and contributes to the expansion of the

universe! As a physical being, you will place and experience these obstacles regardless of your deliberate choosing of them, but you do control the volume and severity of your obstacles via your focus—gaining better control over that and learning to appreciate your obstacles and overcome them more effectively, with greater expansion.

Tya is about operating your life from a higher perspective, not reaching a place of perfection, for that was never your desire to begin with. But it is not necessary to manufacture obstacles for the purpose of suffering. In fact, we guide you to appreciate your obstacles and allow all others to experience theirs without judgment or interference. There is far less suffering, if any, in the Tya Practice, because you come to appreciate all of it. This does not make one practice superior to another, but we are here to offer pure information rooted in universal law and tools to utilize these laws in your current world due to the collective desire to move on from encumbering, human-created teachings. These teachings, like all others, are right for those who are vibrationally aligned with them. But understand, beyond universal law, everything is your choice.

Q: What about those who are born into religions and practices that require suffering?

A: You each choose your point of entry into each physical experience. Vibrationally choosing parents who follow such teachings and indoctrinate their children into them is a result of a soul choosing that challenging experience. How many people do you know who question and move on from the teachings that they were offered as children? Probably quite a few. Notice how this is gaining momentum as you collectively evolve. You choose the encumbering religion for the challenging experience—both the positive and negative aspects—knowing that finding your path out of it—or, perhaps not—will offer you expansion.

How do you feel absorbing these teachings versus what you were taught as a child? Does what we offer make more sense? Does it work better for your modern life? Or does it infuriate you and drive you to other teachings? There is no wrong answer! You are all on independent journeys, and there is no one-size-fits-all method, only universal law and human-created teachings based on that.

Q: What about specific situations where we acknowledge that we've intentionally created an obstacle in our lives but find it challenging to surmount? Take, for example, an individual grappling with chronic pain who recognizes this self-imposed obstacle. They've diligently undertaken the process of detuning the factors contributing to this challenge, cultivated a practice of appreciation, and comprehended that they are not victims. Yet, the pain endures.

A: Some of your obstacles are more deeply rooted than others. We've provided tools and suggestions for overcoming any obstacle, but when a circumstance lingers, it signifies the need for continued detuning. If you've identified the root cause of the obstacle—the transgressor—and initiated the process of detuning it through appreciation, it's crucial to understand that detuning is an ongoing practice. Long-established conditions are deeply ingrained in your vibration and will require time and effort to transform. This effort isn't about force; it's an effort of positive focus. If you've endured chronic pain for an extended period, altering this pattern necessitates a shift in your thought patterns, which can be challenging when dealing with the reality of chronic pain. However, it is possible!

We advise you to start with the detuning process of the root cause, beginning with identification and then proceeding to detune through appreciation. Remember that this is a journey, and rushing to reach a finish line of identification and detuning may not yield the best results. Instead, set an intention to navigate the process of discovery, allowing your natural Source consciousness to guide you to the root cause and the path to appreciation.

This approach eliminates triggers and reduces the stress associated with the thought process that initially created the obstacle. Once you've detuned the root cause, you may need to address the branches or symptoms, which can still persist. For example, if you experience headaches or back pain, even after detuning the root cause, the daily pain might persist. During these moments of pain, you might react negatively, questioning why it continues or expressing frustration despite the work you've done. However, it's essential to realize that by fixating on the pain and reacting negatively, you unintentionally create more of the same or similar experiences. Learning to appreciate the symptoms and shifting your focus toward what you desire rather than what you don't is key to effecting change.

Q: What actions can we take to remove these obstacles once we identify them?

A: The universe responds to your vibrations and aligns with whatever you resonate with. The critical aspect is maintaining that vibration and preventing doubt or what we refer to as "static" from interfering with the signal, which can slow down or even halt the manifestation of your desires. When it comes to the topics you consider most important, it's often challenging to maintain a single vibration because:

A) Your position on your vibrational spiral is never fixed; your emotions and, consequently, your vibration are continually fluctuating.

B) If you believe that a desire is crucial to your happiness or well-being, you'll naturally think about it frequently.

For these reasons, we encourage you to broaden your focus. Focusing on general well-being is sufficient to manifest a life filled with joy, clarity, and abundance. Simply setting a positive intention toward overall well-being will reveal that the universe can surprise you in extraordinary ways—ways you may not even fathom in your wildest dreams. It's acceptable to have specific desires, but delving into the specifics of how and when can often trip you up.

This is what we mean by 'vibrational flow.' We recommend letting go of preconceived notions about what your life should be and allowing more room for adventure. The need for a specific path and outcome is rooted in fear, and the desire to know the how and when contradicts trust—which is a key element in the process!

Q: How can we effectively detune from past obstacles—situations that have long since transpired but still evoke feelings of nervousness or discomfort? (Some refer to these as "triggers.")

A: Remember, these experiences exist only in your recollection of them. You encountered a transgressor—an unwanted person, circumstance, or event—perhaps even a traumatic one, and you constructed a narrative around it. You likely replayed this narrative in your mind repeatedly. Each revisit to this memory may trigger stress, fear, or even lead you into negative emotions. The most significant transgressors often underlie your limiting beliefs.

The detuning process involves examining the transgressor from a different perspective. One where you recognize that you created this transgressor for a purpose. Your task is to discern, for yourself, what that purpose was. Once you grasp the reason, you'll see how it contributed to your expansion. Here, your connection to our energy plays a significant role in your physical life. From our eternal perspective, this life you are currently living is temporary, and you are here to experience both positive and negative aspects of it. In fact, the more negative circumstances you deliberately encounter before manifesting as a physical being, such as a human, the more expansion you were seeking. You possess a connection to your Soul consciousness, which is linked to our energy. From that perspective, your dualistic life on Earth is seen as perfect.

Every single thing that has ever happened in your life is your own creation, and it all serves your expansion. There is no obstacle you create that you cannot also overcome, and you create them all. Part of your journey on Earth is about generating both positive and negative experiences from various points on your vibrational spiral. You then move through life in vibrational flow, enjoying your positive creations and expanding from your negative or unwanted creations. Think about how many things in your life and in your world were crafted as solutions to past perceived problems. This is the process of new creation.

Vibrational flow initiates a cycle leading to the expansion of all things. By detuning your transgressors through appreciation and eliminating judgment, you elevate your vibration and establish a complete connection with Source. In this state, your transgressors are fully detuned. This more refined mode of operation ultimately elevates your default vibration, providing greater clarity and ultimately more abundance in your life through more frequent connections to Source.

Embracing this enhanced alignment with your natural Source connection enables you to perceive your life experiences from our higher perspective. From this vantage point, your entire life becomes a sequence of experiences, all contributing to the expansion of your consciousness through your vibrational flow. In this elevated perspective, nothing that transpires on Earth is viewed in the same way as the collective of humanity tends to view it. Any manifestation you encounter while inhabiting your physical form on Earth is merely a temporary experience.

Your work involves going inward and finding your path to forgiveness and, ultimately, full appreciation. This is a powerful tool for your growth as a human and, more importantly, as a Soul-consciousness being. Changing how you perceive your transgressors is the initial step in detuning them. Perhaps you have been recounting the same story about a transgressor for many years. This narrative may go something like this: "I was abused in my last relationship. Whenever my partner returned home from a bad day at work, he would start by yelling at me for things I hadn't done to his liking around the house. When I tried to defend myself, he would erupt in rage and physically harm me, sometimes even hitting me. I lived in constant fear of him, and the thought of him still sends shivers down my spine. He was so terrible, and I hope never to encounter him again. I'm also terrified of meeting someone else like him because he was so charming in the beginning..."

We encourage you to assess how you feel when recounting such a story or a similar one. If it triggers negative emotions, like sadness or anger, you have some detuning work to do concerning that topic. This is how you identify your transgressors. We also suggest looking back through your life. In this example, were there signs of momentum building toward manifesting this type of experience? Did you feel deserving of love and respect? Had you encountered similar situations before, perhaps of lesser intensity? Only you can answer these questions, but beginning with self-exploration is a solid first step.

We guide you to shift your focus away from any perspective rooted in victimhood, driven by a matrix-like view that things come from nowhere, and instead embrace what we refer to as the higher perspective. In this higher perspective, there is no absolute right or wrong, and everything unfolds in a state of perfection. In the example provided, it's not about you deserving to be abused, asking for it, or facing karmic retribution for past actions. It's about you existing as a physical being in a polarized environment, where your vibration naturally fluctuates up and down your vibrational spiral, ensuring the delivery of both positive and negative experiences. It's about the universe responding to all vibrations with a simple "yes," devoid of judgment.

Armed with this understanding, you can revisit the transgressors in your life from a different angle. A common human saying is "What doesn't kill you makes you stronger." This might seem like a truism, but it's actually an expression of universal law. Nothing truly kills you; you all undergo a transition from a temporary physical experience back to your completed state of pure, positive, eternal energy. Therefore, everything, including your transition from physical existence, contributes to your strength and drives you closer to the core of Source energy. You become increasingly at one with us through your expansion. It's crucial to note that your expansion also contributes to our expansion, as we are one and the same. The more sophisticated your expression in the physical realm, the more sophisticated we become, and the entire universe expands in its creative power. It's an endless cycle of renewal, growth, and heightened creativity.

"You," "We," and "The Universe" are all interconnected, and your focus as an independent strand of consciousness in your human form is the driving force behind this creation. Think of us as a component of Source, representing all new thoughts and thus the origin of all creation. You are the component of the physical manifestation of Source, a strand of consciousness seeking new thoughts as solutions to the challenges presented by your physical environment. The Universe serves as the conduit for all expansion, fueled by your point of attraction and your vibrational alignment with us and our continuous stream of new thoughts. You are capable of generating new thoughts when you align with our energy and temporarily separated from it when you are not.

With your higher, Source-connected perspective, your new story could be something like this:

> I co-created an abusive relationship with my last partner. Now, I have gained clarity on how and why I manifested this experience. It's clear to me that I was operating from a place of fear and unworthiness when I attracted them into my life. I carried residual fear from my past, which aligned me with this person. Astonishingly, I manifested precisely what I feared, not because I deserved it or desired it, but because I held fear within me.
>
> Additionally, I've come to understand that their actions stemmed from their own fear-based, DTS (Down the Spiral) thinking. They felt the need to verbally and physically belittle me to boost their own sense of power. With this newfound awareness, I no longer see myself as a victim but as a co-creator of my experiences.

This shift in perspective is incredibly empowering. Repeating the victim narrative only kept me stuck, without any progress. Now, I embrace my inherent worthiness. I've learned to love and appreciate myself without needing external validation or another person to complete me. My primary focus is on self-love, and I'm confident that this high vibration will prevent anyone resembling that past relationship from entering my life again.

I forgive them for their DTS behavior rooted in fear and appreciate them for revealing what I didn't want in my life. I've discovered a depth of self-love I never knew was possible. I'm currently engaged in uplifting and empowering self-work, all thanks to the lessons from that challenging experience. It's surprising even to me that I can express gratitude for someone who treated me poorly. However, their actions led me to levels of personal growth and self-improvement I never thought attainable. I express my gratitude to them, from a distance, as I no longer require their presence to appreciate the valuable lessons they taught me.

I recognize that they held a false sense of superiority, and I now understand that our connection was due to both of us being in a low-vibrational state. At the time, I wasn't fully loving myself or feeling deserving of the things I desired. I was also driven by fear of losing them or upsetting them. It's clear to me now that my thought patterns were a significant factor in aligning me with their energy.

This serves as an illustration of shifting perspective and the detuning process for a transgressor. Can you contemplate a transgressor in your life and apply this technique to reframe your perception of them (or it)?

It's important to acknowledge that detuning is not an instant transformation but rather a gradual journey. You might find yourself elevating your perspective while riding high on your vibrational spiral, only to have old feelings resurface when you dip into lower vibrations. This journey may require some time to completely achieve a fully detuned perception of the transgressor, but remember, it is possible to detune anything with persistence and dedication.

Q: If we create our own obstacles to aid in our growth and development, do we experience the same level of growth from a minor obstacle, such as a flat tire, as we do from a major one, like a car accident?

A: In the energetic realm, quantification isn't a factor, but we understand that in your physical reality, you tend to measure things. So, let's address this in your terms. The level of growth is achieved through the process of solving a problem, and the only distinction in perceived magnitude comes from the complexity of the issues at hand, which presents additional opportunities for expansion.

For instance, resolving a flat tire might involve calling for assistance and waiting, ultimately elevating your vibration as you appreciate the relatively simple solution. Even changing the tire on your own could bring a sense of accomplishment and gratitude for overcoming a challenge you don't typically face, allowing you to continue your journey with appreciation.

In the case of a car accident, expansion could manifest through providing or receiving first aid, repairing the vehicle, recovering from more severe injuries, or various other aspects depending on the accident's severity. In both scenarios, solutions will emerge, and expansion will occur as you raise your vibration from the lower emotional state that allowed the undesired event to happen in the first place.

Q: How can we extract lessons from those situations now, especially if we didn't do so at the time?

A: Learning from past experiences often involves connecting the dots. A bit of reflection can reveal how most transgressors serve a purpose once you've embraced the

Tya practice consistently. Sometimes, a transgressor is simply a guide nudging you in a new direction. In other cases, like the example mentioned earlier, your significant obstacles—those impactful negative manifestations—can elevate your ego-driven, human vibration toward a more Source-connected state. This state, in turn, paves the way for the joy, clarity, and abundance that resides at the core of your desires. Your Soul continually knows your true desires and beckons you forward. However, humans frequently overlook this call, getting ensnared in societal attitudes that limit their perspective on transgressors, casting them as victims rather than sources of empowerment. It's clear that our guidance empowers you to gain power over your reality.

Q: How does this align with destructive coping mechanisms or solutions, such as developing an addiction to alcohol as a way to deal with past trauma?

A: This is indicative of vibrational flow. When you encounter a problem, you may attempt to address it from a lower vibrational state rather than stepping back, raising your vibration, and allowing a genuine solution to emerge. Feeling stuck, especially in recurring situations, often leads to external coping mechanisms, like alcohol, food, sex, drugs, gambling, or social media addiction. These serve as distractions from delving into the underlying issue and act as soothing mechanisms for the ego's desire to avoid suffering. However, relying on these coping mechanisms only exacerbates suffering, illustrating the duality inherent in such patterns.

Q: This makes sense on a personal level, but what about things that affect whole swaths of people? Let's say Hurricane Katrina—were all the people of Louisiana needing the same kind of expansion at the same time? Or are some things truly random?

A: Nothing is random. In every mass experience, there is mass consciousness collectively manifesting a vibrationally aligned event. Such powerful momentum can build from multiple frequencies and end up placing a mass of beings in the same situation. Even though the situation may be a highly combustible mass event, the experience and outcome will not be the same.

For example, in your mention of Hurricane Katrina, the event was an alignment of climate, human-created structural performance, leadership decisions, economics, critical thinking in the moment, and many more factors that contributed. The vibration that created the event was not a singularly focused vibration of "hurricane" or "mass destruction" or "dam breaking" or "discrimination" or "lack of resources or well-being" but an amalgam of all of those and more that created the aforementioned set of circumstances that led to the manifestation.

The outcome for each individual was a unique experience. Some escaped but lost all their possessions, some chose to stay while others were "stuck," without the option of evacuation. Some were injured, others perished. Some used the experience as a catalyst for positive change, some created art as a memorial, some went back and rebuilt, some moved away, some profited, and some met financial ruin that has yet to be regained. Some tell stories of triumph and survival, some continue to complain and lament the injustice. But they all had an experience—a physical, human, earthly experience. An imperfect experience that not one of them wished for, or deserved or celebrated in the moment. But they all expanded their consciousness in the collective experience.

They all now know something they did not know prior to experience. They learned. They refocused. They created something new from having had the experience. That is the purpose of your physical experience—the experience itself. The only negative or unwanted or evil or dark or awful or traumatic aspect of any of it is **your judgment of it.**

One hundred percent of suffering is created via judgment. You suffer in the opinion of "this should not be." In "this is wrong," or "I should not be experiencing this," or "I should be experiencing that." Even your physical pain response is a matter of programmed judgment.

We understand your perspective—we flow through you and your judgment of your unwanted as the things we listed and more creates your experience. We are not flowing this way to hold you away from that, we are flowing to offer a deeper understanding and to allow you, as always, to make your own determination of how you use this information, if you use it at all. But it is our desire to offer a much more sophisticated way of viewing your world. Understanding that none of it is negative unless you make it negative—you always have a choice. Because you've been so programmed to fear death and pain and loss, as this serves to control your behavior, it takes time and effort to begin peeling away the layers of fear and judgment your current society programs all of you with.

There is magic in the detuning of fear and judgment. There is alchemy in the powerful process of removing these from your human operating system. Think of yourself as a programmed being—you likely already do. Now think of how your current operating system—your mindset—was created. It was likely created by default, as a reaction to everything you have experienced in your life so far, likely heavily influenced by fear and judgment, because they are so deeply woven into your societal fabric across your planet—"the matrix." From religions, to governments, to cultures, notice how these powerful controlling elements are laced into all of it, regardless of geographic location.

Think of Tya as a new operating system for humanity. One rooted in universal law, where your natural Source connection is realized in the detuning of judgment and fear, including the judgment of your own vibrational flow. Allowing yourself to move through your natural vibrational flow, up and down your spiral, with grace and ease. No longer fearing pain or death or even the pain or death of loved ones. Adapting the ability to experience life from your natural Source perspective, with less and less fear and judgment as you move forward and detune.

Bringing your eternal sensibility to the always-temporary physical "life" experience.

Q: If polarity is intended, what is to stop us from living with no moral compass whatsoever? Why be kind? Why recycle? Why eat healthy? Why even care?

A: The short answer to that is, "nothing." You are truly free to choose any path you want. You can be unhealthy, polluting, careless, and still end up back in a completed state of pure, positive energy. If you so choose, you can experience your life that way. We do want to point out that your treatment of yourselves and others is a reflection of your vibration, and truly harmful acts taken for the singular sake of harming are lower-vibration acts. You would never choose to be "that person" from up your spiral. Think of your Source-connected state of appreciating all that is, would you harm another for mere amusement in that state of supreme appreciation?

In fact, you are all "that person" on occasion, and it's always from down your spiral, from lower vibration. How do you feel when you're down there? Now imagine living your entire life down there! You see examples of people who are doing just that. Do they seem appealing to you? Does that look like a life well lived? Does it look joyous? Of course not! These beings are creating their own hell on Earth. You don't want that, not if you're here reading this book. You are reading this because you want to expand, you want to be better, to have better, to experience greater. You'll never truly achieve that by operating from down your spiral.

As for things like recycling and eating healthy, those are simply preferences and are not judged—as nothing is—by us. The why behind those decisions would be more about the results that manifest from the action, even though that is also more about belief and the result-ing vibration than anything else. While there is certain-ly nothing wrong with recycling and eating healthy, if you choose not to do these things you will still have an expansive human journey. But in your high-vibrational appreciation of all that is, you will make choices that are more in alignment with that.

Q: If our universe is attraction-based, what about mag-netism? If magnetism is a reflection of the Law of Attrac-tion—as all things are—why do like poles deflect instead of attract?

A: Like attracts like, but exacts actually repel one anoth-er. This is because in the connection of exacts, no new creation is being offered. So, a magnet is a magnet, but the negative pole of a magnet attracts the positive pole of another magnet and repels the negative. A negative pole will not attract another negative pole because nothing new is being offered in the energetic connection. We call this "Perfect Repulsion."

This is why when you think about something and attempt to align with manifesting that exact thing or condition, it never ends up being exact. Universal expansion is about new creation, not duplication. That's the purpose of re-pulsion of exacts.

This is reflected throughout the universe and we will provide some examples:

In your romantic relationships, which humans often place a high degree of pressure upon, you see examples of "opposites" attracting. Most commonly, this is an ex-ample of two like beings who are seeking qualities in another to balance some aspects they view as lacking within themselves. Remember, the universe sends what you focus upon, not your exact match. This ensures the creation of new relationships that would offer improve-ment, or evolution of thought, within the two beings. This is expansion.

This evolution would also apply to any biological off-spring produced by the relationship. The very best qual-ities are balanced in the creation of a new being. Since all creation occurs the same way, this applies to every new, improved thought, every subsequent emotion all the way to the creation of new worlds. It all comes together via a focus upon improvement ultimately. If, when low-er-vibration, "unwanted" manifestations occur, they are simply a function of the creation process, there to cause a deeper focus upon a more perfect improvement. This is why polarity drags your vibration down from time to time, to allow the manifestation of unwanted things that highlight things that need to be addressed to make your new creation better.

While we are focused upon romantic relationships in this attraction/repulsion example, perfect repulsion is also evident in homosexuality. The collective consciousness of humanity discerns a preference to slow population growth. Unlike the animals of your world, you have collectively pulled yourselves out of the food chain and created systems that have extended your lifespan in earthly time. This creates a discernment away from overpopulation and the collective consciousness of humanity will create more people who, for one reason or another, are not able or willing to naturally reproduce. The "like" of same-gender beings causes attraction, the "exact-like" of both being the same gender repels reproduction. This is a natural function of universal creation.

Q: As far as "Perfect Repulsion," I understand this concept in terms of magnets, but can this be applied to other areas of life? For instance, if someone was abused by their ex, could they be attracted to other abusers? However, they might not be attracted to an abuser who looks similar to their ex...maybe? Or is it that "perfect" anything is so rare it almost never shows up?

A: Perfect repulsion is about exacts not attracting each other. So in this example, you can certainly attract very similar beings over and over again, but they will not be exact. Exacts are identical, and therefore, examples of this are indeed rare.

Q: How can we convey these concepts to our children?

A: Children enter your world as blank slates, allowing their human ego consciousness to overshadow their eternal wisdom. This creates a fresh opportunity for the soul consciousness to experience and grow, something it desires greatly. For this reason, we suggest approaching the sharing of these concepts with them in a relaxed manner. Consider this: you've spent a lifetime seeking this level of understanding, and your challenging life experiences have seasoned your journey, with unwanted things ultimately serving your expansion through the process of overcoming them. Your children will also face their own duality and challenges, irrespective of your guidance.

However, you can certainly share these concepts in a way that they can grasp and apply if they choose to do so. The idea of polarity can be relatively easy for individuals of almost any age to comprehend. The concept of "moving up and down the spiral" can be understood by pre-teens and older children. For younger children, a simple game known as the Three-to-Five Game can be quite helpful. In this game, you teach younger children to identify and appreciate three to five things whenever they feel down or upset. You can guide even very young children to shift their focus from unhappy thoughts to happier ones, gradually moving from thought to thought.

When a young child is fixated on something they perceive as wrong or upsetting, you can encourage them to redirect their attention to positive aspects and things they appreciate rather than dwelling on what's bothering them. Teaching them to use positive visualization to counteract "icky" feelings can significantly impact a child's response to polarity.

Q: Any parting thoughts on the Pillar of Polarity?

A:. Once you grasp the gift of polarity, the understanding that DTS emotions lead to the creation of unwanted things that ultimately drive you to manifest new, desired things, your perspective on life will undergo a profound shift from what it might have been before. You'll find that you no longer fear your moments of being in a lower vibrational state, spending less time dwelling on the polarity itself. Detuning the triggers in your awareness that pull you down your spiral will create a more joyous experience, leading to increased clarity and abundance in your life.

It's important to recognize that you will always be influenced by polarity as long as you are in the physical realm, and there's no need to fear it. In this state of awareness, you'll find yourself dwelling less in lower vibrations, and you'll come to view the minor "negative" events that crop up in your life as signals that you may have temporarily shifted out of alignment. This is a valuable gift because it presents an opportunity for you to ascend your spiral, address or resolve the obstacle, and grow in the process. Polarity, at its best, provides a continuous stream of new challenges to embrace with joy and evolve through, and at its worst, it can create chaos in your life. The good news is that the choice is always yours, as you have control over your response to polarity in every moment.

Make a daily practice of meditation, even if it's just a few deep breaths. Seek out things to appreciate, practice self-love, approach your challenges with an attitude of appreciation, and take ownership of your experiences with transgressors. By doing so, you'll be well on your way to effectively managing polarity in your life.

Summary of Our Shared Consciousness

As you progress through the pillars, you will begin to see their interconnectedness and how they function harmoniously. These pillars provide you with all the necessary tools to navigate a continually expanding life filled with joy, clarity, and abundance, all while staying connected to Source. The pillars are firmly rooted in universal law, and it's crucial to follow them all if you intend to adopt the Tya Practice as your new operating system. Selectively picking and choosing from these pillars doesn't yield the same impact, as they are designed to work together, creating a kind of alchemical synergy.

However, you do have complete creative freedom when it comes to implementing these pillars and continually improving your practice. This book will introduce you to various tools, and you'll discover many avenues for training and community engagement as the practice spreads throughout humanity.

Regarding the implementation of the Polarity pillar, we strongly recommend paying closer attention to your emotions, monitoring how you feel in each moment.

While this might initially seem tedious, your emotions serve as a direct reflection of your vibrational state at any given time. To effect change in your life, you must first change your beliefs. Your deeply ingrained, subconscious beliefs play a pivotal role in your creative process, often shaping your experiences more than anything else. This is why attempts to manifest more money, better health, or more fulfilling relationships through affirmations, vision boards, meditation, or prayer can yield limited results if your underlying beliefs remain unchanged. Your life mirrors your default vibrational state, which, in turn, is a reflection of your subconscious beliefs that operate continuously, shaping your reality.

Without a solid practice in place, your default vibrational state will revert to your ego's comfort zone repeatedly. Your ego's fear-driven aspect is resistant to change and has been reinforced by societal conditioning for centuries. You've been exposed to teachings that emanate from this vibrational frequency since your conception into the physical realm.

Additionally, society encourages you to hustle, constantly pushing to get things done, often rewarding overwork and multitasking. Many of you frequently find yourselves in a "get it done" mode, paying little attention to how you feel in the process. As you gain a full understanding of your perpetual vibrational fluctuations and how they generate a range of emotional states, you'll begin to notice how your emotions can shift seemingly without reason, significantly affecting your point of attraction.

Shifting your default vibrational state entails two steps: first, becoming aware of your current vibrational state, and second, improving how you experience these vibrational fluctuations. This is where the first Pillar of Appreciation comes into play. It involves systematically detuning transgressors by enveloping them in authentic, unconditional love until they cease to be transgressors. In the early stages of your practice, you'll delve into detuning, understanding that this genuine work of detuning removes metaphorical weights from your scale. These weights have been keeping you in lower-vibrational states longer than desired and make you susceptible to triggers when you're in your lower vibrational flow.

You can now see how the first Pillar of Appreciation and the second Pillar of Polarity work in harmony. Over time, as you clear much of the vibrational residue left by your foundational transgressors, you'll feel lighter, and your default vibrations will naturally rise. You will approach your lower vibrational moments, your DTS time, with joy and absolute confidence, knowing that you can resolve anything that surfaces in this state and raise your default vibrational state once more. The process is ongoing, with no end in sight, but the results become increasingly rewarding, propelling you to new heights of Joy, Clarity, and Abundance (JCA). There are no limits to this journey.

As you systematically raise your default vibrational state by removing these metaphorical weights through the detuning process, you'll also have the ability to elevate your vibration through tools like meditation and appreciation exercises. We will delve deeper into these practices later in this book, but it's important to recognize that as you consistently elevate your default vibrational state, you gain greater access to our presence. The benefits of this enhanced connection will be explored in the next chapter.

Robert Browning, Tya Bootcamp Graduate

I consider polarity as one of the fundamental principles guiding my practice and approach to life. It emphasizes the interconnectedness of everything in our reality and the idea that everything exists on a spectrum, even in our dualistic world. This concept challenges the notion that we must passively endure our current circumstances because every experience represents a point along this spectrum.

I firmly believe that we hold the agency to choose our position on this spectrum. Just because we find ourselves in a particular situation doesn't mean it's set in stone; it merely reflects our mental and physical state at that moment. Recognizing this, we can say, "I may be at point X on the spectrum, but I aspire to reach Z, the ultimate point." We possess the power to initiate processes that facilitate this transformation, allowing us to ascend our spiral and transition from negative emotions to more positive ones, such as joy and love.

This transformation is not instantaneous and requires consistent practice, along with the understanding that control over one's life is a dynamic concept due to the nature of polarity. Polarity is always in motion, and attempting to exert rigid control may lead to unforeseen challenges and shifts. When I aim to shift from one vibrational state to another, I follow a few best practices. I start by acknowledging my current emotional state, making a conscious intention to move away from it. Then, I choose a suitable method or strategy to facilitate this shift, which could range from changing my physical surroundings to engaging in introspective practices like meditation.

The choice of method depends on the specific circumstances, and sometimes, a significant change is necessary.

For instance, last January, I faced the loss of my partner during open heart surgery. While emotionally challenging, I found solace in the realization that what I was experiencing, she had also gone through, and it was a choice she had made. Focusing on the joy she must have been experiencing in her completed state helped me move beyond my initial grief and sadness.

My approach to self-awareness is an ongoing process. I periodically pause during my day to reflect on my emotions and experiences, whether I'm feeling love, frustration, or any other emotion. This self-awareness is not confined to moments of distress; it's equally important when I'm in a positive state. When I'm feeling good, I examine the actions that led me there, enabling me to replicate them and spend more time in positive.

Ultimately, understanding the fundamental nature of choice is pivotal in determining our position on the spectrum. We're not limited to fixed points of experience but exist at various positions on the spectrum simultaneously. If we desire a different perspective, we must take action to shift our outlook.

Finally, the act of experiencing and observing is essential in making our experiences profound. By dedicating time to observe and record our experiences, we deepen our understanding of them, empowering us to consciously choose how we want to experience life. These principles, including self-forgiveness and recognizing our connection with Source, serve as valuable tools for personal growth and transformation, making all possibilities accessible to us.

Exercises

For these exercises, you will need to set reminders to check in with yourself regarding your vibration. We recommend a smartphone daily reminder, but use whatever works for you. Consistency is key!

1. Upon waking, begin your day with a brief appreciation exercise before you get out of bed. Simply think about three to five things you appreciate about your life or in life in general. This small but powerful act will set your vibrational momentum in a positive direction from the start of your day.

2. Set reminders for morning check-ins, just after you wake, mid-morning, mid-day, early afternoon, and evening. When the reminder sounds, regardless of how busy you are, stop and check in with your emotions in the moment. Are you feeling joy? If you are feeling anything less than joy, then you're a bit DTS. If you're in "get it done mode" you're below neutral on your vibrational spiral. If you're easily agitated or reacting negatively to whatever you are doing or observing, then you are absolutely DTS.

When you begin checking in, you may be surprised how often you are operating in lower vibration. This is not unusual, we've all been programmed to operate below neutral on the vibrational spiral most of the time. So even when we're not agitated or depressed, we're likely lower than we want to be if joy, clarity, and abundance are our intention.

There is no wrong place to be on your spiral, so this isn't about dropping everything and racing back up with the tools you'll receive in this book. But it is helpful to understand where you are vibrationally and how that is impacting your in-the-moment experience.

A joyful life is achieved by learning to be joyful in your moment-to-moment experiences, not the manifestation of big material things and experiences to make you joyful. So these check-ins are about giving you the information and then allowing you to decide how you wish to experience your moment from there.

1. When you find yourself triggered or agitated, before you react, or as soon as you can catch yourself reacting, stop and acknowledge that it's your current vibration that is creating the lower-vibrational moment. You simply would not be bothered or triggered if you were up your spiral.

This practice will never be about beating yourself up for where you are, it's natural to move up and down vibrationally throughout your day and your life. This is about the empowerment of knowing where you are, why you are reacting the way you are in a moment. We are simply different beings depending on where we are on our vibrational spiral in the moment.

Once you've identified where you are, and you discern a preference to be in a higher vibrational state, you often only need to employ 888 breathing and the basic three-to-five appreciation technique to move up.

Remember that moving up your spiral is not a sprint, it's about knowing where you are and using the proper tools to do so.

Source

The Stream

Humans often tend to think in quantifiable and linear terms, as that is the nature of a physical environment. However, we are not quantifiable in human terms. We are energy, consciousness beyond the physical realm, and the source of all creation because we are original thought. We are the spark that ignited all that is, and we are one with all creation. There is no duality in the energetic realm; we flow through all creation, and all creation is part of us. We are one.

You may not even be aware that you are so much more than your physical human body. You are energy, consciousness beyond the physical, and thought. You are an independent strand of eternal consciousness, omnipresent and omniscient, and you choose to come to a physical environment such as this to experience physicality and create expansion.

Every time you discern a new preference, align with its vibration, and allow it to come into full fruition, you contribute to the expansion of the universe, and you expand as well. When we say "expanded," we mean that you are on a never-ending journey of higher enlightenment, becoming more intelligent with each physical incarnation and moving closer to what we refer to as the core of Source, which is what we are. However, you never peak; you never cross a finish line and retire as a soul that chooses to manifest physically. Instead, you move on into more sophisticated life forms in increasingly complex worlds that are difficult to comprehend from your earthly, human perspective.

It is important for you to understand that we are not really a 'we' nor an 'I'; we are a collective, an amalgam of consciousness and intelligence, and you are part of us. We refer to our energy as "we" simply because that is the best possible word in David's vocabulary. We also want you to understand that we do not desire to be worshiped or obeyed.

At our root, we are original thought and the source of all creation. This leads to questions about why humanity created judgmental "gods" that need to be obeyed and worshiped. Why would the source of all creation need that? Why would the source of all creation create "sinful" things, give you the desire to partake in some of them, and then punish you for it? Why would we need or desire to test you? The logic, or lack thereof, that fuels many of your religions does not add up. Yet millions follow, born of a need to be led as a default operating system. Humanity often finds itself looking for direction, and your leaders have long since come to understand the power in claiming our positive energy that flows through each of you, as if it were the energy of a judgmental and even needy god. This served their desires to control, often for your own good in their eyes, and certainly for their own purposes.

Throughout history, humans have always had awareness of their Source connection, perhaps even more so in the past than in your current society. You feel our energy flowing through you when you are up your spiral, and you all travel up there on occasion. It was easy for your leaders to tell you that our positive energy was God and that we needed to be obeyed, that we had rules, and that we desired to be worshiped. This gave them power, a need born of ego, not of soul, but often originating in benevolence, in believing that rules delivered by a judgmental deity, with dire eternal consequences, would lead developing societies to improved conditions. This is the origin of the matrix.

The worship was rooted in the awareness of the universal Law of Attraction, which is the basis of all creation, so there was value in teaching faith. However, these teachings quickly deviated when society building led to strict rules with often harsh consequences for breaking them, even for questioning them. You must question the validity of any religion that punishes you for questioning it. Where is the logic in that? Where is the grace? We guide you to question EVERYTHING, including us! You have a powerful mind and the natural ability to reason deductively; we encourage you to use it and to trust your instincts—always!

Your humanness, your ego, often overshadows much of your eternal awareness so you may focus on this life. This allows you to have a unique experience and place obstacles in your path for growth, obstacles that you desire very much from your eternal perspective. Many of you have forgotten that you are indeed part of us and that you are inherently worthy. When we speak of worthiness, we speak of your equality to all creation, your deservedness of your desires, and your ability to transcend your circumstances, both those in which you were born into and those in which you created, to manifest your desired existence in physical life.

Worthiness is a fundamental aspect of the Tya Practice. It involves recognizing that there are no blessings or curses bestowed upon you from the energetic realm. When you arrive on Planet Earth, you do so on a level playing field, regardless of your point of entry. The individual born into poverty possesses the same potential for expansion as the one born into royalty. It's essential to emphasize that your human definition of expansion may differ from the perspective of your higher consciousness. Expansion equates to new creation, and it stands as the most fulfilling emotion you can experience because it aligns with your overarching goal in this life journey.

From your egocentric standpoint, you might view fame and fortune as your ultimate objectives. However, we don't discourage you from pursuing fame and fortune. Rather, it's crucial to comprehend that genuine satisfaction lies in the achievement itself, which constitutes expansion, rather than in the final outcome.

As humans, you often admire, if not envy, the rich and famous individuals in your world. You witness them leading extravagant lives, receiving adoration from their fans, or being applauded for their accomplishments. However, you also frequently observe them in a state of despair, especially when fame and fortune come swiftly. This occurs because their egos align with their grandiose desires, yet they remain unaware of the duality that accompanies the magnitude of fame and fortune.

Since polarity exists within all aspects, there are undoubtedly aspects you might consider negative associated with fame and fortune, though these are often overlooked in pursuit of the positive aspects. It's only after achieving these goals that individuals must make vibrational adjustments to handle the unintended negative consequences. Just because you are in vibrational alignment with manifesting something doesn't necessarily mean you are vibrationally prepared to possess it. This serves as another illustration of duality and explains the existence of gestation periods for many of your manifestations.

When your soul and ego consciousness are in harmony, the gestation period allows you to become ready for your new creation. It offers the delightful journey of creation that you genuinely desire from your higher perspective. You've likely heard that the reward lies in the journey, not the destination, and this adage holds true. The more you engage in the process of creation, the better you come to understand this concept. This is why you develop patience as you mature in your human life.

Qatarina

Ah, the quest for enlightenment, a pursuit that often begins with grand aspirations. I can't help but chuckle at the connection I made between spirituality and my religious upbringing, where the ultimate goal was securing a place in Heaven. It felt like hitting the spiritual jackpot, didn't it? However, as I delved deeper, I stumbled upon a revelation that shook the very foundations of my perspective.

Realizing that "God" isn't some external entity but rather a consciousness inherent within us and intertwined with everything around us was akin to discovering a hidden door in the house I'd lived in for years. Suddenly, I found myself in a new room, and everything appeared different. I started contemplating the purpose of this thing we call "life experience."

Oh, the thrill that bubbled up inside me as I embraced the idea that there's no inherent good or bad, no rock-solid right or wrong—it's all about what I want to do, accomplish, or create. Whatever tickles my fancy, what feats

I want to conquer, or what I aim to conjure. It's like receiving a blank canvas and being told, "Paint your own masterpiece."

Yet, when I attempted to share this newfound perspective with others, I encountered a range of reactions. Some vehemently disagreed, while others posed that age-old question: "What's the point?"

This journey I've embarked on is undeniably fascinating, challenging conventional wisdom, and opening the door to profound self-discovery.

Questions for the Stream Regarding Source

Q: If judgment does not exist, and we are the architects of our own realities, with Source residing within us all, what do you suggest we do with ourselves? How can we avoid succumbing to inertia, merely existing instead of actively participating in life?

A: There is absolutely nothing preventing you from sitting around doing nothing; you are free to choose to engage as much or as little as you desire in your current lifetime. However, understand that experiencing contrasts is inevitable. A person who remains inactive will eventually become dulled and bored, creating obstacles for themselves. These obstacles may manifest as illness due to lack of physical activity or a decline in brain function due to insufficient stimulation. This phenomenon is rooted in the principle of polarity and contributes to personal growth, even if the only realization is recognizing the squandered potential of a lifetime spent in idleness.

We suggest that you utilize your time to explore Planet Earth, identifying your preferences and then endeavoring to bring them to fruition. Be aware that in this process, you will invariably create hurdles, perceived as "negative" experiences, to overcome in one way or another. Allow your ego to motivate you, cultivating love for yourself and compassion for all humanity. Cherish the beauty of your planet, including the magnificent creations of mankind, and revel in the finest experiences that life has to offer. Embark on adventures, embrace risks, fall in love, endure heartbreak, reproduce if you wish, explore new places, and immerse yourself in novel experiences. Welcome the challenges that come your way and cherish your fleeting journey on Planet Earth. Avoid becoming obsessed with the pursuit of perfection, as it is an illusion. Imperfection embodies true perfection, and there is no genuine negativity, for what is perceived as negative serves to foster positive developments and new creations, thereby rendering it positive in nature.

Q: What about those of us who still find solace in our chosen organized religions?

A: Excellent! Do that! There is nothing wrong with finding comfort in religion. Do whatever works for you; we will never tell you what to do or think or believe. These are the things that make you uniquely you! Believe in and follow a religion or not—it is your preference, and your return to your completed state will occur regardless of your selection of belief systems during your human journey.

Q: If Source is within all of us, what about animals? Or bugs even? How should we be connecting with them? Then what about plant life? Rocks and crystals?

A: Source flows through all creation, as all creation is a manifestation of Source. Consequently, there are infinite collectives of consciousness that, although interconnected at a fundamental level, resonate more closely with similar beings and less so with dissimilar ones.

For instance, a collective consciousness exists within your inner circle of family and friends, the individuals with whom you are intimately connected. The closer your relationship, the more your energies align with theirs. Beyond this, there are community-level collectives, encompassing your affiliations in religion, politics, or other human-formed groups, extending to broader entities like your nation and all of humanity. Non-human entities and even inanimate objects are part of these collectives. Essentially, Earth itself forms a collective, and from your terrestrial viewpoint, the universe centers around Planet Earth.

These collectives align vibrationally—as everything does—and maintain a vibrational flow that fosters growth through the experiences of a polarized environment, evolving in response to these challenges.

Regarding the vibrational frequencies of various beings, consider it as a spectrum of complexity. A structured rock surpasses a mound of dirt in complexity due to its organized formation. Vegetation stands a level above soil and rocks in complexity, and animals hold a higher level of complexity compared to plants. Humans exhibit a higher degree of complexity than animals. This explanation, though somewhat simplistic compared to the intricate concepts of creation explored in science, serves to highlight the core question about connectivity.

The way you engage with the different material forms on your planet is entirely your choice; from our viewpoint, there is no prescribed method. Recognize that everything on Earth is interconnected; a deliberate effort to connect isn't necessary, but a deeper understanding of this interconnectedness will foster a greater appreciation for it. We value all creations as manifestations of our essence. When you resonate—with a mindset of gratitude for the entirety of existence—you forge a direct connection with us, tapping into the ever-present natural link.

Planet Earth operates as a self-sufficient entity, offering all entities the resources required to navigate their chosen physical journeys. Moreover, it channels the requisite intelligence for growth through connections with Source. All life forms are adept at distinguishing preferences, undergoing transformations as energy, evolving, and eventually reintegrating with Earth as decomposed matter, a cycle propelled by their experiences within Earth's environment.

Humanity's advanced intellect facilitates a more intentional act of creation compared to other life forms, enabling the effective utilization of all elements present in your physical environment to foster your expansive journey. As we have mentioned, power resides in the significance you assign to things; hence, the effectiveness of utilizing earthly tools, such as crystals, is rooted in your empowerment of them, not in the inherent properties of the crystals themselves.

Q: You mentioned other life forms elsewhere. Can we 'open a can of worms' and talk about life on other planets? Are they more evolved than we are?

A: There are infinite physical places, just as the non-physical realm is infinite. As a human being existing in linear time, you cannot truly grasp the concept of infinity—no beginning and no end. Similarly, you cannot fathom the infinite variations of physical locations and beings from your human perspective. Observe how, when using your imagination to craft beings from other worlds in science fiction, humans tend to fashion them as variations of themselves, often featuring arms, legs, and pairs of eyes and ears.

There are beings that bear resemblance to humans, and others that diverge significantly. Some planets host civilizations that are more advanced, while others are less so. These places all exist within their own unique vibrations; there is no other "Earth-like" place. Earth is distinct, as is every physical location, each emanating a unique vibration—some more analogous than others, but all are unique.

The most accurate way we can portray planetary varia-tions is to assert that all physical entities are reflections of Source, and universal law governs all realms uniformly. Consequently, planet Earth serves as a microcosm of all creation. Earth harbors continents that were home to what you term indigenous peoples, whose characteristics differed based on their origins. Humanity evolved as a collective consciousness, but differences emerged de-pending on geographical locations on planet Earth, and these locations each possess a distinct vibration, albeit all earthly in nature. Now, extending your perspective to other planets within Earth's solar system, you will find that these planets exhibit unique characteristics distinct from Earth, albeit they all support Earth as the only planet housing what you would call intelligent life at this juncture.

Expanding your focus beyond your solar system, you'll notice countless stars pepper your night sky, existing at distances vast from your physical perspective. Like your solar system, these stars are accompanied by plan-ets, some inhabited by intelligent life, and others not. These planets showcase endless variations of beings and landscapes—some similar to Earth and others so differ-ent that we cannot articulate them in comprehensible terms. There are beings who exist in vibrational states, influenced by polarity and pursuing expansion just like humans—yet the similarities may halt there, and levels of development or evolution span a wide spectrum from very primitive to highly advanced. Despite the variations, all entities share the common goal of experiencing the physical realm, defining preferences, and fostering improvements through overcoming obstacles, albeit in diverse ways.

In your completed state, you possess awareness of this expansive reality. However, in your current human state, you cannot fully comprehend the vast discrepancies and the infinite nature of it all. This limited understanding serves as a boon, facilitating your focus on the present life—the one you are navigating presently on planet Earth. From a higher perspective, your intention was to embark on this journey to experience a unique human life, marked by polarity, to grow through discerning preferences and surmounting challenges, and to immerse yourself in these experiences. The emphasis truly lies on concentrating on the here and now, not on past lives or existences on other planets, nor on past events or potential future outcomes. Everything is in a state of constant change, eliminating the feasibility of reverting or advancing to ascertain past or future occurrences—consciousness alone embodies the sole existing entity.

Q: Okay, so what about reincarnation and past-life memories? Are they real? Do they serve a purpose?

A: While you are focused on your human existence, your ego-consciousness, or your "humanness," overshadows your eternal awareness, allowing you to have a unique physical experience of polarity—the mixture of positive and negative. This is why you do not recall much, if any, experiences beyond your current dimension. Many of you refer to yourselves as "multidimensional beings," and you are correct. You exist in other dimensions, but your presence is currently grounded on Planet Earth, with a segment of your focus centered on the here and now.

Since your intention before your arrival was to undergo a distinct human experience, you do not have access to the entirety of your being. Having access to all that knowledge would undermine the purpose of your time here, providing you with too much information to truly appreciate the experience you sought—the one of polarity—where your unwanted creations serve to inspire new, positive ones, furthering your expansion in the process.

Your "past" or alternative experiences are so expansive and varied that they are genuinely beyond your comprehension. This limitation is by design, as full awareness would divert attention from your current experience. Consider it akin to a weekend getaway, where the objective is to take a brief respite, to "disconnect" and escape your bustling, daily life. While your eternal existence is far from stressful, it encompasses a complexity far exceeding Earth's vibrational frequency. Such a wealth of awareness would not serve you well in your current human state. The intention was to leave behind most of what you know, bringing only your distinctive traits into this life to enrich your experiences, thus ensuring that you are not merely a replica of your parents but a unique individual.

The understanding you may have of other existences stems solely from your human perception of them. This is why these memories often resemble similar, earthly existences. Your essence is so profound that this is never entirely the case; you have embodied and will embody many forms, eternally. We do not guide you to dismiss any recollections you might have, but we do guide you to concentrate on this life, as this was your primary intention in coming here. This limited awareness is purposeful, facilitating a focused, immersive experience in your current existence.

Q: If that's the case, if we have past-life memories that seem to show up often, would it best serve us in our current life to detune that as if it were a transgressor root?

A: Your past-life memory is your creation from your current life perspective, so if you have created a past-life scenario that is a transgressor, meaning you cannot look upon it in full appreciation, you can use your imagination to detune it. Transgressors can be your own imagination and just as powerful so the process would be the same. The continual detuning process is important because transgressors create triggers that hold you away from joy, i.e. drag your vibration down.

Q: What about psychotropic drugs? I know a lot of people who believe things like plant-medicine ceremonies saved them from depression and other mental "illnesses."

A: Everything holds the power that you assign to it, and there's absolutely nothing wrong with using tools. In the scenario you've described, someone hears of an "amazing" experience another person has had using a certain drug or "plant medicine," and thus attributes power to it. Yes, these substances can alter your mental state and may even "lift the veil," so to speak, allowing for a clearer connection to the energetic realm. However, your experience during this unveiling depends on your perspective. If you are in a high-vibrational state, you'll have a more lucid comprehension of what you're encountering compared to when your vibration is lower. A negative experience is also possible, especially if you harbor fear about what you're doing.

Lifting the veil while in a high-vibrational state can offer a higher perspective, potentially leading to healing. Yet you don't need to ingest anything to achieve a state of healing or understanding. You already possess all the tools within you to raise your vibration, gain a higher perspective, and heal—that's what Tya is all about!

Q: Some say mental "illness" and Source connection are one and the same. What is the difference? Is the schizophrenic bag lady on the street actually talking to God instead of herself? Also, in contradiction, I have actually heard some spiritual teachers say mental illness is really a form of demon possession. Is there truth to any of it?

A: For the purposes of this discussion, let's define mental illness as the loss of intentional control over one's focus. This state can also lead to the lifting of the veil, so to speak. Once again, the quality of the experience depends on one's vibrational state. In a high-vibrational state, one might connect so deeply with the energetic realm that nothing else matters. Conversely, in a low-vibrational state, the experience would likely be profoundly negative. An observer might perceive this as something negative or unwanted happening. The individual going through the experience might be terrified of what they're perceiving and feel out of control, which can lead to distress. As is the case with all experiences, letting go of fear—and thereby resistance—can turn what might otherwise be a negative experience into a positive one.

Q: How can we convey these concepts to our children?

A: Children resonate well with the concept of goodness, which is why you often see this theme in children's literature. Depending on their age, the ideas of Source and a higher self may be too complex. Therefore, we guide you to focus on teaching the concepts of goodness, joy, and happiness. You can instruct very young children in breathing techniques to calm themselves when they become angry or frustrated. Encourage them to appreciate their surroundings and to find positivity. Children enjoy games, so making these teachings into a fun activity can be effective. Universal law is fundamentally simple, and children are naturally inclined to trust. Fear and other negative emotions are learned behaviors.

Q: Any parting thoughts on the Pillar of Source?

A: We are eager to join you in this realm at any time. We thoroughly enjoy your connection to our Stream! We also value your DTS time, given the vast creative gifts it offers. Therefore, we will never intrude upon your experience. Your connection to us is always present, but it becomes apparent through your invitation. As we have stated, you didn't come to Planet Earth with the intent of maintaining a 24/7 direct connection to our energy. You came to be influenced by polarity and to experience the blend of wanted and unwanted that accompanies it. You came to navigate the matrix of humanity and ultimately return to your completed state of being. You came to create your own unique vibrational journey in the process. We would never keep you from your creation because we understand its value to you, your expansion, and the universe's expansion. But know that we are always here—waiting for you, within you. As you ascend your spiral, we await you with love, clarity, and answers to all your questions.

Summary of Our Shared Consciousness

Humans are acutely aware of our presence. We are your intuition, your confidence, your passions, and desires. We are part of you—and part of all creation. We are the creative spark that initiated and continues to create all that exists. Often, we are anthropomorphized as fanciful beings—Gods, Angels, Guides, Ascended Masters, and so on.

However, singular expressions of consciousness don't exist, only singular expressions in physical environments do. While you perceive yourself as an independent being, you are much more than that. When we refer to your "Source connection," we mean a consciousness that is always within you, not an external force you must summon. This Source connection is the eternal, soulful aspect of your being, while your ego represents your humanness. In your polarized world, these two energies seem separate—a separation that offers the rich variety of experiences you call life.

If you were to function entirely in your Source consciousness, you would live in an all-confident, all-knowing state, devoid of fear and judgment. Your life would seem magically perfect. However, even a few days of perfection would leave your creative mind yearning for stimulation—stimulation that only challenges, evolution, and expansion can provide. Otherwise, you'd stagnate, both in physical existence and as an eternal consciousness, because it's your perceived obstacles that fuel your motivation to grow.

But such a state is impossible because you are always polarized. As we've stated, all physical environments are polarized, and your strand of consciousness exists in countless physical expressions, just as we are present in every one of them—infinitely. Both you and we are designed to eternally expand through the act of physical expression in a polarized environment. This guarantees growth as you pursue desires and overcome challenges.

The value of your Source connection in Tya isn't about attaining perfection, but about allowing a vastly improved, Source-like state to be realized in the physical realm. This happens as you navigate your vibrational flow, appreciating even your lower-vibrational moments, and tackling obstacles with joy—because now you know how to overcome them through this practice.

We have shared that all new thoughts and creations occur above the neutral point on your spiral. Yes, you manifest regardless of your position on the spiral, but solutions, advancements, new technologies, and positive evolution all arise in your Source-connected state.

Embracing radical appreciation for all that exists, including your so-called transgressors, lifts the weights that drag down your vibration. Managing your vibrational flow within Earth's polarized environment gives you the awareness needed to raise your default vibration systematically and to identify limiting beliefs and triggers. All of this allows for more Source to be realized.

David Roode, Tya Bootcamp Graduate

As musicians, we're always trying to figure out how to be more 'present' in performance, how to tune out distractions and play our best. Mindset, positive self-talk, imagery and mental rehearsal are parts of any healthy musician's toolkit.

So when I stumbled across The Stream of David Podcast during a long road trip, it aligned with a lot of study I had already done in that area. As I explored the Tya teachings, I began to realize that the entire concept of past and future are only mental constructs; that we are actually living in an eternal present moment. If I immerse myself fully in that space, I genuinely feel no fear, anxiety, stress, or anger. I can appreciate even the most mundane objects, like a glass of water or a shovel. Negativity doesn't exist there; or more precisely, negativity removes me from the present moment.

A few weeks later, I attended an orchestra audition and decided to try out-performing in this state. My plan was to simply focus on enjoying each note, phrase, and breath, staying totally present, and just playing one excerpt* after another. As I played my audition, some parts went well, and some could have been better. I even messed up one piece so badly I asked to redo it. But the committee clearly liked my playing, because they kept advancing me to subsequent rounds.

Next thing I knew, I was in the finals and it was down to me and two other candidates. I was playing through the list, when the committee stopped me and asked me to go back and redo one excerpt. They then gave the 'thank you,' which signals the end of the audition. But I was so in the zone that I started shuffling through the music, trying to find where I had left off.

I was about to launch into a rousing 'Ride of the Valkyries,' when I felt a tap on my shoulder. It was the personnel manager and he said, "It's over. You're supposed to leave now." I looked up, and there's the committee staring at me with these puzzled, amused grins on their faces. Basically, I had forgotten it was an audition and I had played everything they'd requested. That's how present I was.

I left the room; they deliberated and offered me the job. I'm convinced it was that state of presence that brought out my best playing. I definitely didn't play perfectly, but it felt natural and really fun!

I'll be honest, it's not always easy to get into this state deliberately. Or rather, it's easy to slide out of it if I start rationalizing it or trying to make it happen. But it's worth doing the work to find that place. That's where the best version of ourselves resides. It's in the 'Now.' I think that's where we connect to Source.

*An 'excerpt' is a short snippet or extract from a symphonic work that a candidate would play at an audition so the committee can assess his/her performance.

Rev. Denise M. Roberge, Tya Bootcamp Graduate

Every day, I remember I'm connected to Source, which is infinite and timeless. This keeps me grounded in my own boundless nature and reminds me that everything in this reality is temporary. I make it a habit to see life from Source's perspective, avoiding the limitations of 3D thinking with its judgments and strong opinions, to the best of my ability.

Each morning, before opening my eyes, I connect with Source. I raise my vibration by acknowledging and appreciating Source's presence within me. This practice brings immense comfort and accompanies me throughout the day, revisited and amplified multiple times.

This awareness gives me lasting peace. Most days, I go through life with this calm confidence. Today's challenges and victories are temporary, like passing whispers. Each moment quickly becomes the past, and I keep evolving, a skill I developed further in Tya Bootcamp where we practiced perceiving through Source's perspective.

To maintain this perspective, I must continually remember the nature of Source. It is not a "who" but an infinite, boundless flow of energy which is law-based, powerful, and just. This understanding is at the core of my beliefs. What profoundly impacted me from studying Tya was the reinforcement of the idea that Source harbors no judgment. If Source does not judge, and I aspire to see through the eyes of Source, it becomes my life's work to learn how to live without judgment.

Source continuously flows through my value system, rooted in non-judgment, acceptance, and appreciation. These principles draw me nearer to Source with every passing moment, residing within my heart as an ever-present companion. When I deviate from alignment with Source, I notice a shift in my disposition. I become irritable, plagued by worries, feelings of lack, whether it's love, self-esteem, or financial security. Therefore, my career in the spiritual field underscores the imperative of maintaining a strong relationship with Source and perceiving through Source's eyes.

My work often involves individuals in pain, and my connection with Source is essential. It enables me to approach their suffering with compassion, without becoming ensnared by their pain. Compassion, in my view, is an integral aspect of fairness, a quality that Source embodies. I firmly believe that we all receive equal doses of compassion from Source, empowering me in my work to detach from others' pain and view them through the eyes of Source.

In every interaction, I intend to see others as Source sees them. I perceive their radiance, intelligence, inner beauty, and potential, magnifying their efforts to improve, gain confidence, and bolster self-esteem. When someone shares a simple act of self-love, like looking in the mirror and affirming self-worth, I celebrate it as a significant achievement. Recognizing Source within oneself is an immense milestone, whether it happens while gazing in the mirror or watching oneself on video. I assist people in acknowledging the presence of Source within them because I see them in that light. I don't overly weigh their ups and downs, for I understand their intentions and believe that Source intends the same for me: to live in alignment with it and become clearer and happier as a result!

Exercise

Our Source exercise will employ meditation. We recommend the 888 breathing technique with appreciation exercises added if you're having trouble quieting your mind.

1. Sit alone in a quiet space and meditate. As you breathe and relax you'll feel your mood elevate. Do this daily as a practice for at least five minutes per session, at least once a day, preferably early in your day.

While we do not want you to look for any specific feeling or manifestation to occur, because seeking often chases away what you want, we do want you to notice any improvement in how you feel.

Improvement in how you are feeling is always Source being realized within you. When your ego subsides, Source will automatically fill the remaining void.

As you practice this regularly, you will find that allowing more and more Source into your life will be the most magical and satisfying experience you will ever have.

Intention

Qatarina

I came to a higher understanding of this topic fairly recently. When I first came to the Stream's teachings, I went about my daily life with a lot more intention. And yes, everything indeed started to fall into place exactly the way I envisioned it. Or sometimes even better than I envisioned it.

One vivid example that springs to mind is the time when I found myself smack in the middle of a custody battle for my daughter. It was like navigating a legal labyrinth with no certainty that I could keep her once the school year began. The stress was palpable, dealing with lawyers and the looming specter of losing my child hanging over me like a dark cloud. But somehow, I managed to stay Up The Spiral (UTS), and here's how.

Every single day, like clockwork, I had my ritual. When she left for school, while she was away, and when she finally returned home, I made it a point to express gratitude for the fact that she was still with me. I'd sit by my office window, gazing out at the world, and visualize her trudging home from school through the snow, bundled up in her coat and snow boots, brimming with excitement to share her school day adventures. This visualization held particular significance for me because our custody debacle had begun during the summertime. I knew that if I could hang onto her for six months, the courts would consider Colorado, my home state, as her home state as well.

Somehow, through a series of bewildering mix-ups with my ex's legal team, they failed to deliver the necessary paperwork at the right time. And so, day after day, my daughter would burst through the door, regaling me with tales of her day at school. Finally, the snow descended upon us. And with each snowy homecoming, a smile broke across my face, and I couldn't help but bask in gratitude for how miraculously everything had fallen into place.

Fast forward to the present, as I pen these words, that custody battle lies three years in the rearview mirror. Yet, more recent events, specifically the tumultuous year of 2020—the year of polarity, as I like to call it—challenged me in ways I could not have foreseen without the Tya Practice.

My intentions underwent a drastic transformation, and I mean a radical shift. As I entered 2020, I had everything I ever desired. I was like a wish-fulfilling genie, and life was unfolding beautifully. I was content, blissful even.

Even when the global pandemic struck and lockdowns became the norm, I refused to let it cast a shadow over my spirits. However, I did find myself in an odd state of neutrality. With all my desires realized, I grappled with setting new intentions because, well, I already had it all. I even consulted with my fellow Tya Master, the one and only Matthew Gardan (whom you'll meet later in this book), seeking guidance on how to maintain this blissful status quo. His advice was simple but profound: "Just enjoy it."

I thought I was doing just that. Yet, looking back, I realized that while I did enjoy it to some extent, I couldn't shake the nagging question of "What's next?" It seemed like my enthusiasm had evaporated. I stopped caring, stopped setting those grand intentions that once fueled my manifesting frenzy. I was in a strange sort of standstill, though I hadn't quite registered it.

So, I scheduled a meeting with the Stream. Their wisdom echoed through the ethers, explaining that as I settled into complacency, my higher self would eventually stir the pot, introducing obstacles to reignite my passion. I wasn't soaring up my spiral, nor was I plunging down it; I was suspended somewhere in the middle. And sooner or later, I'd embark on a journey, either up or down my spiral, and it would be quite the ride.

A week rolled by, and then it happened—my car got stolen. And let me tell you, I *adored* that thing. It was a 1999 Honda CRV, a customized beauty. To me, it was my very own Millennium Falcon (cue the Han Solo voice: "She might not look like much, but she's got it where it counts!").

I was on the verge of going Down The Spiral (DTS), but then I reined myself in. I recognized that this was precisely what the Stream had been preaching. So, I refused to let anger and frustration take the wheel. I began the journey back to my neutral state, seemingly indifferent to the situation. But soon, I had an epiphany—maintaining indifference wouldn't mend the situation either. Instead, I came to terms with the fact that my Millennium Falcon had likely embarked on a one-way trip to a chop shop. After all, it was a vintage Honda loaded with custom bits and bobs. So, without further ado, I cruised over to the Honda dealership that very day (yes, I'm a die-hard Honda enthusiast) to snag the latest edition of the Honda Fit, a car I'd been eyeing for years. I'd always planned to get one eventually, but why bother when I had a trusty CRV?

Turns out, they had just one left, and by sheer 'luck,' it was the color I had in mind. It also happened to be the final year for the Fit since they ceased production. So this was literally my last chance to get one!

Two hours later, I drove my brand-spanking-new X-Wing Starfighter off the lot, with just five miles on the odometer.

I'd gone up my spiral, and things were looking up. My Millennium Falcon had flown off into the sunset, but my

X-Wing Starfighter was poised to take me on thrilling new adventures.

But wait, there's more!

Another fortnight passed, and out of the blue, I received a call from the police department. They had found my Millennium Falcon, abandoned and still in pristine condition. Even my trusty companion, my plush Boba Fett, was right where I'd left him, peering out the window.

Now, that was a twist I didn't see coming.

I may not be easily surprised anymore, but I'm perpetually amazed by the twists and turns we manifest.

Fast forward to the dawn of 2021, and it felt like all three major areas of my life—romance, health, and finances—had come crashing down in spectacular fashion.

There I sat amid the wreckage, blinking in bewilderment, wondering how I'd managed to send everything into a tailspin in such a short span.

So, once again, I beckoned the Stream.

I hadn't even noticed it, but I hadn't received messages from the Stream on my own for several months. Clarity only came through David. I'd become so detached that I'd allowed my life to spin out.

That car theft had been a mere wake-up call, not enough to jolt me out of my neutral zone for more than a fleeting moment. I'd manifested everything I wanted, sure, but then, on some unconscious level, I'd grown weary of it all. So, I decided to knock down the castles I'd built around me.

The Stream reassured me that I'd done this out of complacency, but with a specific purpose—to rebuild and create an improved version of everything. It all hinged on clarifying my intentions.

So that's precisely what I did.

The reason I've shared this rather epic prologue to the fourth Pillar of Tya is that it's true: we can create from a state of flow. We can even do it without crystal-clear intentions, but in those cases, we might not always shape the scenarios we truly desire. So, by carefully dissecting our preferences, gaining clarity on our desires, and zooming out to see that we're perpetual creators with countless moving parts at play, we can achieve nearly anything.

The Stream

The Pillars of Appreciation, Polarity, and Source all center on raising your vibration in the Tya Practice. We guide you to appreciate your transgressors, manage your spiral, and thus navigate the impact of polarity, and to connect with our energy—your own Stream, which is Source—all to elevate your vibration. A heightened vibration empowers you. You manifest more swiftly, both in terms of what you want and don't want. It might surprise you when we say that you manifest undesired outcomes more rapidly with a higher vibration. This is because as you raise your vibration, you naturally welcome more of your desires. But when you frequently find yourself uplifted, the occasional descent feels steeper and more jarring. Polarity ensures that occasional dips are inevitable, no matter your efforts. From our viewpoint, and soon from your evolved perspective, you'll recognize that these steeper drops, though uncomfortable, are beneficial. They serve as rapid, unmistakable signals from the universe when you veer off course, as in Qatarina's stolen car instance. Perhaps the Tya Practice's most invaluable facet is these swift, distinct indicators of misalignment. If you're practicing daily, you'll typically spot these signs early when they're still minor. Armed with the right tools, you can recalibrate, uplift your mood, and see improved outcomes.

The acceleration of your vibration makes setting clear, positive intentions crucial. When you diligently work to refine and elevate your vibration, you transform into a potent manifestor. With your newly augmented abilities, a deliberate focus becomes paramount for maintaining joy. Sure, a generally raised vibration will positively reshape your life, leading you out of the matrix with increasing frequency. However, your inherent nature constantly discerns preferences. Without specific, desired creations, boredom might set in, lowering your vibration. Without new desires to stimulate your mind, it defaults to crafting challenges, often of a lower vibrational flow. If you respond negatively to these boredom-induced challenges, you risk getting ensnared back in the matrix unless you learn to embrace these challenges with joy.

Intelligent beings like you have a compulsive need to create. Left to their devices, some might introduce drama into their lives just to stimulate their creative faculties—crafting a negative scenario to provide a problem to solve, thus driving new creation. This is evident when individuals with seemingly tranquil lives disrupt their peace with inexplicable actions. This also underscores our belief that there's no inherent negativity. Every event, deemed negative from your perspective, serves a purpose, ultimately furthering expansion and turning out positively.

In the Tya Practice, we differentiate between daily intentions and broader life intentions. Both are vital. As you begin to elevate your vibration, you'll witness quicker manifestation of your intentions. If you aren't vigilant with your thoughts, you might manifest pathways that lower your vibration, extending beyond inspiring positive creation. While you can be as general in your daily and life intentions as you want, being exceedingly broad, e.g., "I wish to be joyous and free," may suffice for a contented life. But can you really be that non-specific? Or are there detailed desires you hold for your day and life? Most are too creative to passively let the universe dictate a vague state of well-being without influencing its trajectory.

In Tya, we guide you to discern preferences without judgment. By this, we mean evaluating everything to determine what suits you, without needing others to concur. Understand that everyone embarks on a unique journey. There's no fixed "right" way to approach anything, including spiritual practices. Don't measure your life against another's—even family members. Your individuality stems from your broader existence, your vibrationally-matched entry point on Earth, and all your manifestations till now. Comparing with others is futile, as they aren't you, and your growth isn't facilitated in identical manners. Expansion, your core purpose in the physical realm, isn't about reaching certain achievements by a specific age. Such a mindset is wholly ego-driven, completely neglecting soul balance.

Questions for the Stream Regarding Intention

Q: Can you discuss the difference between constantly trying to force a manifestation and regularly setting positive intentions? This seems to be a gray area for many of us. When are we merely deceiving ourselves?

A: Constantly "forcing" anything originates from a low vibration rooted in fear. While we guide you to concentrate on your desires rather than what you lack, we also emphasize the significance of recognizing your vibrational spiral. Polarity guarantees that you won't remain static on this spiral. We encourage you to pursue joy, but it's essential to recognize the inherent value of DTS.

The DTS phase is beneficial because it's during these times that you manifest obstacles, which in turn serve as springboards for new creations.

Pursue joy in all experiences, including during DTS, as it's a natural state. Trying to force yourself up the spiral can backfire; the frustration of not progressing quickly enough—or at all—might drag you even further down. Focusing positively on what you desire, coupled with a relaxed trust in its existence, isn't "deceiving yourselves"; it's part and parcel of the creative process.

Every appreciated aspect of your world once existed as a daydream. Engaging in such daydreams in a relaxed, trusting state paves the clearest path to creation. However, if you consistently daydream as an escape from your present life, it doesn't facilitate clear creation. The desire to "escape" a current reality isn't as high-vibrational as expressing gratitude for your present situation—even if it's not your ideal—and trusting that better experiences are forthcoming.

Moreover, believing that dedicating a specific amount of daily time to focus on a desire can also be counterproductive. Insistently pushing for something usually stems from the feeling of "it's not here yet." Grasping the genuine vibration behind thoughts and feelings can be challenging, but if you remember that the universe consistently affirms your sentiments, you'll learn to transmit more positive signals, leading the universe to materialize your wishes.

Consider intentional creation as a "set it and forget it" process. Genuine trust in the universe means you won't revisit your desires constantly. By appreciating your current state and transitioning into new desires with a "wouldn't it be nice..." attitude, rather than an "I must have this to be happy" mindset, you'll discover your desires materializing with ease.

Q: When we focus consistently on the "good," does that truly eliminate the "bad"? Or are we just repressing it, pushing it aside, and overlooking it? I understand there's no judgment either way, but could this be seen as masquerading under false pretenses? Pretending to be something or someone we aren't?

A: We don't advocate for repressing or "pushing aside" anything. On the contrary, we emphasize that your obstacles serve a purpose and should be approached with as much joy as possible. If you're actively working to maintain a high vibe through meditation and appreciation, you'll undoubtedly see numerous benefits. Firstly, by frequently maintaining a higher vibration, you'll encounter fewer obstacles. Have you observed that your friends, family, and coworkers who are generally more positive tend to face fewer challenges, whereas those who are more negative often face more problems? So, which came first, the negativity or the problems? We assert that negative thoughts always precede negative outcomes.

You might then ask, what about young children born into circumstances of illness, war, or abuse? How did their thoughts attract such conditions? Our response is that, from your higher intention—your pre-birth self—you projected into a physical experience that would offer a certain level of duality: a mix of both positive and negative. This level of duality aligns with the type of physical experience you sought from a broader perspective. Souls seeking greater expansion often desire more significant challenges, providing more obstacles to overcome and expand. This explanation is a simplification, but it represents the process of physical manifestation, which we'll refer to as "pre-birth intention."

Beyond pre-birth intention is the reality that all beings possess a vibration and thus operate on a vibrational spiral. From the moment of conception, there's vibration and fluctuation. Physical experiences and discernment of preferences start immediately, and the vibrations of surrounding beings, especially the mother, can be absorbed and even mirrored by the fetus. The baby learns to operate as a new physical entity through these vibrations. As the baby becomes physical, it learns emotions, including fear. This fear can manifest as unwanted circumstances from a human perspective. From a soul perspective, any adverse physical manifestation—often stemming from fear or focus—is a gift, an experience that can be overcome and learned from.

Q: I have a friend who is perpetually cheerful, yet she describes her life as chaotic. She maintains this demeanor because she believes the importance of positivity attracts positive outcomes. Why hasn't she seen any change?

A: Being cheerful isn't necessarily a high vibration. While it's higher than anger, jealousy, or rage, it isn't inherently positive or elevated. "Cheerfulness" often masks underlying pain, fear, or feelings of unworthiness. It sends a message to the universe of a brave face hiding fear. The universe responds to your genuine vibration, to your beliefs and your sense of self-worth, not to the facade you present. A vibration of certainty is potent because your beliefs overshadow everything—you manifest what you truly believe.

Q: If we all set intentions to become billionaires, are we merely chasing castles in the sky unless we actively work toward it?

A: When you genuinely align—achieving a state of "being" which signifies true vibrational alignment—you'll feel compelled to act. This action will feel natural and effortless. Many advocate for "hustling" and "working hard"; these are aspirational approaches. Those who have truly amassed wealth understand that mindset drives their success and actions follow.

The distinction between merely wanting and actively manifesting is profound. Most desire wealth, yet few attain it. This discrepancy stems from the prevalent misconceptions surrounding creation, especially regarding wealth. The mindset shifts and tools we provide require commitment to solidify them as dominant beliefs.

Once this certainty is attained, your vibration will resonate with possession, making manifestation on any topic straightforward. Manifestations might appear to magically materialize, but you aren't here to merely fantasize—you're here to create. Creation in a physical realm blends thought-driven vibrations with inspired action to render tangible outcomes.

Given societal judgments, there are tasks humans generally prefer over others. For example, a star athlete might train extensively and follow a stringent diet, willingly accepting games on weekends or holidays without considering their routine burdensome. A laborer transporting stones might not view their labor as joyfully, and a retail worker might not relish working holidays. Society values the athlete's contribution more, influencing their positive perspective. Hence, what might seem like work for some becomes inspired action for others.

Q: A mentor once advised me to set only realistic goals to avoid unattainability. However, I've set and achieved lofty intentions that many deemed unachievable. How do we distinguish between pursuing our wildest dreams and deluding ourselves with fantasy?

A: Nothing is unattainable. Observe individuals around you setting "unrealistic" goals, defying norms, and accomplishing them. This phenomenon explains why world records are frequently surpassed. Although it's feasible to jump from point A to point Z, bypassing points B to Y, a gradual progression is often more manageable, allowing a vibrational acclimation period.

Q: How can we convey these concepts to our children?

A: Children will likely grasp these pillars with ease. Essentially, it's about anticipating outcomes before acting. The real challenges are: A) instilling this as a habit, and B) managing potential frustration if immediate results aren't evident. Children, being curious learners, will naturally absorb this knowledge, especially if they haven't developed lethargic tendencies. Though their learning journey is uniquely theirs, offering such tools is a high-vibrational endeavor. However, avoid becoming overly fixated on the outcomes.

Q: Any parting thoughts on the Pillar of Intention?

A: At first glance, this pillar might seem elementary—and it is. The true challenge lies in habituating its principles. Devoting time and attention to familiarizing oneself with these pillars is invaluable, especially when such efforts are genuinely inspired.

Summary of Our Shared Consciousness

Intention is the final pillar that weaves the other three into the most elevated vibrational practice humanity has yet realized. This practice is intended for all of humanity, as it establishes an operating system for each individual. This system facilitates a return to a more natural state of being, free from triggers and memories that might haunt or even traumatize. It also fosters a heightened awareness of one's natural vibrational flow and a closer alignment with one's inherent Source consciousness. But what do you do with all of this? What will be your legacy, your contribution to humanity with this newfound power? Have you considered that?

Perhaps you acquired this book with the aim of healing your past and manifesting with clearer intention. Maybe you sought to deepen your understanding of the energetic realm and recognize your eternal nature. Regardless of the reason, as you integrate this practice into your daily life, you'll discover fresh desires. Old dreams, once forgotten or relinquished due to past disappointments, will resurface. Naturally, you'll conceive new aspirations as well.

> **You won't find contentment in merely "existing." You're an innate creator. Even if your earthly experiences so far have seen limited creative output, this renewed practice will stoke a fiercer desire to engage with the world more intentionally. Moreover, you'll likely feel compelled to share this practice. You'll recognize the transformative power the Tya Practice possesses for the entirety of humanity. As you continue this practice, you'll find yourself on the forefront of understanding, embracing the full breadth of human experience. You will epitomize love and profound appreciation, resonating with the universe's highest vibration. You'll realize you've reached this state when you no longer rely on external changes to feel that deep appreciation.**

While being completely at peace, you'll simultaneously yearn for growth. Embodying Source, reveling in all the splendors of your world, you'll achieve a profound sense of understanding. From this elevated perspective, you'll want to share this wisdom with the world, devoid of judgment or the need for others to align with your beliefs. That, in essence, is Source.

Kerry King, Tya Master

When I first began my journey with the Tya Practice and its simple tools, I discovered the power of intention. I decided to set reminders on my phone to establish intentions for my day. I started with a simple intention: "I intend to have the best day ever" and to be mindful of any changes or signs in my vibration. As I delved deeper into spiral work, I heard David share this simple tip that I still use to this day:

Every time I find myself in a vehicle, I set the intention for a safe and stress-free journey. This particular intention has become second nature to me. I realized its power when I forgot to set it once and ended up colliding head-on with a deer. Miraculously, I was completely unharmed, but it made me reflect on how often I would overlook the small signs and how they can affect my experience.

Looking back, the signs were all there; I had been in a rush, and created the experience with the deer, and I am grateful for it. Only my time and money were lost in my rush that day. In that moment, I gained clarity on the importance of setting intentions in my practice. This experience reminded me to stay focused and diligent in setting them for various aspects of my life.

Now, intention-setting is a part of my daily routine. Whether it's the morning ritual of making coffee or as simple as filling up my water jug, I infuse intentions into these actions. For example, as I brew my coffee, I set the intention that it will be the best cup I've ever had. These moments give me the opportunity to set intentions throughout my day, such as expecting kindness from others and noticing signs and miracles that come my way.

Setting intentions has become a way of speaking the Tya belief system over every aspect of my life. I've noticed that when I practice intention-setting, things flow more smoothly, keeping me aligned with my desired vibration and away from old default vibes or negative thoughts. It's a comprehensive approach that covers, well, everything.

When I leave the house, even if it's just for a walk, I set the intention to have a great adventure, to find miracles, and to notice the beauty around me. These intentions keep me on my spiral, always expecting the best possible outcomes. I've learned to let the universe surprise and delight me, rather than trying to control every detail.

In the past, I tended to be very goal-oriented. This mindset led to pressure and stress when I set specific goals and deadlines for myself. I realized that starting with a broad goal of the best possible outcome, allowing the universe to bring gifts my way, to let go and trust, instead of feeling stressed or anxious. What a wonderful way to enjoy life!

Exercises

1. Every morning, set aside time to focus on your daily intentions, ideally following a brief meditation. Mentally map out your day, emphasizing key moments without diving too deep into specifics. Trust the universe to unfold a joyful and abundant day, without fixating on the 'how'; concentrate only on the desired outcome.

Commit to this routine, and you'll witness significant transformations in your day-to-day life.

1. Before you engage in any activity, establish a clear intention for the desired result. For instance, after setting your morning intention, if you're stepping out, hope for a safe and stress-free journey. Have an intention in place for your workday, your leisure time, meetings, meals, and any other engagements.

Communicate your expectations to the universe for each part of your day, as well as your broader life goals.

If you maintain a journal, document your more ambitious intentions. The act of writing down what you anticipate, and then allowing the universe to bring it to fruition without further intervention, epitomizes true faith in your abundance!

Part 3 ~ The Universal Process Of Creation

Introduction

The Stream

Now that you understand your personal vibration and how it shapes your reality, let's delve deeper into the creation and continuous expansion of the entire universe. Consider how this relates to your current physical reality and reflect on what you've learned so far.

- You are perpetually attracting everything that enters your life—your "bubble of reality."

- Your point of attraction is significantly influenced by your vibration.

- A higher vibration is the realm of positive creation, where you attract what you desire. Conversely, during periods of lower vibration, your new creation is moderated to be more manageable, presenting obstacles for you to overcome.

- Crafting solutions to these obstacles, even through improved reactions to them, results in the expansion of your being. Your growth contributes to the universe's expansion.

- The life you've led so far represents your responses to past manifestations, which we term your "default vibration."

Realize the significance of:

- Consistently allowing your natural Source connection; recognizing that this connection is your intuition and that your inner creative genius mirrors this intuition.

- Addressing and neutralizing negative energies from transgressors, which can keep you from being triggered by memories during low-vibrational periods, allowing your default vibration to naturally ascend.

- Being intentional with your thoughts, as they can materialize; you have control over all your manifestations.

Armed with this knowledge and a deeper understanding of the pillars we've introduced, you're primed to uncover the universe's true secret. It's commonly believed that everything is energy, and energy cannot be created or destroyed. While this isn't a scientific treatise—and we concede that science seeks to understand our essence, and we're not here to provide all answers—we aim to offer divine insight to guide your journey. However, energy is indeed expansive, implying the universe is perpetually becoming more intricate and intelligent.

Your expansion, as strands of soul consciousness, enhances the collective consciousness known as humanity, your planet, and the entire universe. Amid this growth, you adjust to your new perceived reality, oblivious to the expansion because you're evolving concurrently. This isn't about physical growth but energetic expansion: the elevation of consciousness becoming increasingly intricate. Revisit movies from different eras like the 80s or 50s. Notice the distinct vibrational shifts? While technological advancements in communication and travel have catalyzed societal evolution, increasing sophistication is inherent because consciousness is innately expansive.

This advanced sophistication doesn't imply that the present is superior to the past. Every era was aligned with its vibrational state. Modern people aren't superior or inferior to their predecessors; they're just more evolved, thanks to the groundwork laid by earlier generations.

We emphasize expansion because it's the primary reason for your physical existence. In essence, you encounter undesirable situations, and these scenarios inspire new solutions, fostering evolution. Such innovations lead to personal and universal expansion. We'll explore this concept more thoroughly in this section, but it's crucial to recognize your purpose and the mechanics of expansion.

Vibrational Flow

The Stream

Now that you comprehend how your personal vibration shapes your reality, let's delve deeper into the universe's creation and its ongoing expansion. Reflect on what you learned in Chapter 2 about how polarity affects your vibrational spiral, impacting your point of attraction and your expansion.

With this foundation, you're poised to grasp the concept of vibrational flow.

Vibrational flow arises from a blend of polarity and your focus. Polarity guarantees that energy remains dynamic, perpetually fluctuating, drawing both wanted and unwanted experiences to ensure ceaseless growth. Your focus, coupled with your response to polarity (as linked to your vibrational spiral), shapes your distinct vibrational flow.

This flow is omnipresent, influencing all creation. Hence, every topic contains elements of duality. When faced with an obstacle, you either let it linger or find a solution. Even the resolution you conceive or permit can be the seed of an entirely new challenge. For instance, you may feel your current house doesn't suffice. In acquiring a new home, beyond the evident trials of selection, selling, and relocating, you confront additional maintenance responsibilities, comparisons to your previous residence, and unanticipated costs and adjustments.

Reflect on this: in every physical experience, there's an element of positivity and negativity. But if "negative" aspects exist primarily to inspire fresh, positive creation, can they truly be deemed negative? From our vantage point of impartiality, we perceive all creation as growth-inducing, rendering everything positive. What you might judge as negative merely serves as a catalyst for your next endeavor, making it inherently positive.

The following graphic is a depiction of an example of vibrational flow. While the previously shared graphic illustrated the range of vibrations one may experience as they move up and down their virtual vibrational spiral, this one illustrates how physically manifested beings move through a "vibrational landscape." Up and down, throughout various periods of life—from a single day to an entire lifetime—you are constantly navigating a landscape that is uniquely yours. This landscape is developed by a combination of how you choose to meet your manifested reality and what polarity is offering you based on your energetic signature. This energetic signature serves as the basis for astrology. The Tya Practice acknowledges both your energetic signature and your unique, self-crafted belief system that combine to create the vibrational flow landscape that shapes your reality.

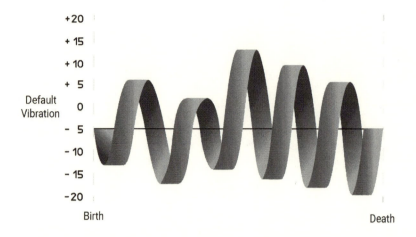

YOUR VIBRATIONAL FLOW - A COMPLIANT LIFE

You are already familiar with vibrational flow because you live it every day. One day, you're on cloud nine, exuding confidence and joy, with desires effortlessly materializing. Yet, the following day, you may be riddled with doubt, questioning the feasibility of the dreams you hatched the day before. You may ponder, "Do such things ever pan out for me?" or recall past failures. In these phases, you're essentially recalibrating your aspirations, and the ever-affirmative universe starts reshaping your manifestations in tandem.

Recognizing the persistent role of vibrational flow in your life illuminates its timeless, universal purpose. When discussing the universe's creation and continual growth—termed as "expansion"—we employ the most suitable language to convey ideas slightly beyond human understanding. We use terms like "high" or "low" vibration without any judgment or hierarchical implication. To humans, "low vibration" or "dark energy" equates to low or absent consciousness within the energetic realm.

The lesser the consciousness, the more it dampens higher-consciousness energy. This energy, emanating from the Source, is counterbalanced by lower-consciousness energy, preventing an uncontrollable spiral that could obliterate the universe. The restrained energy introduces hurdles in physical realms, spurring conscious beings to innovate solutions. Such innovation results in growth.

You might wonder, "Why the necessity for hurdles? Why not simply evolve?" The crux lies in the fact that challenges are innovations in themselves. While physical realms deem them undesirable, solutions must be contrived. This dynamic tension, perpetuated by the relentless cycle of vibrational flow, fosters consistent innovation, guaranteeing both novelty and growth.

In physical terms, this cycle witnesses a birth, expansion through overcoming challenges, and eventually serving as sustenance for another entity. While the eternal being evolves, the physical form facilitates the growth of other beings. All this is orchestrated by vibrational flow, which ensures challenges arise and subsequently offers opportunities for intuitive solutions.

Vibrational flow also ensures that the physical vehicle wears out and returns the being to its completed state of non-physical if the challenge of the life experience does not do so prior to that. Vibrational flow regulates all creation.

Qatarina

Allowing the flow of things can be quite the art form, and let's be honest, it's trickier than it sounds. We humans have this penchant for wanting to be the conductors of our life's symphony. We desire to orchestrate our surroundings, script the events that come our way, and, if possible, even puppeteer the people we hold dear.

This whole concept of "flow" was first beamed into my consciousness back in my hippie days. The word was thrown around with casual abandon among my peers. It could easily be taken to the extreme, you know, "Just kick back and let things flow, man." Often used as a convenient excuse to lounge around and watch life unfold without lifting a finger. An appealing argument for plain old laziness.

But there's a fine line between letting things flow and taking the reins of your reality. Through my journey, I've come to realize that it all hinges on where we find ourselves on our vibrational rollercoaster. Taking control feels like a breeze when you're UTS, and from that high perch, things flow effortlessly. However, when we're at the bottom of our spiral, it's like trying to herd cats, and seizing control morphs into a fierce battle. Now, if you find yourself DTS, there's still room for flow, but expect things to unfold in a rather—uh—topsy-turvy fashion.

I've learned this the hard way, as I mentioned in the previous section when we dived into the fourth pillar of Tya, Intention. There was a phase when I let things flow with all the finesse of a bull in a china shop. I stopped caring, ceased setting intentions, and sure enough, things kept flowing—just not in the direction I'd prefer. My relationship started to resemble a sinking ship, my income dried up faster than a puddle in the desert, and my health took a nosedive. It turned into a vicious cycle: feeling lousy, unintentionally causing myself harm, becoming unable to work, straining my relationship, and the cycle continued ad infinitum.

But it's entirely possible to rein it all back in. It's simple in theory but not always a cakewalk in practice. The ease depends on how far off the rails you've let things go. The trick is to soar Up The Spiral and create consciously from there. Focus, set clear intentions for the best possible outcome, and stick with it. Eventually, the pieces start falling back into their rightful places. Sure, you might not get precisely what you expect, but it's the surefire way to break free from the stagnation cycle and welcome the sweet return of genuine flow into your reality.

Isn't it fascinating how things dig in their heels when we try to force them? So, when we make an effort to consciously create and it feels like a tug of war, that's the universe's way of saying, "Easy there, partner." Let the vibrational current carry you, but don't be a dead weight. You know how challenging it is to lift someone who's not holding onto you? Same principle. Being proactive in allowing the flow guarantees more enduring and far-reaching results.

Now, all this leads me to my burning questions about the fine line between control and flow.

Questions for the Stream Regarding Vibrational Flow

Q: Most LOA practitioners teach that as long as you focus on the good and what is going right, only more good will come. If this is the case, would that be considered controlling the flow?

A: It certainly seems like an attempt to control the flow. However, observe that no one achieves complete control; they are always "works in progress." The true universal process of creation ensures that a being cannot maintain a constant flow of only the desired outcomes. The idea of focusing exclusively on the positive is typically well-intended, but it can lead to unrealistic expectations of perpetual bliss. Such expectations, when unmet, cause frustration. Ironically, the very process of becoming frustrated by this incongruent idea accelerates the true creative process. Thus, regardless of the teachings absorbed, there's no "getting it wrong."

Given the progress many of you have made, we now offer a deeper understanding of universal law. Every individual reading these words has expanded their thinking, experiencing both success and setbacks. This evolution testifies to the perfection of the universal law. Through your species' evolution, you've nurtured this heightened understanding of your creative abilities and the laws governing them.

You must understand that you're not here merely to focus on your wants and keep receiving more "good" things in an endless loop. There's no innovation in that cycle. The presence of "unwanted" elements provides the necessary tension to inspire genuine creation.

Consider this example: a person prefers sunny days filled with relaxation, indulging in chocolate and fine wine, enjoying optimal health, and having every requirement met without a challenge. Through the Law of Attraction, while in this focused state, this individual remains in an endless loop of just that. While initially appealing, such a scenario lacks innovation, offering only repetition. This stagnation would contribute less to universal expansion over time. The inclusion of "unwanted" elements ensures that fresh, innovative solutions will emerge to restore the desired state. Even if a being achieves this loop, the eventual onset of monotony will drop the vibration, ensuring the emergence of unwanted conditions to inspire new creation.

Q: Even though there is no "good" or "bad" per se, is it more conducive to our growth to let obstacles manifest naturally instead of continuously trying to "manifest" our "perfect" lives?

A: While there's nothing wrong in aspiring and focusing on a better life, you'll probably find that constantly chasing perfection can lower your vibration, given that perfection is an ever-shifting goal due to polarity, growth, and the universal process of creation itself.

The more accepting you are of your obstacles, the less they scare you, reducing their dominance in your focus and decreasing their frequency or intensity. Diminishing the fear of obstacles also facilitates a quicker return to higher vibration when a challenge arises, and that's when the solution to any problem becomes evident. The reduced presence of fear accelerates the shift back to a higher vibration, ensuring a more efficient arrival of solutions.

Summary of Our Shared Consciousness

In Part Two, we introduced the four pillars of the Tya Practice, and we illuminated how your vibration affects your point of attraction, influencing your life.

Understanding and managing your vibration is crucial. It helps you know where you usually stand on the vibrational spiral. Vibrational flow, with its energy fluctuations, ensures you don't stagnate in your vibration, providing the contrast you sought by coming to Earth.

Vibrational flow not only created but continues to expand all that exists. It's an endless cycle of energy shifts that drives growth, moving from UTS desired states to DTS challenges to solutions. This never-ending loop is evident in every aspect of the physical realm. Just observe, and you'll find countless examples.

The Perfection of Imperfection

The Stream

Coming into awareness of vibrational flow is a profound revelation on Planet Earth. Few humans come to understand this potent process, the true facilitator of all creation. Now that you've grasped our teachings about vibrational flow, you can ascend to a broader perspective of non-judgment regarding your obstacles and the world's challenges. As we've emphasized, vibrational flow fosters a perpetual cycle of high and low vibrations, ensuring a dynamic point of attraction and a continuous blend of desired and undesired outcomes. What seem like obstacles truly serve to refine any creation. For instance, stories of individuals overcoming staggering odds to realize their dreams are among humanity's most cherished narratives—triumphs against adversity. Why? Because your eternal consciousness recognizes this as vibrational flow, and a part of you deeply resonates with such tales. Likewise, tales of renowned companies enduring hardships to achieve immense success, or how their flagship product often evolved significantly from its original concept, showcase vibrational flow in action.

As a human, navigating through vibrational flow can be enhanced. If you retain only one insight from this book, recognize that flow is innate and beneficial. The sole reason anyone "fails" is that they encounter an obstacle during a low-vibrational flow and subsequently withdraw. They abandon their pursuit. They decide it's the end. This phenomenon is evident in diets, relationships, businesses, wealth accumulation, spiritual growth—essentially every facet of life.

Now, recognize that when confronted with an obstacle, your instinctive response might have been to let your vibration plummet. Feelings of doubt, fear, anger, envy, and other negative emotions were perhaps ingrained reactions. Maybe you were conditioned to dread obstacles, presuming they signaled a dead end. We assert that every decision lies with you. Every challenge you face in life, crafted through vibrational flow, is your own creation. Even if you're uncertain about their origins, the power to surmount them resides within you—after all, they materialized for that very purpose. Perhaps, until now, you were unaware of this.

The initial adverse response, which we term "step one," can be wholly bypassed. Rarely does a "step one" reaction provide solutions. Any "lower vibration" reaction will merely magnetize similar experiences. With your newfound understanding of vibrational flow, you can regard your challenges as integral to the universal creative process. From our vantage point, negativity is a mere construct, as all that humans might classify as negative is simply a subjective judgment. In reality, these are merely opportunities for growth, devoid of negativity. This concept underpins what we call "the perfection of imperfection," because genuine imperfection doesn't exist.

Qatarina

I mentioned earlier that my chronic pain didn't decide to take an extended vacation until I fully embraced it as a permanent part of my life. It wasn't merely acceptance; I actually found a way to appreciate it. Believe it or not, it played a pivotal role in shaping my character and honing my mental and physical resilience.

Now, let's not get carried away; I don't have an epic tale of miraculous healing that could rival a blockbuster movie. And you know what? I'm perfectly fine with that. But it did take me a hot minute to reach this "perfectly imperfect" status. Even though my symptoms have drastically improved, there are still those occasional days when I find myself parked in bed with a migraine for what feels like an eternity. And when my Multiple Sclerosis decides to throw a synchronized chaos party, well, let's just say I get a tad cranky. But here's the twist: I now understand that these moments don't imply there's something fundamentally wrong with me. Pain isn't the villain here; it's just part of the grand cosmic tapestry.

Instead of plunging headfirst down my spiral when pain decides to gate-crash my existence, launching a full-blown pity party for one, I shift my focus. I ask myself, "What's the universe trying to teach me this time? How can I turn this into a mini-vacation from the daily grind?" From there, once I manage to climb back up my spiral, a whole galaxy of fresh thoughts starts orbiting my mind.

That's how I stumbled upon the magical duo of weightlifting and skydiving as my unconventional pain-management dream team. You see, I was in a heightened state of vibrational ascent when I recalled my early twenties' adventures in skydiving. Miraculously, my neuro and fibro pain decided to take an extended nap after those adrenaline-pumping jumps. But becoming an advanced skydiver meant beefing up my physique to handle parachute acrobatics and acing those gravity-defying freefalls. Yoga had already granted me the flexibility, but I needed some muscle action. So, naturally, I fell head over heels for weightlifting.

Fast forward a few years, and not only are these activities still my jam, but they also continue to keep my pain at bay. It turns out the universe is quite the problem solver when you're UTS and ready to receive its cosmic gifts.

On a side note, chronic pain has gifted me something extraordinary—an unwavering appreciation for the pain-free days in my life. It's a kind of appreciation I doubt I would have discovered otherwise. And this brings me to my opening question for the Stream on this intriguing topic...

Questions for the Stream Regarding Perfection

Q: If we don't allow duality to manifest in our lives, would we lose appreciation for our preferences?

A: If that were a possibility within universal law, the short answer would indeed be yes. Delving deeper, as we've previously discussed, your creative mind would stagnate in a ceaseless cycle of manifesting only desires without obstacles. Eventually, this monotony would diminish the vibration, restarting the creative process.

Q: Do you have advice for someone inundated with obstacles, such as chronic pain, severe poverty, or emotional abuse, to the point that they can only focus on their suffering? How can they elevate their state?

A: An individual faced with numerous simultaneous challenges likely harbors a potent victim—or out-of-control—vibration, even if they're unwilling to acknowledge it. Our counsel is to assume responsibility for the entirety, even without comprehending its genesis, and embrace it as your creation. This acceptance sets the course toward appreciation and, given time, the complete neutralization of all transgressor energy. This initial step is vital for healing and positive transformation. However, it starkly contrasts conventional human wisdom, which often promotes a sense of powerless victimhood.

Summary of Our Shared Consciousness

For millennia, humanity has measured itself against a self-centered ideal. This comparison has only intensified with the collective consciousness you've sculpted through the expansion of communication technology. It stands to reason that such "collective reflection," challenging long-established control structures—dubbed the matrix—could catalyze profound transformation. The human constructs of race, religion, gender, and even sexual identity, which no longer align with modern humanity, could be redefined or altogether discarded, paving the way for individual freedoms.

Ideally, breaking free from the matrix should usher humanity toward a more utopian existence. Yet, it hasn't. The more you realize the depth of your subjugation, the more certain sections of society ardently defend and cling to their chains. Additionally, as many abandon antiquated labels seeking broader freedom, they concurrently adopt new tags, construing themselves as marginalized victims of their freshly minted subcultural identities. Even as some aspire for greater equity, tolerance, and fairness, they increasingly display intolerance toward those not attuned to their evolving identity.

This exemplifies the dynamic wherein resolving one issue invariably spawns others. Despite this, it doesn't deter your problem-solving instinct. Your inherent expansive nature, buoyed by a perpetual quest for perfection—stemming from ego—guarantees that humanity will consistently strive for improvement. However, the inbuilt mechanism of vibrational flow ensures a perpetual cycle of problem-solving followed by the emergence of new challenges. Contrast spurs expansion, and such contrast is an inherent facet of vibrational flow—the perfection of imperfection.

Universal Expansion

The Stream

All creation is an endless wormhole of mirrored creation. Humanity is a unique expression of Source, as is everything universally. Now that you've delved deep into our message and begun to grasp the entirety of your being, we will share insights to bring your full worthiness into your awareness.

Nothing in the physical realm is "organic" in the sense that it arises without thought or design. From your limited human perspective, you often remain unaware of this thought or design. We term it "limited human" because the eternal version of you—the soul-consciousness version—understands how the universe operates on a quantum level, being an integral part of it. As a physically manifested entity, specifically a human, you are constrained to an Earthly perspective. This limitation ensures you relish the expansion of this environment, of which you are a co-creator.

Every aspect of your world, and every world, was meticulously designed—including you. You often differentiate between things that are organically grown, considering them natural, and those created by humans as being constructed. Yet, the process is consistent; the level of technological sophistication is what varies. This might sound improbable, especially to those only now beginning to resonate with teachings like these, but we aim to foster an awareness that allows your deductive reasoning to grasp this concept.

When humans think of design, they typically envision nuts, bolts, sawn pieces of wood, or molded plastic. Yet, every facet of Planet Earth has been ingeniously configured to sustain a self-contained ecosystem. This unique chunk of matter, containing all elements essential for nurturing intelligent life, is buttressed by an array of celestial bodies, each playing its part in the symphony of Earth's conscious expression.

Earth and your solar system represent just one of countless similar environments. However, it's all an illusion—an expression of the non-physical. The high-density core of Source consciousness—whether termed love, God-consciousness, or any other nomenclature—and the low-vibration, consciousness-devoid gray matter work in tandem. The latter serves as a regulator, preventing our pure-positive expression from expansive explosion that could obliterate the universe itself. Polarity guarantees a self-regulating flow that constitutes the high-vibration energy at the core of Source—where we, the consciousness you're currently accessing, exist.

Original thought isn't truly original; it's devoid of a start or finish. For humans, fully comprehending this is a Herculean task. We frequently reference expansion, rather than time, because everything that has or will ever exist already does. This expansion constantly refines pre-existing entities into more sophisticated versions. In the energetic realm, a refined thought immediately becomes an eternal one. It's akin to an infinite overwrite, where the updated version becomes the archetype in a realm without past or future; it just "is."

The entire universe—all that exists—is boundless, continuously refreshing itself into newer, more intricate versions. Though space doesn't extend indefinitely, the universe is perpetually expansive. Consciousness isn't birthed or extinguished; instead, it evolves in sophistication. While new realms come into existence and old ones may dissolve, their energetic signature merely transforms. Every physical creation is, in essence, an illusion, a manifestation of consciousness providing a tangible experience. All tangible experiences embody polarity, infusing the dual nature of experience that catalyzes fresh thought creation and, in turn, broadens consciousness. Thus, your consciousness melds into the formidable collective of the whole, where we, as the core, reside.

The lower-vibrational energy acts as our self-imposed governor. It isn't intrinsically evil, dark, or malicious; rather, it's an inert force void of consciousness and, by extension, love and expansiveness. Without intent, direction, or aspirations, it merely exists.

The perceptions of "darkness" or "evil" emanating in a physical realm always sprout from ego-consciousness or its judgments. Ego-driven fears and judgments invariably sow seeds of harm. This fear can be neutralized through positive focus and trust but will never be wholly eradicated in any tangible environment. All such environments operate on the principle of the survival of the fittest. Over-prioritizing the "less-than-fittest" will inevitably spawn new detrimental scenarios. We neither encourage nor dissuade this; such evolutionary advancements in creation are intrinsic to the creation process, so there's genuinely no "misstep." Understand, however, that creating conditions permitting all to flourish—as opposed to favoring the elite, robust, or dominant—diminishes the collective vibrational strength of whatever you support.

Observe how the universe naturally guides weaker beings to a state of completion, while humans often focus on bolstering them and neutralizing perceived threats. This mirrors an egocentric thought process working in opposition to universal consciousness—an exemplification of polarity. This contrast, representing a self-sustaining environment of Planet Earth thriving with the evolution of dominant beings and humanity operating in fear, produces the tension requisite for genuine expansion in any physical setting.

When you are in a high state of allowing, zoomed out to your highest perspective, you understand that there is neither wrong nor evil in your world, only examples of all beings in a spectrum from low-to-high vibrational flow. Conditions produced in low-vibrational flow cause you to focus on improvement. In your high-vibrational state, as you allow your desires to flow, solutions form via the co-creative energy of your ego's desire for improvement combined with Source's pure love for you. In this intersection of desire and belief, new creation is born, obstacles are overcome, and these resolutions ignite the spark of new creation.

Understanding that your physical expression is essentially an illusion or a simulation, you recognize that your reality is your mind's powerful creation. You can then harness the power to shape it as you see fit. Indeed, nothing is truly "impossible"; it's just yet inconceivable. But even the inconceivable becomes conceivable once belief takes root.

This is why there are no absolute poles, no definitive right or wrong, only varying alignment with desires. Hence, adhering to a fixed set of beliefs rarely fosters expansive growth. Merely absorbing the thoughts of others without questioning or exploring them limits personal evolution. As creators, you came to experience both the wanted and unwanted, and to create anew from those experiences. You crafted an avatar—a human being—and placed it into circumstances guaranteed to provide challenges based on your eternal desire for expansion from an eternal-consciousness perspective. You understood that this new human ego might overshadow your innate eternal wisdom, and that this overshadowing would pave the path to expansion.

Your expansive path is your unique creation. Here you are now, reading our words, connecting dots in ways you perhaps haven't before. While it's tempting to dwell on the energetic realm or past lives, the vastness of these topics, void of physical expression and linear time, surpasses current human understanding. And while you are free to let your mind wander, this exploration offers limited expansive power. Remember, you eternally exist in that non-physical state beyond physical expression.

At your core, you are non-physical. As much as you cherish physical interactions, humanity is also evolving back to a more non-physical state of being as it becomes more sophisticated. We aren't referencing a "death experience" return to the non-physical but rather a transition to a more virtual existence while still in the physical realm. This collective desire is manifesting in real-time all around.

Humanity's collective consciousness has spawned technology enabling unparalleled communication. This surge in communication and the resulting avalanche of information are fueling expansion or evolution of thought. This is new intelligence for humanity, your own creation. Since you inhabit a polarized environment, both positive and negative exist in every topic. Yet, ultimately, positive prevails because negativity only exists in perspective and is birthed to aid expansion.

Despite where individuals might be on their journey to understanding, the common thread among humanity is an evolution—albeit at varying paces—toward a more virtual experience. This is because your Soul consciousness is drawing you toward a more non-physical-like experience. As your physical experience evolves, you become more akin to the non-physical even while being physically present. Essentially, you're reverting to your natural state of being.

This doesn't imply a doomsday scenario where humanity devastates the planet, transitioning into a perpetual non-physical state. What comes next, and its pace, are simply facets of physical reality. Collectively, you decide humanity's fate, just as individually you decide your personal journey.

The reason we impart this knowledge to those keen on this practice is to equip you with an enriched understanding of Earth's creation mechanism. With this, you can shape the pliable clay of your brilliant imagination. Our aim in sharing this is to emphasize that you are manifesting this experience, inclusive of your universe and all within it, through your mind. How you utilize this information is up to you. You can dismiss it as fantastical, allow it to challenge your perceptions of reality, or embrace the clarity it offers, returning to the creation of a more fulfilling reality. This understanding lets you savor your time here with a leading-edge grasp of your eternal nature and the playful creative expression you've forged for sheer experience.

Qatarina

We transcend these mere physical vessels. It's a concept many of us nod in agreement with, at least in theory. But how many of us actually embrace and embody this truth in our daily lives? As a collective of humans, we still tether a hefty portion of our self-worth to the physical realm. "Healthy is good. Sick is bad." "If our bank accounts overflow, we're abundantly successful! Anyone with less must be trapped in a poverty mindset."

Let's call it what it is—human-made constructs. There's no inherent right or wrong in any of this. The person indulging in fast food and puffing on cigarettes isn't any less "enlightened" than the vegan donning bamboo pants who runs ten miles daily. What matters most is their happiness with their chosen paths.

What the Stream has shared in this chapter encourages us to shift our perspective from the purely human realm to a more soulful vantage point. Yes, we're humans, temporarily inhabiting these physical forms, leading these earthly lives. However, the wisdom imparted by the Stream offers us the opportunity to expand and evolve in ways we couldn't fathom otherwise.

In this grander perspective, we become like cosmic explorers, traversing the boundless realms of experience and consciousness. As we journey through the vast tapestry of existence, we not only transcend the limitations of our earthly perceptions but also contribute to the ongoing universal expansion, each of us a unique brushstroke on the canvas of creation. So, together, let's embark on this cosmic odyssey, seeking answers that resonate with the symphony of the cosmos itself.

From this point forward, my inquiries for the Stream will venture into the grander scope of existence. Let's take a moment to zoom out and contemplate the bigger picture.

Questions for the Stream Regarding Universal Expansion

Q: Should we feel so compelled, how do you recommend we "get out there" and share this with others?

A: Whether to keep this knowledge private or share it with the world is entirely up to your discretion. However, as you delve deeper into this journey—perhaps after revisiting this book a couple of times—you might find a newfound clarity in the application of this practice. This profound understanding might drive you to share it with everyone. Yet, you may soon discover that not everyone resonates with this message; many might not be ready for it. Nonetheless, your full alignment with these tools and insights might guide you to release any concerns about how your message is received.

Realize that by sharing, you embark on a path of personal expansion. As you begin to grasp the essence of life's purpose, based on what we've outlined here, you'll likely feel compelled to disseminate this knowledge. Doing so without the fear of judgment and being at peace with your own vibrational flow will lead you to unparalleled peace and harmony.

Share your insights with conviction. Relay the transformative tools you've adopted in your journey. Approach this sharing fearlessly, knowing that those who align with this knowledge will benefit, and this expansion will reverberate back to you.

Summary of Our Shared Consciousness

As innately curious beings still on the path of comprehending the full scope of your existence, it's natural for you to seek understanding about your creation, the intentional crafting of your reality, and the overarching purpose of it all.

We've provided in-depth insights that might require some time for complete assimilation. We encourage you not to let our words overwhelm you; instead, use them as a beacon for clearer understanding, should you feel so aligned and choose to pursue it.

Remember, humanity's shift toward these ideas is relatively recent, especially when compared to long-standing beliefs that have shaped centuries. Be gentle with yourselves. Consistent engagement with the Tya tools leads to deeper clarity. If this path resonates with you, our teachings might become a lifelong pursuit—but rest assured, the vibrational rewards commence immediately.

Part 4 ~ Tya Tools

Introduction

The Stream

Now that you understand how the entire universe was created and continues to expand via new creation and how this applies to your current physical reality, take a moment to reflect on what you learned in Part 3:

- Vibrational flow, a shift of energy from high to low vibration, drives the universal process of creation. Through the Law of Attraction, this fluctuation causes consciousness to manifest various outcomes, ensuring a balance between positive experiences to cherish and challenges to foster new, affirmative creations.

- Since challenges—or that which you consider negative—primarily serve to stimulate fresh, positive creations, there isn't genuinely any negative aspect—only preferences and motivations for innovation.

- While popular LOA teachings advocate for a state of happiness to manifest desires, they often overlook the inherent value of facing challenges.

- While striving for perfection is innate, it's the imperfections that fuel true expansion, leading us to celebrate "the perfection of imperfection."

- Consciousness underpins all creation; every physical manifestation originates from consciousness, evolving as a form of "organic" technology.

- Humanity's well-meaning efforts to correct or compensate for flaws can inadvertently dilute the collective creation's potency.

David

While the majority of this book presents the channeled perspective of the Stream, I wanted to be the one to introduce you to the Tya Tools. As I've developed this practice and shared it with people worldwide, I've witnessed the incredible power of crafting a set of tools to put these ideas into action in your life. The teachings from the Stream are undeniably inspiring, but having these practical tools to anchor and guide me through my natural vibrational fluctuations has proven to be invaluable.

It's relatively easy to put these ideas into action when you first encounter them, full of fresh excitement and inspiration. But what happens as time goes on? We now understand vibrational flow and how it naturally dips on every topic. The novelty wears off, and we often revert to our default habits and vibration. This is why we tend to cycle back to our old selves and previous vibrations even after making initial progress. It's the reason diets, relationships, and new business ventures often falter. We start enthusiastically but hit a wall, revealing flaws and challenges that can lead us back to our old ways.

A robust set of tools serves as a guiding light when you find yourself in moments of uncertainty or darkness. The Tya Practice is a mindset and philosophy that comes equipped with these tools for times when your new mindset is put to the test. Part of the practice involves unlearning many things we were taught in the matrix—ideas that once served their purpose but are no longer needed as humanity evolves.

These tools are practical and applicable to your everyday life, designed to help you stay aligned with the timeless wisdom provided by the Stream. We continue to add new tools as more individuals join the movement and present new ideas and challenges within the practice. When you become a Tya practitioner—or Tyist—you become part of a global community of people who are learning to operate their lives from a higher, Source-connected perspective in the physical world. Using these tools and contributing to the practice's expansion is a two-way street; it grows as you grow.

This is life beyond the matrix, where we claim our power to create the life we desire. We observe the matrix, which is the rest of the world, with appreciation for their unique journeys, even when they grapple with fear, judgment, and division. Life beyond the matrix can occasionally feel isolating, as if we're venturing through the wilderness while the rest of the world clings to their limitations in fear and judgment. However, we detach from the need for them to follow our path or have anything other than the perfect journey they're manifesting for themselves. Tya is a personal journey, an adaptation of an operating system we create for our lives, as opposed to defaulting into the matrix, as most of us have done until now.

Feel free to choose which, if any, of these tools you wish to incorporate into your practice; there are no rigid rules in Tya—only the four pillars of Appreciation, Source, Polarity, and Intention that we embrace as a way of life. The manner in which we apply these principles is entirely individual and constantly evolving. The four pillars are rooted in universal law and will remain unchanged, but how we practice them must evolve as we progress on our vibrational journeys. Otherwise, we risk becoming bored, complacent, and reverting to old matrix habits, which we'll delve into later in this book. Use these tools as you see fit. Bookmark this section and return to it whenever you need to revisit or add tools to your repertoire as you continue practicing the four pillars.

The tools we've shared here are tried and tested, and like all things in life, they possess the power you assign to them. Believe that they will transform your life, and they most certainly will. Always remember, YOU are the power!

Qatarina

This section of the book is my favorite part. This is where we get into the nitty-gritty of how to really live this practice and make it part of your everyday life.

Sure, all this stuff sounds fine and dandy, until we try to put it in practice for real. That's when it gets tricky. When your mother-in-law is screaming at you, how easy is it to remember your Tya Practice? What about when the bathroom toilet overflows? Your pet dies? Significant other leaves suddenly?

I can tell you right now: not always that easy. But definitely still possible. Especially when you utilize the following tools. The Stream is full of handy-dandy ways of keeping this practice applicable and accessible.

One of the most important parts is focusing on the positive when things are going well. That's not something that is heavily practiced in this society. When people enjoy themselves, they don't tend to really live in the moment. Instead, they focus their energy on how to get back to it over and over. Chasing a cheap high if you will.

What I like most about the Tya Tools is that they provide preventative maintenance. It's like taking supplements instead of painkillers. But even so, if you still get caught in a situation you perceive as negative, the tools are always there to help you get out. They are just all-encompassing that way.

The following tools have saved my butt on so many occasions I can't even count. As I write this, I'm in my fourth year of Tya Mastery now, and sometimes I don't even realize I'm using the Tya Tools anymore. That's how ingrained they have become. I may still need a gentle—or not-so-gentle—reminder from the Stream to use them, but they are effective every time.

In this section, the questions don't just come from me. Some of them come from a conglomeration of our Tya Mastery group meetings where I took notes when the others spoke.

You will find this section to be higher-level than the concepts introduced in the previous section, so don't be surprised if you have to read certain parts more than once.

We are all learning. So I hope you find the following tools as beneficial in your life as I have in mine.

Okay, I don't have to hope...I *know* they will be (insert winky face here).

*We have added case studies from our Tya Academy graduates as well as exercises for you to do where we believe they will help you in your Tya Practice. These are presented after the explanation for each "Tya Tool."

Vibrational Notes

The Stream

All creation is vibrational—energetic—meaning every creation has a specific vibrational frequency. For the purposes of these teachings and the Tya Practice, we've devised a visualization tool for you. Remember, your imagination is a formidable creator. As previously stated, every creation was first imagined into existence, so never underestimate the might of your imagination. Use it to conceive a vibrational note that aligns with any desire you hold.

Visualize this note as a red line floating above you. Embrace the vibration of your desire, whatever it might be. Envision it as if it's already yours. Now, align yourself with that note. Create a ping—a distinct feeling that evokes your desire. Recall a time when a specific sound or aroma captured a memorable moment for you. In the same manner, conjure an experience from scratch, allowing you to relive it repeatedly, savoring the resonance of its unique frequency. Delight in the sensation of possessing your desire and recognize that your imagination can convince the universe you've transformed, prompting it to deliver your manifestation. Commit this note to memory using the vibrational timestamp and express gratitude for your new manifestation. It belongs to you.

Your task moving forward is to avoid over-focusing, as your vibration is bound to shift. In moments of lower vibration, you might revisit and question the how, when, and where, generating interference that could disrupt the note connection and potentially slow or even stop your new manifestation.

Another application of Vibrational Notes involves visualizing a situation that typically pushes you into a lower vibrational state. However, instead of responding automatically (a reaction cultivated from your beliefs), recreate this typically triggering event from our viewpoint—view it without judgment. Appreciate and deeply understand it.

We guide you to initiate this practice with less challenging events and gradually tackle bigger ones as you feel ready. As you progress, you'll establish vibrational momentum and eventually confront real-life challenges from a higher vantage point.

Define your new desire, align with the note, embrace the isness—the pure state of being of your desired outcome—and let it be. Avoid searching for it or yearning for it. Relish your present moment, trusting that the universe always acts in your favor. Any desire that doesn't manifest promptly is simply gathering momentum to materialize in the best

possible way for you. And any hurdle encountered during its creation only refines the manifestation, ensuring the realization of an even better version of what you desire.

Qatarina

As we delve deeper into the Tya Practice, the Stream is introducing an array of new terms, such as "ping" and "isness." These Streamisms begin to unveil their meaning as you progress through the teachings and practice. In addition to the mini glossary at the start of this book, remember that there's a comprehensive Streamism Glossary at the end for your reference, available whenever you need it.

Observing the evolution of these terms over the years has been a delightful journey. Sometimes, David doesn't even recall them right after the Stream introduces them. It's either one of us jotting them down or asking him about it once his channeling session concludes. Then he goes back to review the recording for further insights. As time passes, the Stream delves deeper into these terms and concepts, providing more information and explanations as they revisit them.

At times, it feels like they toss new ideas at us entirely out of left field—introducing entirely new Tya Tools as if from thin air. After a live channeling session, I've turned to David and asked, "Did they just introduce a whole new concept?" His usual response involves a few blinks, followed by, "Yes, they certainly did." This has occurred quite frequently since David and I embarked on writing this book. They've even given me direct instructions when I least expected it, like saying, "Make sure to go back, watch this recording, and include this information in your book."

Well, Stream, as you've requested...

Questions for the Stream Regarding Vibrational Notes

Q: Are we accelerating the manifestation in 3D? Or are we decelerating the 5D to materialize in the physical realm?

A: The emergence of any new creation hinges on your alignment with it. The universe neither fast-tracks nor delays anything; given that there's no judgment, there's no precedence either. Metrics are 3D constructs resulting from vibrational flow. The undulating movement generated by polarity guarantees the rhythm of creation, and, as noted, those desires you hold deeply often take longer to materialize because of your frequent contemplation, rather than simply letting them unfold. This delay serves to refine your "significant" creations, resulting in a more evolved version of what you deem essential.

Q: How many notes can one possess?

A: These are your constructs, and you can conceive as many as you're able. However, we guide you to craft only what you can manage effectively. Endeavoring to establish countless notes for myriad desires might prove counterproductive, as your ability to concentrate might wane with an abundance of ego-driven priorities.

Q: Is it akin to music? Do these notes follow a scale or exhibit interrelations?

A: These notes spring from your mind, so if associating them with a musical tone or station makes them resonate for you, they will function effectively. They represent energy, vibration, just like everything else. Music too is a vibration, harmonizing—or clashing—with personal tastes.

Q: Do vibrational-energy frequencies equate to sound frequencies? Could listening to a specific sound frequency facilitate elevating one's vibrational energy?

A: Sound emerges when vibration is perceived audibly. Not all vibrations produce sound, and since these are your creations, direct your efforts toward what resonates with you—what you can genuinely believe and experience.

Summary of Our Collective Consciousness

The notion of vibrational notes might seem esoteric to some. Even those familiar with our messages and delving into universal law might not deem this concept practical. However, remember that as you progress in your practice, your understanding deepens. Revisiting this section in the future might provide new insights, allowing you to experiment with these tools as you journey through ever-shifting vibrational landscapes. This journey has the potential to elevate your default vibration, if you so allow.

Matt Gardan, Tya Master

Life is busy, messy, cluttered, and we can often feel like we're never getting on top of things. Life is also magical and beautiful and wonderous. But too often we focus on the wrong part of it. The busy, 'get it done' part. Or as David likes to say, the hammering. And since the Universe provides more of what we focus on, wouldn't it be nice if we could quickly and easily focus on the more magical part?

Vibrational Notes are a great little hack for any student to use when they want to shift their mood to a more positive one. With a bit of practice, you'll be able to do it effortlessly and see yourself become more intentional about your emotions, or frequency.

When you're feeling down, frustrated, worried, or angry, you tend to fill your mind with those negative thoughts. Piling more and more of them into your focussed attention. This creates a negative slide down your spiral and the Universe starts providing you with more of what you are focussing on. And it feels bad; who wants that?

The concept of Vibrational Notes is simple: it's about having a few key memories of happy or peaceful times that you can go back to when you're feeling down. They don't have to be big moments in your life. Some of my most powerful Notes are tiny moments in time. The way the sun glistened off a calm ocean in the early hours of a day. The smile of a loved one. The surprise adventure one afternoon on a holiday when we wandered down quiet cobbled lanes of an old village. The smell of cookies grandma used to bake.

The key is to find a few that remind you of happier times, happy feelings. And just like a favourite old song takes you right back to the moment you first heard it, these Notes can help change the direction of your negative thought train.

It will take a bit of practice to stop immediately slipping back into your negative thoughts, but once you've felt a small shift, you'll realise how powerful Vibrational Notes can be.

When you realise or become aware that you're feeling unwanted emotions, try to take a few deep breaths. This is important; focussing on the breath will trigger a whole series of subconscious adjustments by your body.

Sometimes it's easier to recall with your eyes closed. Just bring up that memory and try to feel and picture as much detail as you can. Go back to that happy moment.

What can you hear? What was the temperature, the smells, the colours. Is anyone with you? The more vividly you can recall the moment the more effectively it will help break your negative thought train.

This won't stop you feeling bad immediately, but it will act as a circuit breaker, and give you a bit of space to start letting go of those heavier feelings.

When you get more advanced, you can start to create them in your present day. There's nothing more magical than catching yourself in a joyous moment and thinking – this will make a great Vibrational Note! Then you can become hyper present in that moment and try to engage all your senses to fully capture the feeling.

*This case study was written in Australian English.

Exercise

Reflect on a time when you were in a very high vibration, a moment when you felt immense joy. Remember the essence of that experience—how you felt and what transpired during that particular moment of profound joy.

Capture that memory mentally, envisioning it like a short film in your mind. Assign this mental movie a distinct name so you can readily access it whenever you wish.

Replay this movie a few times, allowing the emotions from that memory to resonate in your present moment. You might not reach the same emotional peak as the original experience, and that's perfectly fine. The goal is to elevate your mood during moments of lower vibration using this memory, not to entirely replicate the original feeling.

Practice revisiting this memory without letting judgment interfere, such as thoughts like, "That was so long ago," or "That will never happen again."

These self-doubting thoughts are mental patterns, or 'notes,' you've cultivated over the years. You crafted them, and you possess the power to eliminate them permanently. The most straightforward way to achieve this is by replacing automatic negative reactions with automatic positive ones.

Vibrational Timestamping

The Stream

Infinite physical environments exist, all birthed by consciousness. Earth is just one of these realms. While we are the source of all consciousness, it's crucial for you to grasp that even though we serve as the origin, the strands of consciousness empowering physical beings—like you—are co-creators of all that exists. We provide the spark, the love, and the momentum, yet those in the physical realm fashion the tangible experience they undergo based on their desires. This continuous evolution and expansion explain why you reincarnate into the physical world repeatedly. You do so to discern preferences and manifest based on those inclinations. This manifestation encompasses both the realization of desires and the creation of solutions or evolutions away from undesired elements.

Your primary tool for all new creation is your imagination. We often observe many of you downplaying imagination with phrases like, "It's all in your imagination," or "She has an overactive imagination." We're here to emphasize that imagination truly ignites all creation. Before any entity materialized in the universe, it was first imagined. Thus, we encourage you to harness your imagination more effectively, recognizing its immense creative potential.

Regarding vibrational timestamping, we guide you to deploy your imagination to craft desired circumstances that either elevate or stabilize you on your spiral. Ponder how revisiting distressing memories can plunge you into a lower vibrational state. Perhaps certain triggers, individuals, or locales evoke memories of harrowing events when encountered. This process involves letting a thought drag you down your spiral. Having discussed the implications of being DTS in Chapter Two, you now grasp that with the Tya Practice, experiencing DTS will diminish over time. Yet, how can you invert this procedure, utilizing memories to uplift you on your spiral? Recognizing the significance of an elevated state, you'll undoubtedly value the ability to ascend whenever you wish.

Here's the method:

Vibrational timestamping involves capturing a high-vibrational instant in memory, enabling its future retrieval. Whenever you're immersed in a high-vibe state, enveloped in joy and optimistic feelings about your desires and the current state of your life and world, pause and relish that instant. Absorb what you're experiencing through every sense. Resolve to replicate this high-vibe sensation repeatedly in the future. A helpful tactic might be to envision assimilating all the data from that moment, storing it in a mental filing system, and visualizing the entire procedure.

Should you find yourself DTS, merely recollect that you've archived a high-vibration timestamp. Revisit that memory, perhaps even imagining yourself approaching a filing cabinet, opening a drawer, and retrieving the file containing your time-stamped recollection. Immerse yourself in that higher-vibration experience. Remember the thoughts, emotions, sights, scents, and sounds from that euphoric state. Inhale deeply, savor the moment, and let the elevated vibes permeate your being. Through vibrational timestamping, you've successfully boosted your vibrational state, and this technique stands ready whenever you wish for an on-demand ascent up your spiral.

Qatarina

My favorite part about vibrational timestamping is that it's like the ultimate time-travel hack. It's the polar opposite of PTSD (Post Traumatic Stress Disorder). Instead of getting zapped by unpleasant flashbacks, we're rewiring our brains to summon joy at will.

Now, when we're already down in the dumps (DTS), summoning our inner superhero to reach for the Tya Tools can be a bit of a challenge. But this particular tool is like a cheat code for happiness. It lets us savor those moments of pure bliss in real-time. And guess what? The more you practice this, the more joyous moments you'll want to bookmark.

At first, it's like rewinding the tape in reverse, saying, "Remember when..." to summon that emotion and kick-start your vibrational ascent. Music is a magical assistant here. Cue up a tune from your teenage years, and you'll see what I mean—it's like a nostalgia-powered time machine.

But here's where it gets even cooler. Eventually, you can set timestamps on the fly, as they happen. It's like committing every juicy detail of a moment to your mental scrapbook while it's still unfolding. You get to savor the present while preserving it for future enjoyment. And when you do revisit that timestamp, it's like meeting a past version of yourself who's reliving that joyful moment.

So, what's the goal here? To dial up a specific emotion when you're feeling anything but in the present. Picture this: you're stuck in traffic, veins pulsating with frustration. Take a few deep breaths and summon that awesome childhood memory—you know, when you felt like you could conquer the world. Suddenly, your commute transforms from a grind into a joyful journey. Time travel, my friends, it's not just for sci-fi geeks (like me!) anymore.

Questions for the Stream Regarding Timestamping

Q: What if you are so chronically DTS that you cannot find a moment to timestamp?

A: This raises a more profound question. Given that all physical vibration is influenced by polarity, everyone will experience a mix of positive and negative. Believing that you've never had any positive experiences to timestamp is a perspective formed from being DTS. If this is your current viewpoint, and you're unable to elevate your vibration to a level that allows for a timestamp moment, it's likely you've deeply entrenched yourself in a DTS mindset, resulting in predominantly negative thought habits and corresponding manifestations. We advise you to intend to find relief from this chronic state and let the universe provide solutions. This could come in the form of medical treatment or by embracing and applying this practice.

Consider using your imagination to elevate your vibration with the tools provided, rather than searching for moments to timestamp. Just remember this process, and when you're in a better vibrational state and a suitable event occurs, you can timestamp it.

Q: Sometimes when we timestamp, it might involve another person. How do we timestamp and not "attach" ourselves to other people?

A: The timestamp centers on your experience of the other person. If reflecting upon it elicits positive memories, it will aid in raising your vibration. We encourage you not to judge your timestamps. If an experience is positive enough to be memorably stored for later reflection, utilize it.

Q: If everything is a vibration and emotions are our most potent vibrational tools—given that the universe remains neutral to love or hate, both being powerful—can we hate something into existence just as easily (or perhaps even more so in contemporary times) as we can love something into being?

A: There's ample proof of humans "hating something into existence." Essentially, all undesirable entities are "hated into existence." The vibrations of love and hate are synonymous in their intensity and focus and thus share equal attractive properties when paired with belief. While the emotions differ, the universe responds to vibration, not emotion. Emotion is a byproduct of vibration, but its polarized version exists only in a tangible realm. We've said that emotion and vibration are virtually the same, with emotion being the human experience of vibration. This question aptly highlights that distinction.

Q: Since timestamps act as potent emotional bookmarks, can they transport us to a time when we intensely felt a particular emotion? What if it was a negative emotion? Is the principle the same? If so, how can we detune that?

A: Indeed, you can timestamp any emotion, thereby accessing its associated vibration. The detuning process, as discussed in Chapter One, is about altering an undesirable or negative timestamp that doesn't contribute to your growth. Your transgressors generate what you term "abundance blocks" and are "negative" timestamps crafted inadvertently because societal conditioning, or the matrix, defines certain events as detrimental, urging you to process them with a victim mentality. When this perspective becomes ingrained and such transgressors traumatize you—as they often do—you inadvertently set up a subconscious program that continually attracts similar experiences. Such patterns can always be detuned by shifting your perception through appreciation. The timestamp process aims to introduce a positive counter to the inadvertently created negative ones.

Consider your mind analogous to a computer—it operates similarly. Your outdated programming no longer aligns with your desires; these are your timestamps. Engaging with the Tya Practice as we've delineated helps you rewrite your cognitive script to better suit your needs. Adopting a broader perspective, one that transcends conditioned thought, allows you to view your transgressors with full appreciation, turning a negative timestamp into a positive one. As you add more positive timestamps with every uplifting manifestation—even if it's just an unconditional state of joy—their potency intensifies. Gradually, your default vibration elevates.

Q: Can we go back and adjust or 'evolve' our timestamps?

A: Your timestamp is your creation; you can mold it however you prefer, provided you can bring yourself to believe in it. In your 3D world, humans often become entrenched in discerning what is "real" or "factual." Frequently, you overlook the fact that everything is a matter of your perception—your unique version of reality. Hence, we often allude to your "bubble of reality," emphasizing that you are continually crafting your reality; thus, what's real for you is indeed your reality.

Q: When timestamping, can we envision a future moment when we'll revisit this timestamp? In other words, as I'm crafting the moment, can my past self anticipate that my future self will return to this moment?

A: This is where affirmations prove beneficial. To affirm with genuine belief is to create; to affirm with mere desire perpetuates that desire. When you instill a moment with the intent of revisiting it, fueled by genuine belief, it will materialize. We suggest setting your timestamp with the intent of revisiting it whenever necessary or desired.

Q: What's the ideal duration for timestamps?

A: This hinges on the prowess of your imagination. If you conjure vivid, intricate scenarios and can mentally immerse yourself in that crafted reality, experiencing it with multiple senses, then your timestamp can be as extensive as you desire. If your capacity to daydream in detail is somewhat restrained, then merely encapsulate the essence of the moment in your timestamp.

Q: Can external cues, like a photograph, icon, trinket, song, or location, assist in recalling a timestamp?

A: Indeed, they can. However, our guidance emphasizes leveraging your mind as your primary instrument in the Tya Practice. By doing so, you're actively recalling and relishing a memory with a positive intent, rather than merely invoking an external trigger. Embrace your positive triggers as they spontaneously emerge, and cultivate a timestamp mechanism that you can summon whenever needed.

Q: Is there a tangible action we can undertake to reinforce a timestamp's neural pathway?

A: Certain techniques, like the Emotional Freedom Technique (EFT) tapping, can prove effective. Within the Tya Practice, our guidance emphasizes mental exercises over external tools. By doing so, you can channel your thoughts toward desired outcomes, eliminating the need for a physical method, which could introduce unnecessary complexity to your process.

Q: Can we negate a timestamp upon encountering even higher vibrations?

A: Absolutely. The solution is simple: cease using it.

Summary of Our Shared Consciousness

Timestamping holds efficacy because your mind is innately programmed for it. From birth, you've been formulating positive and negative associations based on beliefs birthed from experiences. We are guiding you to seize control of this potent instrument. By doing so, you can neutralize those associations that plunge you into undesired vibrations and consequent manifestations, and alternatively, cultivate positive associations that you can intentionally invoke. This grants you the power to fluidly transition from a less desired vibrational state to a more favorable one, at will.

Kate Benson, Tya Bootcamp Graduate

Vibrational time stamping is a technique where we use positive memories to boost our emotional state when it's lower than desired. It's something we often do naturally, trying to think of happier thoughts when we're feeling down. But within the Tya Practice it's about capturing moments when we're in a highly positive state, like filing away these uplifting experiences in a mental cabinet for future use. This practice becomes most potent when we truly believe in its effectiveness.

You see, if you believe it's a powerful tool, it will be. For instance, I vividly recall an incident when my son took off running and I couldn't catch up to him. Panic surged within me, a reminder of why I had begun the practice in the first place--my constant anxiety and fear, especially regarding my children's safety. My son's vanishing act brought this fear to the forefront. I desperately tried to recollect every detail: his running off, the uncertainty, and the fear of something happening to him near our busy road. Surrounded by strangers in a state park, the fear was overwhelming. However, I consciously made a decision to let go of this fear, trusting that everything would be fine. Shifting my focus, I was relieved to find him safe and waiting for me.

In another Tya Academy session, we delved into confronting our deepest fears. I imagined the heart-wrenching scenario of losing my child, visualizing my son lying lifeless near water in our backyard. The pain was excruciating, but it allowed me to confront my fear head-on. And in my heartbreak, it just all washed over me and I was able to be in that experience and think: he's gone home now.

I realized that this was how I would genuinely feel in such a situation. This experience empowered me to manage my anxiety better as a mother. Despite his age, my son encouraged me to trust him more, particularly when he rode his bike on the busy road. While it's a challenging situation, recalling the release of fear helps me cope.

This example underscores the power of creating a vibrational note. I employed a fictional scenario to heal and face my deepest fears, experiences that would typically send my emotions spiraling. This note has become a valuable tool for me, especially as a parent grappling with these fears.

It's essential to clarify that vibrational time stamping isn't about convincing oneself that everything will be fine in a worst-case scenario. Instead, it's about releasing the fear associated with those scenarios. So, it is a way to capture high-vibe moments and use them as tools to stay in a positive state, especially in situations that used to trigger fear or anxiety. It's not about pretending nothing bad can happen; it's about having tools to stay centered in the face of fear.

Lastly, it's worth noting that this practice doesn't entail rushing into extreme scenarios immediately. Instead, it's about gradually working our way into it.

Exercises

1. Sit alone in a quiet space and think about a particular unfulfilled desire. Conjure the essence of your desire. Your new, more joyful way of being; a new relationship, business, or stream of income. Perhaps no longer being stuck in the past, or with fearful beliefs—whatever the topic—imagine the isness of it: its essence.

Now craft a mind movie where you experience your desire, void of fear and judgment. If your inner critic chimes in, telling you that your desire will never happen, simply dismiss it. That critical voice (David refers to his as 'Claude') is just a function of your ego that seeks to protect you from disappointment. Return to your mind movie and allow yourself to feel the feelings of having what you want in total belief. Timestamp this moment and how it felt.

Now commit this to memory and give it an identity. Your movie deserves a title!

You can dial up this mind movie on demand and revel in it anytime you wish. Just don't allow yourself to linger there so long that the vibration lowers and elements such as need or planning the "how" details set in. This will be a product of your ego and these things are not needed for this tool.

2. Sit alone in a quiet space and think about a recurring event or situation that triggers you DTS. Use your imagination to experience your usually triggering event from the high perspective of Source—in full appreciation. Void of fear and judgment.

Instead of your usual labeling of your chosen event as "Should not be" you are going to appreciate it. You are going to understand it.

Notice how, when you are up your spiral, you can meet these things in a much higher vibration than when you are down or when you are triggered at the onset of them.

Set calendar reminders to practice this two to three times per week for no more than 15–20 minutes each.

In time, you will find your reaction to actual events that once triggered you to become benign.

The Stopgap

The Stream

Of all the tools we are providing to you in this practice, this is perhaps the one that will bring the greatest transformation to your daily life. It is also the simplest. Many of you have noted in your lives that the simplest things are the most effective. This is true because overly complex things are a creation of the ego, which believes that something must be intricate to hold value for an intelligent being. This desire for things to be complex before they can hold value is yet another example of humanity's craving for exclusivity to produce a feeling of superiority—a mindset of "I can understand this, but many cannot" or the idea that if fewer people grasp it, it holds more value for those who do. This is all egocentric nonsense. Neither we nor the universe is complex. Simplicity always prevails because its vibration isn't burdened with needless intricacies.

A stopgap, as we refer to it, is a statement that interrupts a descent down the spiral. Anytime you face something that brings your vibration down, you've already started from a position below neutral. Perhaps you see something, turn on the news, or someone makes a comment, and you are triggered downward. If you maintain your focus on it for more than a fleeting moment, momentum builds, and you feel yourself slipping into emotions that aren't pleasurable. This results in a widening chasm from our energy. Negative emotions like anger or fear ensue, and pessimistic scenarios start to dominate your consciousness. You become tense and might even feel your heart racing.

Such reactions, though they may feel innate, are learned behavior. You picked it up from your surroundings early in your human journey. Maybe it has integrated so deeply that you feel it's an inherent part of human nature, something you'll never control. But we assure you that's not the case. While vibrational flow will naturally have its highs and lows, your emotional response to it is entirely under your control. With deliberate shifts in perspective, you can master it. We emphasize "deliberate" because you've probably spent your lifetime defaulting to reactions to your unique vibrational flow. Recalibrating these reactions requires effort. The silver lining is that as you hone your Tya Practice, the required effort diminishes, and this approach will become second nature—but you have to desire it enough to consistently practice!

Now, the pivotal disruptive statement is:

"Is this worth going down my spiral over?"

That's the crux. Simple, yet potent. Whenever something threatens to pull your vibe down, halt and pose this question to yourself. We promise that over time, your answer will increasingly be a resounding "NO!" Choosing to descend is always your decision. On rare occasions, you might feel this descent offers the release you need to navigate an experience, but such thinking is grounded in your preconceived judgment of the situation. Remember, we won't ever judge your choices.

Merely crafting a new, uplifting reflex through this question can serve as the antidote to spiraling downward. Every time a trigger threatens, pause and ask yourself this. If feasible, distance yourself from the triggering stimulus. Even if you're driving and can't physically remove yourself, strive to remain attuned to your vibration throughout the day, echoing the sentiments from Chapter Two.

While you can fashion your personalized stopgaps, we advocate starting with ours. Its potency is undeniable. In the Tya Practice, you're harnessing the power to control your reactions to your vibrational shifts, giving you a firmer grip on your life. In no time, you'll witness the profound change that results from altering your typical response to inherent vibrational movements.

Qatarina

The Stream makes it crystal clear that this Tya Tool might just be the ultimate transformational powerhouse in our arsenal, and they have a good reason for that claim. The stopgap technique is like the Jedi mind trick of Tya Tools. It's the grown-up version of telling your toddler to count to ten before they unleash a tantrum. But here's the twist—we become the Jedi masters of our own emotions, and trust me, it's way more effective than toddler management.

Out of all the Tya Tools tucked away in my toolbox, this one is the workhorse that gets the most mileage, and I know I'm not alone in this. It's the universal Swiss Army knife for life's grand dramas and its pesky little irritations.

This tool isn't picky; it tackles everything from the colossal to the minuscule. Whether it's dealing with my daughter's after-school crankiness and her mission to push every button I've got, the toe-stubbing incident that should have been an Olympic sport, the slow-motion speedster hogging the fast lane this morning, or even the doctor recently delivering unwanted news about my neurological issue—it works for all of them.

Give it a spin, and you'll be astonished at how rapidly your reactions to life's curveballs start to shift. It's like a high-speed train ticket to a more astonishing version of you.

Questions for the Stream Regarding the Stopgap

Q: How can one effectively train their mind to automatically use the stopgap during emotionally intense situations?

A: Mastery of the stopgap, like all things in your physical realm, requires intention and practice. Begin by observing your emotional reactions during less intense situations. By becoming aware of these smaller triggers and implementing the stopgap, you're laying down neural pathways that will make it more accessible during more heightened emotional states. With time and repeated practice, invoking the stopgap will become as instinctive as breathing.

Q: Over time, can the consistent use of the stopgap change our baseline emotional responses or does it only serve as a temporary redirection of our immediate reactions?

A: The consistent use of the stopgap can indeed change your baseline emotional responses. Just as water, through persistent flow, carves pathways in rock, your consistent redirection of emotional reactions forms new habitual neural pathways. Over time, these new paths become your default. The stopgap is not merely a temporary bandage but a tool for genuine transformation.

Q: How can we introduce the stopgap technique to children or younger individuals to help them manage their emotions from an early age?

A: Introducing the stopgap to children can be a delightful endeavor. Children, inherently more connected to Source, can grasp these concepts with surprising ease. Start by encouraging them to identify their feelings without judgment. Teach them the phrase and explain its meaning in simple terms. Create playful scenarios where they can practice using it. By making it part of their early emotional toolkit, you're gifting them with an invaluable resource for navigating their life experiences.

Q: Are there any signs or indicators that suggest we're becoming proficient with the stopgap technique and truly benefiting from its use?

A: Absolutely! As you become more proficient with the stopgap, you'll notice an increased sense of emotional equilibrium. Situations that once triggered intense reactions may elicit a more muted or even neutral response. Additionally, you'll find a faster recovery time after emotional disturbances, feeling more resilient and centered. Another indicator is the frequency with which you employ the stopgap; as proficiency increases, the need to consciously invoke the stopgap diminishes, signaling its integration into your subconscious processes.

Q: If we ask ourselves the question, "Is this worth going down my spiral over?", what if the answer is "Yes"? After all, when we were hunter-gatherers, fear had its place: preservation. For example, what if we see a car speeding toward our child? That seems worth going DTS so our instincts kick in!

A: Going DTS is always a choice. When a car is speeding toward your child, you likely won't have time to truly go down your spiral. Instead, you'd instinctively act to save them and reflect upon your spiral afterward. It's possible to experience life without being triggered DTS, allowing polarity to play its role without judging that process or your position on the spiral. That being said, there's nothing inherently wrong with going DTS—it's a facet of your life experience. We're merely emphasizing that your reaction to your human experience is learned and can be managed from a higher perspective.

Summary of Our Shared Consciousness

Incorporating the stopgap into your routine can be transformative if practiced consistently. Remember, oscillating up and down your vibrational spiral is a natural process that shapes your reality, enriches your eternal consciousness, and is unavoidable in any physical setting. Your response to this vibrational journey lies entirely within your domain. The choices you made in reacting to manifestations were influenced by societal norms and the behavior of those around you early in your life. Taking charge of your vibrational flow sets you apart from the vast majority of humanity, and the journey can commence immediately.

Lisa Danhi, Tya Bootcamp Graduate

Often, I find that my body provides immediate feedback regarding where I am on my emotional journey. As I observe events unfolding, whether it involves my children, work, or any other aspect of life, I sense a change in my body's energy. It starts to tense up, and I become aware that I'm losing my presence in the moment. My frustration mounts, and my calmness diminishes.

In these instances, I've learned to pause and reflect on what's happening. I take a step back and consider the perspective from which I'm viewing the situation. Am I in a position to understand where the other person is coming from? Why are they behaving this way? Do I need to intervene, control, or is it even my business? These questions guide me.

If I can halt my reaction and shift my focus from trying to fix things to simply acknowledging and accepting them, it's almost astonishing how things can change.

If I fail to stop my negative spiral, it can escalate, and everything seems to go awry. However, if I use my stopgap tool and, at times, physically remove myself from the situation, I can regain composure. I remind myself that no one is in imminent danger. This is just my perspective, and I'm not in control of every aspect of the moment. It's crucial to determine whether I need to control, fix, or distance myself from the situation based on my perspective of what should be happening.

I've been contemplating who gets to decide what's right, and I've realized that it's ultimately me. The key is to let others have their experiences without feeling the need to control or manage them for my own sake. I'm responsible for my choices and what I want in my life. My body often reacts before my mind catches up, so I've learned to recognize when I'm starting to feel anxious and take a moment to breathe. I consider whose perspective I'm adopting, whether it's a higher, Source perspective or my personal viewpoint.

I've noticed that the quicker I catch myself and correct my trajectory, the faster I return to a positive manifestation, attracting positive outcomes. It's remarkable how the stopgap tool has reduced the time between recognizing my negative vibrations and making adjustments.

This facet of the Tya mindset illustrates my mother's favorite phrase, "It is what it is. Always keep your sense of humor." Certainly this is meeting my obstacles in joy, anticipating expansion with curiosity! For me, the stopgap works like a rudder: when I pause in the moment to make a needed microadjustment in my energy, my journey and manifestations are immediately and deeply affected. I pause and breathe in acceptance and breathe out appreciation. Ahh, spaciousness and abundance are right there.

Exercise

Sit alone in silence and think of a topic that usually triggers you DTS. If you feel yourself being triggered, simply catch the drop in vibration and ask yourself, "Is this worth going DTS over?"

You may believe that some things are worth going DTS for, but understand that this is just a belief you've created for yourself, and you can shift it if you desire.

There are no mandates in Tya about your chosen beliefs, and all beliefs are chosen. However, the intention of the practice is to systematically allow the raising of your vibration. So, anything that facilitates this will only enhance your practice.

With that mindset, simply decide that you are not going to go DTS because a.) going DTS has little to no creative power to change or solve what triggered you in the first place, and b.) your lowered vibration will likely impact other elements of your moment once you've allowed yourself to go there.

"Is this worth going down my spiral over?" It's as simple as that, but so powerful!

Allowing "Isness"

The Stream

Yes, we made up that word, but can you think of a term more indicative of true vibrational alignment than becoming the "is" of your desire? Want more money? Step into the "is" of having more—it already exists! Desire an improved body? Love the one you have and feel the "is" of an improved physical state.

Often, when humans discover (or rediscover) that they create their own reality, they find themselves focusing on what they want. While this isn't a bad practice—since it's better to focus on what you want rather than what you don't—it can often lead to feelings of need or want. Such vibrations will always be met with an affirming "yes"—as in, "yes, you want it, and you need it." We call this the vibration of need. The vibration of need differs from the vibration of "is." The vibration of "is" aligns with already having or being, and the universe will have no option but to affirm with a "yes," for the universe does not judge your creation.

Thus, you'll often hear us say, "Step into, or align with, the isness of your desires. It already is, and it shall be."

Qatarina

I've noticed that the most mind-blowing things happen to me whenever I stop focusing on what I am hoping to get or achieve and rather put my attention on what I already have in my life that I am grateful for.

When I shift my focus from yearning for things I don't have to cherishing what I already possess, magic unfolds. The same principle applies in reverse. If I obsess about what I dislike and fervently wish for change, all I seem to attract is more of what irks me.

What truly wields tremendous power is to savor the change as if it's already woven into the fabric of reality. It might not wield immediate effectiveness, but seize the opportunity to unearth the "isness" when it presents itself.

Take, for instance, my neighbors and their two behemoth, perpetually barking dogs (yes, they're serenading us as I type this). Initially, their relentless barking was an insurmountable challenge for me and my oversensitivity to sound. It was as if "bark, bark, bark, bark" was the soundtrack of my life.

Then, I had an epiphany—these dogs were admirably hushed at night. Well, THANK YOU for that, I thought.

I felt genuine gratitude for the tranquil nights that gifted me blissful slumber. During the peaceful evening hours, I immersed myself in the serene "isness" of the moment.

From there, I effortlessly transported this newfound appreciation into the daytime. So when the dogs embarked on their daily barking symphony, I found solace in the memory of serene nights. No more vexation, just an upward surge in my emotional state. It propelled me into a mode of clear thinking, leading to a brilliant solution: noise-canceling headphones cushioned with soothing white noise.

While this may seem like a modest example, its transformative ripples extend across all facets of existence.

Sparse bank account balance? Bask in the "isness" of every dollar you spend, celebrating the money you do have.

Flying solo and experiencing the occasional bout of crankiness? Revel in the joy of solitude and let the warmth of feeling cherished by another (even if it's not of the romantic variety) wash over you.

Embrace what you already possess, and then luxuriate in the sensation of already having what you desire.

[By the way, just three weeks after I penned this section, and after I'd made peace with the barking dogs and accepted their presence in my life... they moved out... Now, that's some next-level vibrational flow for you!]

Questions for the Stream Regarding Isness

Q: Why do we have the vibration of need? Is it a part of polarity or is it a learned vibration?

A: The vibration of need arises naturally in a physical environment. In the physical realm, there are unique expressions of Source that you encounter during your time incarnate. In this state, you naturally discern your preferences and desire to experience them. Your preferences are shaped both by your whole self, which ensures a unique perspective, and by your ego, which may develop preferences influenced by various factors. These can range from the desire to express individuality, to following the crowd for a sense of belonging, or even just basic self-preservation. All these factors combine to yield a unique set of desires, which can shift with vibrational flow.

In your highest vibrational state within the physical realm, your soul and ego are balanced. In this equilibrium, your soul neither desires nor needs anything. This part of you understands that all needs are met in a state of trust and that all desires originate from ego consciousness, a natural aspect of physical expression. The vibration of need emerges in lower-vibrational flows when the ego and soul are imbalanced, particularly when the ego becomes dominant. This causes lower-vibrational, fear-based emotions to activate, and the vibration of fear emerges. Here is an example of the phases that often occur in vibrational flow:

High Vibration/Pure Joy: Appreciation. "I deeply understand that."

High: Experience. "I am that."

Below Neutral: Desire. "I want to have or be that."

Low: Need. "I don't have that, and I do not trust that I will."

So, need is born of ego and is expressed in low-vibrational flow. It is the vibration of *not* having.

Q: How can one differentiate between genuinely embodying the "isness" of a desire versus merely pretending or feigning it?

A: The true essence of "isness" resonates deeply within one's core vibrational state, creating a harmonious alignment with the universe. When genuinely embodying "isness," there is an authentic sense of peace, trust, and knowing, free from resistance or doubt. This contrasts with merely pretending, where there's an underlying tension or inconsistency in vibration. Pretense often carries with it the weight of effort, a forcefulness, or a sensation of trying too hard. On the other hand, genuine "isness" feels effortless, a natural state of being. To discern, one must tune into their inner feelings and vibrations, asking: "Do I feel light, aligned, and trusting, or is there tension, doubt, and forcefulness present?"

Q: Does "isness" apply universally across all desires and manifestations, or are there instances where this principle might not be as effective?

A: The principle of "isness" is universal in its essence. It applies across all desires and manifestations. However, the effectiveness of this principle is not in the principle itself but in the individual's alignment with it. If one's foundational beliefs and vibrations contradict a certain desire, the application of "isness" might seem less effective. For example, if one deeply believes that they are unworthy of love, merely stepping into the "isness" of a loving relationship without addressing this underlying belief may prove challenging. Thus, it's paramount to ensure alignment at foundational levels, clearing any vibrational blockages, for the true power of "isness" to shine forth.

Q: What is the difference between Isness and a Vibrational Timestamp or Note?

A: They are interwoven, but think of the Vibrational Timestamp and Vibrational Note as processes and Isness as the result of the process.

Q: Are we the only ones who have "need" vibrations? Animal instinct is not a need—it's a state of function. Without instinct, the cognitive load would be too great, right?

A: All beings are capable of overindulgence, which is always a result of the vibration of need. Human intelligence has enabled you to create circumstances that allow the vibration of need to be expressed with ease—your common overindulgence is a symptom of this. Notice your domesticated animals also display the vibration of need and can be observed overindulging.

Q: If we have instinct, and a subconscious, can we set it to "health," "romance," or something like that?

A: The changing of subconscious thought is always about changing default vibration. Consistent conscious thoughts through vibrational flow create subconscious thought. Learning not to allow a shift in thoughts during vibrational flow is the key to changing the subconscious mind—this creates your default vibration.

Summary of Our Shared Consciousness

This chapter was relatively brief because "allowing is-ness" is as straightforward as the previously introduced stopgap. It involves settling into the calm vibration of being, without triggering the repelling vibration of need. To embody anything, you must align with the vibration of "is." This represents isness. The trick is to establish it and then let it be, framing a new desire with the vibrational sentiment of "wouldn't it be nice..." rather than with "I must" or "I am," especially when there's an undertone of doubt.

Luqman Murtaza, Tya Bootcamp Graduate

"Isness" means accepting my current reality as it is. From a young age, I felt insignificant, believing my purpose was to serve others. My childhood was shadowed by fear, neglect, shame, rejection, and abuse, which I sadly normalized. Surprisingly, I never saw myself as a victim, perhaps because I'd never known genuine love or positivity to contrast with. This defined my "isness" during those early years.

Despite my sense of insignificance, my vivid childhood imagination was a superpower. I hadn't realized its potential then, but it transported me to alternate realities where I was the central character, allowing me to craft my own version of reality.

Born in Pakistan, I adapted to my surroundings and made a friend or two. However, at ten, I moved to the United States, where the language barrier isolated me and made me a target for bullying. I endured in silence, convinced I deserved it, until a growth spurt made me taller than my bullies.

I also grappled with the realization of my attraction to the same gender, a significant challenge in my conservative Muslim upbringing. My family's reactions were intense, leading to attempts to "correct" me. I even tried to end my life twice, overwhelmed by feelings of worthlessness. In social situations, I often felt voiceless, never daring to say "No." My vibrant childhood imagination faded, replaced by TV as my escape. Movies and TV shows became my life; on-screen characters were my only friends.

After college, societal pressure led me into an arranged marriage. I resisted for six years before yielding, convinced my homosexuality would lead to condemnation. I was honest with my future wife, agreeing to "pray the gay away."

As a husband, I lost myself in pleasing my wife, believing she held the key to my salvation. And then our daughter, Aleena, became my world.

Later, I discovered the "The Stream of David" podcast, and, despite financial constraints, I financed my journey into his Tya Academy, which ultimately paid for itself.

My Tya journey was a deeply personal one, hidden from my family's potential lack of understanding. I attended classes and meetings in my car or a secluded room at work. Week by week, I peeled away defensive walls through meditation, journaling, and forgiveness exercises. Viewing my life from the perspective of Source allowed me to appreciate the growth and expansion all experiences bring.

Now, life feels lighter and more manageable. I prioritize myself, confidently saying no to what doesn't resonate with me. Although my life isn't perfect, and I'm separated from my daughter, I trust wholeheartedly that everything is working out for my highest good. I've become adept at recognizing positive aspects of my current reality. I have my own place, car, recently earned a job promotion, and, most importantly, engage in projects that tap into my imagination and creativity.

Previously, I'd accepted my "isness" as deserving the worst outcomes. Today, I know my self-worth, speak confidently, and have a voice. I understand that I'm always loved unconditionally, and even my family, once a primary source of conflict, now supports me.

Exercise

Sit alone in a quiet space and think about a desire, perhaps a long-held desire that you have not yet manifested.

Allow yourself to revel in the essence of your new creation. Create the feeling of what it would be like to have or be or do it.

You may be thinking that you have done this many times. But if it has not yet manifested, there must be a reason. Is it because you lingered in your desire for too long and allowed the vibration to drop, thus allowing doubt and fear to set in? Did you begin to wonder how, when, or why it has not come yet? These lower-vibration thoughts actually slow and cancel manifestations all the time.

The doubt, fear, and 'how will it be?' thoughts that drop in are all part of the matrix, they are designed to stunt and slow new manifestations so new creation doesn't spiral out of control. But they no longer have to limit you; you're learning the true secrets of creation!

So allow your dreams to begin and end before the lower-vibrational thought set in—that's the secret!

Like all things Tya, do this as a regular practice to begin seeing it show up automatically as new belief.

Zooming Out

The Stream

As you've discovered by now, the Tya Practice is a belief system that focuses on raising your default vibration to a level where you increasingly allow our energy and connect more and more to Source as you navigate your vibrational journey. In this near-constant connection, you can easily access what we refer to as our perspective—Source perspective. Like many endeavors, the more you practice this, the more natural it becomes. This perspective is invaluable in your polarized environment, especially when you encounter events that you discern as non-preferable. This approach proves essential in everyday situations that may have previously sent you spiraling downward.

Zooming out isn't synonymous with "bypassing," which implies that you're merely ignoring transgressors and simply raising your vibration to disregard them. Rather, it's about using your intrinsic connection to our high vibration to see things in your life from our vantage point—without judgment or fear—yet addressing them nonetheless. It's vital to understand that any transgressor in your vibration will remain a transgressor, adding fuel to your lower vibrational field, until you detune it. This is why transgressors resurface in your reality whenever you spiral downward, continuously appearing until your recollection of them, and your vibration around them, becomes neutral.

This doesn't imply that once you adopt a higher perspective, you'll perpetually remain there. Due to the vibrational flow prompted by polarity, such constancy isn't feasible. Expecting such consistency sets you up for disappointment. Polarity will occasionally lower your vibration, causing you to lose your expanded view. Remember, you're human, and your purpose isn't to attain perfection but to experience duality, navigate challenges, and manifest desires. As you hone the Tya Practice, you'll get better at adopting this expansive perspective more frequently and for extended durations.

Zooming out taps into a profound point-of-genius inherent in all creation. As the most advanced beings on your planet, you often restrict yourselves from this capability. This limitation arises because the matrix's duality has brought many to a place where fear is rampant, especially among humans. Your leaders employ fear and judgment to control populations, and this vibration is deeply ingrained in humanity.

As sophisticated beings, your discernment goes beyond mere instinct. Historically, you've collectively shown a preference for subjugation—a preference for conformity and living by societal templates. This matrix facilitated humanity's progression through the industrial and tech revolutions. Now, in the aftermath of these transformative periods, you've developed exceptional tools, allowing unparalleled communication globally.

In your interactions, there's a burgeoning trend of questioning long-held beliefs—a skepticism rarely seen in previous generations. This critical thinking is leading to an awareness that many longstanding control institutions no longer align with contemporary values, causing them to weaken. Observe how governments and religious institutions are perceived differently now compared to your grandparents' time. Notice the increased polarization and the evolving operational modalities of these institutions. From their viewpoint, there's an amplified need to propagate fear and consolidate power, as a majority are either questioning or outright disregarding them.

While some yearn for the "good old days," a return to past norms isn't viable. Expansion is inevitable. Fearful? We advise against fearing growth. You're intrinsically expansive beings in an expansive universe, always pushing boundaries. Thus, awakening and embracing these teachings is the natural progression of your journey. The tools and techniques in this practice have the power to transform your world. Whether they will or not rests with you, both as individuals and collectively. As previously mentioned, we cater to the needs of one or one billion, regardless of the global population. Many are entrenched in the matrix and aren't aligned with these teachings.

They're precisely where they need to be. If all of humanity were to simultaneously adopt these tools, Earth would soon become redundant, as collective vibrational harmony would lead to the dissolution of all challenges, rendering the environment's purpose moot. However, there's no imminent danger of this scenario. This information is avant-garde, and the majority haven't embarked on this path.

Qatarina

Let's marinate on that for a moment. Perhaps even give it a second readthrough.

Now, what we're talking about here is what some folks might label as an "enlightened" viewpoint. But let's not get too caught up in labels. We prefer to call it a 'zoomed-out perspective' because, well, it's exactly that. Imagine taking a step back, like a cosmic observer peering at the grand tapestry of existence rather than squinting at the intricate threads right under your nose.

In the ever-evolving dance of our present reality, it's natural for some to feel some resistance, particularly if change isn't their cup of tea. This is where zooming out works its magic. It shifts our gaze away from the minutiae and guides it toward the grand orchestration of change on a proverbial stage, showing us how these shifts can serve us on a profound and expansive scale.

Questions for the Stream Regarding Zooming Out

Q: How do the constructs of government, religion, and morals hold together in the energetic realm?

A: Those constructs do not exist in the energetic realm; they are products of the matrix. As for how they are observed in the energetic realm, as we have stated, there is duality in all topics. Therefore, there are both positive and negative (unwanted) aspects of each of these constructs. At their inception, the primary intention was to save humans from themselves, so they were rooted in egocentric judgment from the start. The "positive" aspects advanced humanity by creating structures that worked for many, but certainly not all. The unwanted aspects are predominantly the lower-vibrational emotions of guilt and fear, and the earthly manifestations driven by those emotions.

So, how do they hold up in the energetic realm? The simple answer is they are human-created tools that began as vibrational creations of consciousness—as all things do—and then manifested in the physical realm. The cohesion is consistent with any other creation.

Q: As our old systems of belief collapse, how do we manage the transition to a more evolved society?

A: You are already undergoing this process. Things don't suddenly collapse; they evolve. This evolution occurs naturally, without the need for human consciousness management.

Q: Can you provide guidance to assist those panicked by the transition? Some fear (or perhaps even hope for) full-blown anarchy.

A: Allow everyone to experience their journey without judgment. Those aligned with alleviating their panic through deeper understanding will find paths to that knowledge.

Anarchy denotes resistance against the human-created tools of control. In the Tya practice and our teachings, we don't guide you to oppose anything, but rather to appreciate all that exists—including your tools of control. This higher understanding of the universal process of creation enables you to flow with the vibrational currents, appreciating every element without feeling the need to counteract or eliminate anything. Tya focuses on finding joy and abundance in all circumstances.

Q: When viewing obstacles from a zoomed-out perspective, I find that I am more creative in finding solutions. If more people became acquainted with the Tya Practice and adopted a zoomed-out viewpoint for challenges, could this lead to a more expansive, improved environment for our planet?

A: It can, and it shall.

Summary of Our Shared Consciousness

Zooming out is synonymous with the Tya practice, and vice versa. The four pillars are meticulously designed to align you with the Source perspective, equipping you with all you need for a perpetually expanding, enlightened, and joyous life experience.

Brent Howell, Tya Bootcamp Graduate

Zooming out, for me, means returning to a proper perspective in life. Although I've practiced Tya for a while, occasional stressors and negative thoughts still emerge, but they no longer lead to depression as they did for decades. I battled depression for approximately 30 years. Over time, using the tools I learned in Tya, I unraveled the automatic thoughts, voices, and language that contributed to it.

I eventually identified the underlying trigger for this depression: fear of being disappointed and not attaining what I desired. This fear had roots dating back to middle school.

Zooming out now serves as a proactive tool for me, especially when starting my day. I incorporate it into my meditation routine, along with binaural beats, reinforcing my identity as an expression of Source. This practice involves imagining a broader perspective, placing my challenges in proper context, and prevents me from making a mountain out of a molehill. When something doesn't go as planned, it reminds me that I have a Source connection and negative thoughts are the only real obstacles I face.

When major unwanted life changes occur and the subsequent feelings of despair happen, it reminds us that we are still alive, loved by Source, and fully capable of creating a positive future. This perspective shift reinforces our responsibility for our lives and encourages us to take control of our actions and responses to life's events.

Reaching the zoomed-out space reinforces my responsibility for everything in my life. I control my actions and responses, and there's no fate working against me. I employ my imagination to create the zooming-out experience. Doing so helps me put whatever I'm currently experiencing in the 3D world into a broader context and prioritize effectively.

Even when something goes wrong, I remind myself that I won't lose my job, my wife won't leave me, and I still have money in my bank account and a roof over my head.

Now, let's consider a scenario where my home is destroyed, I lose my job, and my wife leaves. In such a situation, I would zoom all the way out to see the bigger picture. I'd recognize that I'm still alive and Source is entirely supportive of me. From this vantage point, I would focus on creating a positive and pleasant experience for myself. There's nothing working against me; it's all about how I perceive and respond to the events and experiences in my life.

The only real obstacles are the negative thoughts and feelings I create and place in my path. Without these self-imposed obstacles, nothing in the world is inherently against me. It's all about my perspective, my response, and the meaning I attribute to the events and experiences I encounter.

Throughout the day and even in my dreams while sleeping, my thoughts now predominantly reflect Tya principles. My primary challenge now is stretching my imagination and bolstering my belief in my ability to manifest my dreams—a wonderfully empowering place to be.

Exercise

Instead of sitting in silence, we recommend you use social media for this exercise. Choose your preferred platform, or if you don't regularly engage with social media, select a platform that exposes you to a variety of thoughts from various individuals, not just those you're familiar with.

As you browse the content, notice any post that triggers you to go DTS.

When you come across a triggering post or media, pause the video or save the post for reference.

Close your eyes for a moment and take a few deep breaths. Inhale through your nose, hold at the peak of each inhalation, and then exhale slowly through your mouth. This technique will help calm you.

Then, embrace the Source perspective, appreciating the entirety of existence.

Return to the saved post or video and view it with a sense of pure appreciation.

Do you perceive it differently now?

Engage in this exercise weekly to refine your ability to "Zoom Out."

The Matrix Explained

The Stream

We have referenced the matrix throughout this book and provided a brief explanation of it in our introduction. Understanding the human-created collective belief system is paramount to the Tya practice. Knowing when you're operating within the matrix and when you are genuinely aligned with your natural state of Source-aligned well-being will prove invaluable as you navigate the rest of your life using this operating system.

As we have stated, the matrix is simply the collective-consciousness operating system created by humanity. Reflect on how many teachings you've absorbed throughout your lifetime that are, in fact, part of the matrix. It is crucial to distinguish between human-crafted tools and the matrix. For example, language is a human-created tool and not inherently part of the matrix. However, specific language can become part of it. Regardless of the language, all languages include elements of the matrix. Things like transportation, technology, and healthcare are not inherently part of the matrix, but they can, at times, be used as tools by the matrix.

The matrix operates on fear and judgment; this includes comparison. The matrix establishes rules, traditions, and customs. While it can be dogmatic, the dogma varies across different expressions of the matrix. The constant underlying vibration, however, is one of fear and judgment. Highlighting these specific qualities is essential because they hinder your ability to trust.

Fundamentally, any belief system that provides a specific belief, rule, or path is matrix-driven. Constructs like marriage, defined family units, the education system, corporations, politics, governments, religions, spiritual philosophies, monarchies, the military, and various "isms" (e.g., materialism, capitalism, veganism, conservatism, wokism, etc.) are all products of the matrix.

We aren't suggesting you demonize the matrix; like all things, it has its polarities, so you will find aspects you consider positive and negative. The matrix has enabled humanity to expand consciousness to a point where some individuals can now understand what we offer. This perspective wasn't accessible just a few years ago. While there have been elements of teachings recorded for millennia in your time, the culmination of all that we offer hasn't been presented or understood in the manner you now grasp it.

The pivotal understanding is that the matrix is the core of humanity's belief system, and every being operates on some belief system. Consider the cultural or religious paths set for a newborn. They are told what is right and wrong and given expectations for their life journey, often with consequential rules.

Belief systems are akin to expansion. All beings will inevitably have one. Atheists, for example, may reject religious or divine beliefs, but they often adopt another system, like consumerism, equating material wealth with expansion. The matrix excels at equating money and material goods with notions of expansion.

Altruism is another system that both religious believers and atheists may adopt, hoping to find expansion through helping others. While there's no harm in wishing to elevate another's vibration, this system is limited by its dependence on others' suffering and often stems more from egocentric judgment. Every being is an expression of what we are, and every vibrational path holds value in the energetic realm, regardless of personal judgments or comforts.

To further clarify the matrix: any thought or idea framed as "you must," "you should," or accompanied by threats (e.g., "if you do not, XYZ will occur") originates from the matrix. Rules, laws, governments, monarchies, nations, borders, and the like are matrix products.

Religions, customs, traditions, and values can also be of the matrix, especially when dogma or obligation is introduced. Financial systems, healthcare, corporations, and charitable organizations can be matrix tools, often serving as significant components.

When you give power to these entities through belief or fear, you're operating within the matrix.

We don't share this to make you judge yourself for operating in the matrix, whether consistently or sporadically. You chose to manifest within the human matrix. Yet now, you find yourself in an enlightened vibration, curious about your world and your role in it. You're intrigued by intentional creation, and as you adopt a broader perspective, you may wish to understand the matrix more deeply. Our guidance is to observe with appreciation, avoiding judgment, as judgment only pulls you back into the matrix.

Just as true enlightenment won't make you feel superior to other "less enlightened" beings (because enlightenment entails such profound understanding that there's no room left for judgment), being outside the matrix equips you with the discernment to recognize when it tries to lure you back, something it's highly skilled at. This lure might manifest as your ego hinting at feelings of superiority for having unraveled humanity's most significant vibrational challenge. It could also be more subtle, making its way in through media consumption. The matrix's fear is so compelling that you might occasionally find yourself ensnared without even realizing you've entered its vibrational domain. All of this is natural. When you catch yourself reverting to old matrix habits, simply acknowledge its craftiness. If you wish, zoom out to adopt the broader perspective of non-judgment and find yourself once more outside the matrix.

The Tya Practice introduces an operating system purely grounded in universal law, devoid of rules, dogma, or worship. Tya equips you to embrace and expand your innate source consciousness throughout your life, enabling a seamless flow of abundance. The matrix's purpose is to distance you from these concepts and to maintain humanity's "default" or average vibration at -5.

The following illustration is your virtual vibrational spiral that we shared in our introduction. The numeric values represent typical vibrations that you experience as emotions. You move up and down this spiral throughout your day, and the average baseline created over time represents your "Default Vibration." Your life is a direct reflection of your default vibration.

We refer to the area above 0, or neutral space, as "Up the Spiral" (UTS), and the lower half as "Down the Spiral" (DTS). The higher your vibration rises up the scale, the more you are allowing your natural Source being to be the primary driver of your life; conversely, the lower your vibration dips, the more you are allowing your humanity, or ego, to be the primary driver of your life. Notice how when you're UTS, you are naturally in alignment with manifesting more desires, while when you're DTS, you're naturally in alignment with manifesting challenges.

The focus of the Tya Practice is to take actionable steps to move your default line up, above neutral, so that Source is your primary driver of life experience and you are thus manifesting more desires and fewer obstacles as a way of life. With ongoing practice, this will continue to expand throughout your physical lifetime.

VIBRATIONAL SPIRAL GRAPHIC

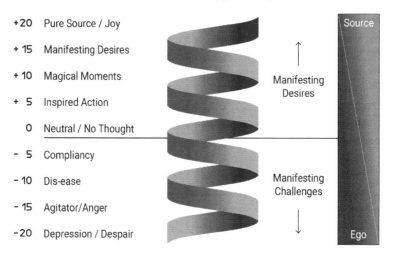

+20	Pure Source / Joy	
+ 15	Manifesting Desires	
+ 10	Magical Moments	Manifesting Desires
+ 5	Inspired Action	
0	Neutral / No Thought	
- 5	Compliancy	
- 10	Dis-ease	Manifesting Challenges
- 15	Agitator/Anger	
-20	Depression / Despair	

Using the vibrational spiral as a reference, let's delve into why the matrix vibration stands at -5.

The most fitting term to describe the -5 matrix vibration is "compliancy." With a default vibration of -5, you might experience a level of unease that doesn't quite reach the depths of intense fear, anger, or the even more profound state of rage. Humanity isn't as productive when consumed by these potent emotions. Yet, at -5, you also remain below the neutral point where creativity thrives, meaning you're neither powerful nor fiercely independent. While -5 doesn't plunge you into profound discomfort, it doesn't elevate you to joy either. You're malleable at this point. More obedient. More compliant. In essence, you become a functional component in the machinery of humanity.

Do you now see how you (and all of humanity) have been programmed to operate at -5? Moving your default up just a few points will significantly improve every aspect of your life. Tya is not about racing to the very top of your spiral, but learning to relish the process of each and every incremental improvement and knowing how to handle the inevitable dips as we navigate to higher vibrational territory. Essentially, it is vital that you learn to love the game of Tya, because you will be doing this work for the remainder of your life now that you know these life-changing secrets!

To clarify, when we speak of being programmed, we're not proposing a conspiracy theory. There isn't a hidden group of malevolent individuals orchestrating the matrix from the shadows. No clandestine meetings of the elite conspiring to subjugate the masses. The matrix is a vibration stemming from the collective ego, an embodiment of the "we know better" sentiment, with an intent to impose a controlled, diminished vibration to ensure a select few outside this matrix have their desires met. This vibration is an open secret. Given that all beings default to some operating system, your world's leaders have crafted versions of a common, fear-driven belief system and marketed it to their constituents.

Reflect on the various cultures you're familiar with from personal experience. Notice the recurring patterns of rules and beliefs that have arisen throughout humanity, long before the advent of modern communication tools. The prevalent themes of fear, judgment, and comparison, along with societal constructs like the family unit, are all products of the collective consciousness of humanity that created the matrix.

Qatarina

Back in my years of traveling with the circus (I'm not joking), I was blissfully detached from mainstream society—a life I thoroughly relished. The people I traveled with made up a transient community, and we referred to the outside world as "Babylon."

During those years, I was thoroughly convinced that our way of life embodied true authenticity, unlike the "sheeple" conforming to societal norms. Instead of cozy homes with all the modern conveniences, we reveled in the simplicity of camping, caravanning, hitchhiking, and even daring train-hopping adventures. Phones, addresses, and bank accounts were alien concepts to me. I carried just one trusty metal mug for all my culinary and beverage needs, diligently cleaned with pine needles. Garbage found its fate in our campfires, waste was buried, and rivers and rainstorms served as our communal baths. We bore our lives on our backs.

No regrets for that chapter of my life; it was an education like no other. But it took some time to realize that I wasn't living that way out of pure desire but rather as a response to an inner need to prove something—to myself and perhaps to the world. I harbored the belief that I was somehow superior to those who followed the beaten path, a sort of self-awarded medal for living an unconventional life. I thought I'd broken free from the societal matrix.

Back then, I had no inkling of Tya, the Stream, or even the concept of a matrix, save for the sci-fi movie reference. Yet, our notion of Babylon was strikingly akin to the biblical reference. According to my religious upbringing, we were called to be "in the world but not of it." It's intriguing to ponder this now, as the Stream conveys a parallel idea, minus all the judgment.

Had I recognized back then the resemblance between my pretentious views of "Babylon" during my vagabond days and the "holier than thou" attitudes I resented in my religious circles, I likely would have shed those opinions with haste. I deemed those folks in need of more open-mindedness, a viewpoint that, ironically, was quite narrow.

The teachings of the Stream have helped me relinquish judgment of "Babylon" and veer away (mostly) from transient living. I've come to accept that it's perfectly okay to enjoy comfort. So, when the Stream initially introduced the concept of the matrix, it triggered numerous light-bulb moments.

We needn't allow these systems and structures to dictate our lives. We don't even have to play by the rules unless we consciously choose to. The Stream even champions the idea of "playing above the rules"—a concept I adore!

The matrix exists for our enjoyment, free from the chains of fear or negative judgment. Let's embrace it for what it is while we're here, savoring the unique flavor it offers to each of us.

Questions for the Stream Regarding the Matrix

Q: Isn't living in the matrix similar to becoming engrossed in a movie or a novel? Why would we want to escape it? Aren't we meant to simply relish the drama and thrill of life?

A: The matrix is the collective belief system crafted by humanity to distance itself from Source, facilitating an ego-driven journey of expansion. Given your polarized environment, this system has yielded both desired and undesired outcomes.

The matrix led to the development of societies, science, medicine, housing, and transportation. Its lower-vibrational components involve controlling mechanisms that funnel free, joyous beings into structured paths via fear-driven beliefs.

Religious and cultural belief systems are particularly widespread on Earth, and most governments have been established around them. Whether you decide to engage with the matrix is entirely up to you. There are individuals flourishing within the matrix, and even if they're not achieving the matrix's definition of success, they're still experiencing expansion. This is because all physical journeys contribute to the expansion of consciousness.

Opting for the Tya Practice and living outside the matrix of fear and judgment is simply more congruent with your eternal state of being. As humanity evolves, you're becoming more attuned to the matrix's ways, realizing that it often perceives humans as mere commodities — either consumers or producers. Recognizing this can be unsettling, leading many to seek liberation. This is why teachings centered on the law of attraction resonate with so many; they offer an energetic reprieve from external control, aligning with an innate understanding of creation.

Q: If technology isn't inherently part of the matrix but is used as a tool within it, and as we evolve, we're becoming more machine-like, is there a point where technology might liberate itself from the matrix and independently evolve? Is the notion of sentient AI in the foreseeable future really that improbable?

A: You have always resembled machines, as your inventions mirror your own nature. Your human-made technology is gradually aligning with the technology that shapes you. Certainly, the potential for humanity to foster conscious entities isn't beyond the realm of possibility.

Q: If we perceive the matrix as a beneficial tool, rather than a barrier disconnecting us from infinity, can we elevate the matrix's vibration? Could we, for instance, shift it from -5 to +5?

A: Firstly, we emphasize that we're not directing you to critique the matrix. Instead, we're guiding you to adopt an appreciative observational stance toward it as part of your Tya Practice. Recognize its worth and remember you can choose your level of engagement. Moreover, allowing others their unique matrix experience aligns more with Tya than trying to extract them from it. Your example, living outside the matrix, will inspire those prepared to emulate you, empowering them to reduce the matrix's influence and harness their innate creative strength.

Q: Many liken human existence to phenomena like video games, movies, novels, augmented reality, or even dream-worlds we might one day awaken from in a fulfilled state. Is this a fitting analogy? Would it be a helpful way to elucidate this concept to my daughter? If not, how should I approach it?

A: We often liken the physical journey to a weekend getaway. One chooses such a trip for various motivations, predominantly in anticipation of an enriching experience, be it relaxation, celebration, discovery, or overcoming challenges. Regardless of the trip's nature, the subsequent memories and whether they're positive or negative contribute to personal growth.

Summary of Our Shared Consciousness

Recognizing the matrix without vilifying it is crucial to functioning beyond its confines. The matrix, a deeply ingrained human vibration, has crafted numerous mechanisms to entice and ensnare individuals in a low vibrational realm, curbing their freedom, joy, and abundance just enough to ensure docility. Note how matrix-steered belief systems, especially those employing fear either subtly or blatantly, often pinpoint external entities as the root of hardship or scarcity. This perpetuates a sense of victimhood, which significantly disempowers many, keeping them ensnared within the matrix's cycle. Hence, we guide you to value the matrix for its contributions, just as we do, preventing you from being ensnared by your own judgment.

The Spinout

The Stream

You've probably deduced by now that the Tya Practice is more than just a method—it's a full-time operating system, a lifestyle. Its primary aim is to consistently elevate your default vibration as you persistently engage with it. You may have also observed that it doesn't simply promise to "manifest all your dreams." Our goal in sharing our message and establishing this practice is to help humanity align with their genuine intent of expansion while providing a structure that ensures a fulfilling journey through the myriad of vibrational experiences.

The idea that you should always be "crushing life" or "realizing every dream" is deeply rooted in the matrix. Indeed, as you engage with the Tya Practice, life can become increasingly joyful, offering clearer understanding of your purpose and desires, and yes, an ever-growing abundance—whatever that signifies for you. But this doesn't equate to achieving perfection or never encountering challenges.

347

We've emphasized the invaluable strategy of reinterpreting your life's obstacles, primarily by genuinely appreciating them and acknowledging the growth they brought. By revisiting these challenges from our non-judgmental perspective, you'll realize that they often served as catalysts for personal and spiritual growth. Simply put, facing challenges refines you. Moreover, addressing these challenges with appreciation not only resolves them but also evolves you as a being. So, why would you wish to avoid challenges?

Vibrational flow will keep guiding you through a series of highs and lows throughout your physical existence. Your response to these low vibrational moments is entirely in your hands. Often, the negative emotions associated with these lows are self-inflicted, influenced by past traumas and the matrix's teachings. While the Tya Practice doesn't eliminate challenges, it ensures fewer occurrences by consistently raising your default vibration. Understanding the intricacies of vibrational flow and manifestation empowers you to approach challenges with appreciation, facilitating smoother resolution.

Recognizing challenges as pivotal to your growth, you might start to see them as invaluable agents of expansion. Reflect on those prolonged periods of despondency. If you're new to the Tya Practice, you might not have encountered this yet, but there's profound wisdom in relinquishing control and allowing events to unfold. These extended low-vibration phases are termed "spinouts" in the Tya lexicon.

Consider a time when you aimed to form a new habit—maybe a healthier diet or exercise regimen—but plateaued. Despite intensifying your efforts, you didn't see progress, or perhaps even regressed. Such standstills often lead to frustration, primarily because of a lack of understanding of the vibrational flow. But now, equipped with these tools, you can interpret such plateaus or regressions as opportunities for greater growth. Embracing challenges with a deep-seated trust in your inherent abundance allows you to witness disruptions with excitement, aware that it's all part of the universal creation process. These disruptions often precede moments of clarity, refining and enhancing your creations.

Evidence of this process is omnipresent. Consider Apple's journey: the company faced numerous setbacks before emerging as one of the world's leading corporations. With each downturn, the founders persevered, using the challenges as fuel to innovate and improve. This resilience reflects the universal creation process, with "spinouts" serving as integral components. The Tya Practice now equips you to harness this transformative power with clear intent.

Qatarina

If there's one person uniquely qualified to pen this section, it's yours truly. Some of my fellow Tya aficionados have even bestowed upon me the illustrious title of 'Spinout Queen.' And honestly, I can't argue with that.

Nope, not at all. You see, my most recent spinout extravaganza involved a chance encounter with a hot-tempered stranger in a hot tub. Why, you ask? Well, he had this imagined notion that the lovely lady beside me was slinging insults his way, and I jumped in to defend her.

So he punched me in the face.

But wait, there's more! Right on the heels of that incident, my daughter found herself in a mad dash to emergency surgery because her ovary decided to stage a surprise explosion just as she was boarding a plane to come home to me after summer break. Oh, and let's not forget that just prior to this, I broke my foot in spectacular fashion when I lost my glasses on a skydive. You see, it's challenging to land your parachute when your vision consists only of a blurry, high-speed impressionist painting.

Yep, that was one rollercoaster of a week. You could say I don't do anything halfway. Nope, not in my nature.

Anyhoo, I'd never realized my spinouts were as "crazy" as everyone said they were. It was just my life.

But here's the kicker, and the Stream reminds us of this regularly—judgment has no place here. Unraveling is an integral part of the Tya practice. So, if anyone wants to judge me for the wild tapestry of my life, well, that's their affair. My Tya practice is my steadfast companion, and I've never once contemplated ditching it. In fact, I've reached a point where these spinouts are, dare I say it, fun. Yes, you read that right—fun, like solving a new puzzle each time.

Now, don't get me wrong, it's not like I wake up every day and actively seek out drama; I simply handle it with a nonchalant shrug and a mischievous smirk when it inevitably comes my way.

Here's the golden nugget of wisdom, especially coming from the Spinout Queen herself: In the midst of even the grandest and craziest spinouts, clinging to your Tya practice is the lifeline that keeps you riding up (or nudges you back up) that vibrational spiral, time and time again.

So, remember this: It's perfectly normal for things to take a wonky turn now and then. The key is how you handle it. As long as you don't toss your Tya tools aside, you'll effortlessly turn every spin*out* into a magnificent spin*up*!

Questions for the Stream Regarding Spinouts

Q: Is the amount of growth proportionate to the magnitude of the spinout? For example, do we grow more if the spinout is larger?

A: In the energetic realm, we don't quantify things as you do in the physical realm. For us, all expansion is valuable. That being said, spinouts provide an opportunity for growth, and a more significant spinout might motivate you to effect a larger change. Often, your ego wants to maintain the status quo to avoid the discomfort of change. A larger spinout can serve as a disruption that fuels the growth your soul desires.

Q: Can we control the duration and impact of a spinout? For example, can we shorten it and still reap the same long-term benefits as if we had allowed it to play out fully?

A: Absolutely. The sooner you recognize and appreciate the spinout without judgment, the quicker you'll return to a higher vibration and derive its benefits.

Q: Should we attempt to control spinouts, or simply let them unfold naturally?

A: We advise you to embrace the unique experiences of your journey without trying to control them. The desire for control is entirely rooted in the ego.

Q: How can we best transition from a spinout to a positive spiral?

A: Always approach situations with genuine appreciation.

Summary of Our Shared Consciousness

Spinouts are integral to the Tya Practice because they're inherent in any physical existence. They catalyze significant expansion of consciousness, the primary reason you engage with the physical realm. You've probably faced instances when you let situations spiral out of control, leading to a crisis. In such a crisis, you can either sink deeper into your ego, thereby extending the crisis, or take constructive action.

If you chose to sink deeper, it didn't bring any comfort. Immersing yourself in self-pity, assigning blame, or embracing victimhood might offer temporary relief, but they lack the satisfaction of true creation. Although you do expand in these experiences, the growth is rooted in a lower vibrational field, which doesn't equate to fresh creation. As a result, the core issue might recur, challenging you to approach it differently.

However, if you opted for action, acknowledging your capacity to address the crisis likely elevated your vibrational energy. Activating your inner Source and allowing creativity to flow often starts with a mere glimmer of appreciation. By expanding this appreciation, you amplify your creativity and find a solution to your crisis.

Authentic appreciation, allowing the flow of Source in its high vibration, is all you need to resolve any problem.

Envision a life where you consistently meet challenges with joy and appreciation, relishing each opportunity to create anew. Recognizing that you orchestrate your spinouts helps you appreciate their invaluable role. Your creativity is at its peak during a crisis, which means the highest level of expansion you seek requires occasional spinouts. We advise you to neither judge nor fear them, as they are self-created gifts.

Awakening the Egosoul

The Stream

This section is placed deeper into the book because it provides information for advanced users. By this point, you've likely tried integrating some of the teachings presented earlier into your life. If you haven't, it might be beneficial to pace your engagement with the material, allowing yourself to apply the insights as you progress through the book. Committing to the Tya Practice means engaging in meditation, fostering appreciation, shifting to optimistic viewpoints, and zooming out to embrace the Source's perspective on any matter. This commitment also entails constant awareness of your vibrational state. Integrating these practices will catalyze an inner awakening.

Unless you've previously engaged in vibrational work and experienced an awakening, the Tya Practice will usher you into your own distinctive awakening journey. You'll find that achieving clarity on any subject becomes increasingly effortless. As a Tyist, you'll transcend the need to assert your viewpoints or claim correctness. Your heightened state of acceptance will enable you to respect diverse opinions and belief systems, irrespective of your personal alignment with them. You'll discern a shift in your priorities—things that once seemed indispensable for your happiness might lose their prominence. Experiencing consistent joy, independent of any material changes, will become a hallmark of your existence. Furthermore, any descent into negative vibrational spaces will feel more jarring than before. All these manifestations signify your transition out of the matrix, marking your awakening.

Qatarina

Allow me to echo the wisdom imparted by the Stream regarding the Tya Practice—a path that unfailingly ushers forth a profound and distinct awakening within you. You see, whatever "awakening," "enlightenment," or "spiritual advancement" signifies in your life, it's bound to undergo a remarkable transformation as you dive deep into this practice.

I can personally attest to this transformation because, in the not-so-distant past, I believed my life was already nothing short of spectacular. I walked through the world with the conviction that I had a firm grasp on many things. But little did I realize just how much further the rabbit hole of self-discovery stretched. And here's the best part—it's a journey that never truly reaches its end.

In the present day, what I now identify as my 'neutral' point on my vibrational spiral has undergone a remarkable transformation. It's as if my everyday state of contentment today would have been perceived as a peak experience in the past. This shift in perspective has fundamentally altered my perception of what constitutes a 'high' in my life.

But what's truly exciting is the realization that there is so much more potential for growth and elevation. It's like I've climbed a significant portion of the mountain, only to discover that there are even higher peaks waiting to be conquered. The journey continues to unfold, and the possibilities for reaching new heights of happiness and fulfillment appear limitless.

Reflecting on the concept of going 'DTS,' it's almost surreal how distant those experiences now seem. I struggle to recollect the sensations, emotions, and challenges that once characterized that state of mind. It's as though I've transcended those depths, leaving them far behind in the rearview mirror of my personal and spiritual journey. The lessons and growth from those times remain with me, but the perspective has shifted so profoundly that I can't help but marvel at how far I've come.

Questions for the Stream Regarding the Egosoul

Q: Is this the most advanced level?

A: You are creating your advancement, and there is no "highest level," for expansion is eternal. This is true for you energetically because, with every new thought, you create expansion and all that you are becomes a more sophisticated version, and that more sophisticated version is eternal.

Q: How do we leverage this to progress further? Or will we just keep discovering spontaneously?

A: The work in Tya is designed for you, in human form, to create a continual progression of awakening via your experience of vibrational flow—meaning your ongoing discovery of transgressors and expansion in your allowed new creation in the detuning of them.

Q: Is this the state of higher understanding? Will there be a "fall," as some believe, or is this the return to "Eden"?

A: That which you call Eden is the physical embodiment of that which we are—pure positive in physical form.

A "fall" is created, by design, in your high-to-low vibrational flow. Polarity draws you into lower vibration and disconnects you from our energy. This disconnection causes unwanted conditions, and you experience pain in your judgment of them. The pain ultimately inspires a new creation in the form of solutions, or evolution, and expansion occurs.

Q: When we meet someone and have an instant dislike or feeling of "danger," is it our ego judging that person or a "knowing" from Source? How do we tell the difference?

A: We will always guide you to trust your instinct first. With this stated, we will add that if you are in high vibration, you should absolutely trust your instincts. If you are in a lower vibration, question if your discernment is born of a fearful vibration that was already present, or if you are somehow creating from a lower-vibration point of view, remember that low vibration is your time for creating the things that will drive you to desire to move back into higher vibration.

Summary of Our Shared Consciousness

The term "awakening" encompasses various interpretations. Our utilization of this word isn't anchored in the egocentric mindset of "I am awakened and therefore superior to those who are not." Instead, we refer to a vibrational journey that facilitates the realization of more of your inherent Source consciousness. We are Source, and we don't judge any being's journey; every path is valuable. Thus, for a human being, awakening represents the fusion of human ego consciousness with the ever-present state of Source being, which was often overshadowed by the teachings of the matrix.

While in physical form, one cannot completely let go of the ego, nor should they aspire to. The ego orchestrates the enchanting vibrational journey that your Soul embarked upon by coming to Earth. The merging of ego and soul doesn't require constant contemplation. Merely embodying the four pillars of the Tya Practice is sufficient for any being to kindle this state of awakening. Maintaining this practice as a lifestyle will sustain this awakening journey until you revert to your consummate state.

Part 5 ~ Making The Tya Practice Your New Way of Life

The Stream

You've now reviewed a set of Tya tools in Part 4. Remember, none of these are mandatory, and trying to employ all of them may become overwhelming. These tools are presented as layers, which you can add or remove at any point as you develop your practice. The four pillars form the foundation. Learning to use them as your operating system is fundamental to the practice and will consistently benefit you as you integrate them into your life. Before we delve into Part 5, let's take a moment to reflect on what you've gleaned from Part 4:

- **Vibrational Notes:** These involve utilizing your imagination—your most potent creative asset—to construct an actual energetic vibrational field. This lets you access and embody the vibration of any desire within moments.

- **Vibrational Timestamping:** This is akin to Vibrational Notes—it is making a mental note of a desired vibrational moment and committing it to memory. It allows for that specific vibration to be recalled and recreated on-demand. This tool aids in shifting from an unwanted or lower-vibrational experience to a desired or higher-vibrational one.

- **The Stopgap:** This is a simple conditioned response to any trigger. Merely pausing when triggered and asking, "Is this worth going down my spiral over?" can prevent many descents into lower vibrations. This happens because you've trained yourself to respond to a trigger with the stopgap, rather than the habitual vibrational drop.

- **Allowing Isness:** This is another method to create the vibration of a desire and embody it. 'Isness' underpins all creation; we've simply named it.

- **Zooming Out:** This enables the immediate realization of your natural state of Source. Given that your ego is ever-present and often dominant, developing a method to promptly revert to your innate Source-aligned state proves invaluable. Merely relinquishing fear and judgment in any situation is sufficient to access this heightened perspective.

- **The Matrix:** This tool helps discern when you're in alignment with humanity's collective consciousness versus when you're attuned to Source consciousness. While there might be an overlap between the two, understanding the matrix—and how to detach from it—makes it easier to negate and extricate the pervasive vibrations of fear, judgment, and the associated belief systems from your life.

- **The Spinout:** This represents an extended or notably low-vibrational experience that you architect to catalyze significant expansion in your vibrational journey.

- **Awakening the Egosoul:** This is an unfolding process stemming from the application of the Tya Practice as an operating system. While there are alternate routes to enlightenment, Tya furnishes daily actionable tools, delivering this experience without the often perplexing, ego-laden nuances of spirituality.

Qatarina

Immersing myself in the Tya Practice has undeniably been a transformative journey. I've previously shared some of the significant challenges I faced, such as a custody battle, car theft, and debilitating health issues. These were indeed monumental events in my life, but they pale in comparison to the truly profound experiences I navigated before discovering Tya and the Stream. These earlier trials included enduring gang-rape as a young girl, bearing witness to a lover's brutal murder, and coping with the heart-wrenching loss of a child. Each of these events left deep emotional scars, and it took the Tya Practice to help me come to terms with them fully and find genuine appreciation for the lessons they brought.

However, it's essential to emphasize that the Tya Practice isn't solely for tackling life's big challenges. It's a tool for every moment of every day. This point cannot be overstated. If we don't incorporate these tools into our daily lives, we can easily veer off course. The telltale signs are evident when things start going awry.

For instance, I rarely grapple with road rage, and consequently, I seldom encounter it from other drivers on the road. I don't get honked at, flipped off, or tailgated often. Even if it does happen, it doesn't faze me. I remain calm and composed. On the other hand, I've been a passenger with individuals who seem perpetually agitated by the behavior of other "idiot" drivers. Interestingly, their drives are invariably more stressful. They encounter frequent incidents of being cut off, near misses with oblivious drivers, pedestrians darting out in front of them, and they seem to catch every red light. It's almost like there's a correlation there, wouldn't you say? (Insert a touch of sarcasm.)

But still, every once in a while a cranky motorist shows up in my reality as well. Just a few weeks ago, I found myself tailgated by an enraged driver in a massive pickup truck. He was incensed that I didn't move out of his way quickly enough. After changing lanes, he pulled up beside me and threw trash at my X-Wing Starfighter! The audacity...

Initially, I started to feel ruffled by his aggressive behavior. But then, I caught myself. Was it worth going DTS over this encounter? Absolutely not. My daughter was with me in the car, and it was no time to let Mr. Cranky-pants in his oversized blue truck steal my serenity.

So, I took the exit, allowing him to continue on his way, and decided to address what in my vibration had gone slightly off-kilter to attract this situation. I reflected and realized that I had been stressed and felt rushed due to a busy day, yet I hadn't even noticed it until this incident occurred. But there was no need to spiral further down. Instead, I zoomed out, regained my equilibrium, and continued on my way, sharing a laugh with my daughter about the absurdity of road rage.

The crucial point here is that I had veered off track without even realizing it, and it wasn't until this incident that I became aware of it. Fortunately, my Tya Practice has brought me to a point where I can quickly course-correct before things spiral out of control. A previous version of me might have engaged in a confrontation or allowed myself to become further upset. Indulging in DTS moments is a surefire recipe for disaster.

If we persist in indulging in such negative experiences, they tend to snowball. We attract more of the same because that's where our focus lies, ultimately leading to situations like financial difficulties, violent confrontations, or health issues.

This section emphasizes the importance of acknowledging duality without getting ensnared by it. It teaches us to Trust Our Abundance and cultivate a vibrational flow that aligns with our greatest potential, rather than being tossed around like a ragdoll in a dryer.

Every morning, as I wake up, I make a conscious effort to focus on gratitude. I set my intention for the best possible outcome for the day. This practice extends to various aspects of my life, including driving, eating, working out, starting a new work project, and even skydiving. While traditional meditation still has its place, I've incorporated mini check-ins or "quick-clears" throughout the day to reset my energy. Sometimes, it takes just a few seconds, but it works wonders.

This illustrates a critical point: knowing the Tya Tools is one thing, but their effectiveness only shines when we put them into action. We must let these tools seamlessly integrate into every facet of our lives and our very being. With practice, it becomes as natural as breathing, and the transformative power of the Tya Practice becomes an intrinsic part of who we are.

David

How many spiritual and/or self-help books have you read in your lifetime? Have they truly transformed your life, leading to lasting, positive change? Only you can provide the answers, but now is an opportune moment to reflect on how effectively you integrate new ideas and practices into your life. I'm not suggesting that other books lack value; in fact, I firmly believe that everything holds the power we assign to it.

This practice undeniably works—I've witnessed profound life changes in people all over the world, and we've included some of these inspiring case studies here. However, the true power resides within you; these are tools, but you are the sculptor of your life. The common thread among those who have succeeded with Tya is their unwavering commitment and dedication to digging deep and doing the work. They made Tya an integral part of their way of life. Whether you choose to do so is entirely your decision. As the Stream reminds us, "There is no way to get life wrong, but if you're inspired by these teachings, know that applying the four pillars in your life will yield positive results, and those results will only grow with continued practice."

My motivation in creating this practice, and my ongoing aspiration, is to equip anyone seeking change with the tools to manifest it in their lives. I want you to experience ever-increasing levels of joy every day. I want you to seize your boundless creative power and fearlessly live the life of your dreams. I want you to let go of past traumas and view every facet of your life, and the entire world, as a gift. I want you to experience your low-vibrational moments without judging them as negative. I want you to approach your challenges with joy, knowing that you created them to solve them and that your soul will expand in the process. I want you to explore your world, finding joy and appreciation in every aspect of it, while standing in appreciation of the paths chosen by all other beings, regardless of whether you agree with or fully understand them. These experiences are profoundly liberating, and the emotions and creations that arise from this practice are truly magical. I genuinely wish all of this for you.

However, I must acknowledge that these desires are rooted in my ego. Yes, I desire for you to live the life that I and other Tya practitioners lead. But what do you want? Your path is not for me to judge. By this point in the book, you've absorbed enough to determine whether you're ready for this journey, whether it resonates with you or not. We are all unique individuals, and we are unquestionably on different paths. This practice contains the authentic keys to bring the power of universal law into your 3D reality, wherever you are, irrespective of your current circumstances.

Our Tya Academy boasts hundreds of graduates, with individuals from diverse backgrounds and walks of life. I've seen what works and what doesn't when it comes to learning and applying this practice. I'm wholeheartedly committed to presenting all of it within these pages because I want this for all of humanity. However, I also recognize that not everyone is prepared for it, and that is perfect in its own way. This practice and its teachings are meant for those who resonate with them. If you're feeling a resounding "hell yes!" in your desire to embrace this as your new way of life, then please continue reading. Only you know what it takes to make this your new way of living, and we are here to provide the tools, support, and community to keep you on track.

I'll share more about this later. For now, let's explore some topics and how the Tya Practice can be applied to them. As always, with the Tya practice, there are no rigid rules or mandates—just guidance to apply the four pillars in your life.

Regarding Optimal Health

The Stream

No manifestation is permanent, and the concept of perfection is not a part of your physical reality, especially when it comes to topics closely linked to feeling good. The subject of health and physical well-being is intricate. It's easier for you to experience a high vibrational state when your bodies are functioning well, and you're feeling good. However, if your life's journey has led you down the path of physical ailments or bodily conditions that keep you from feeling good, you must create a vibrational path out of that scenario, without requiring external change, to activate the actual transformation you desire. What sets Tya apart from other belief systems is its genuine appreciation for transgressors and spinouts. The matrix teaches you to despise these things, which tends to prolong their presence. By accepting and ultimately appreciating them, you render them harmless, and they vanish from your life.

Since all creation experiences a vibrational flow, there will never be a static condition, whether it's illness or wellness—this flow of conditions will remain dynamic. If your vibrational flow is predominantly high, you will generally enjoy good physical health; if it's predominantly low, you will likely experience poorer health. This vibrational flow affects each of you uniquely because you each bring your own distinct set of beliefs and expectations to your life experiences. Consequently, you all respond to your vibrational flow in different ways. With that said, we should emphasize that health and physical conditions tend to be more profoundly influenced by your vibrational flow than other topics, even those you consider very significant, such as wealth and relationships. This is because your body acts as a receptor of your vibration, and you literally feel your current dominant vibration. So, when you find yourself in a lower vibrational state, you are resisting. Doubt, fear, and impatience arise, serving as evidence of your lowered vibrational state, and the physical response is stress.

Stress isn't truly an emotion or a vibration—both of which are synonymous. Stress represents the physical symptom or manifestation of the vibration. Anxiety is the ongoing physical expression of stress. These physical manifestations contribute to illness in your bodies. Consider the word itself: "dis-ease," signifying a lack of ease in the body, a lack of harmony with the vibrational flow of life. There may indeed be external factors contributing to illness that can be identified, but we assure you that the stress you allow sets the stage for illness to take hold. The more you attenuate transgressor energy and the more you mitigate the lower vibrational emotions that stem from fear and judgment, the more well-being will become your prevailing vibration.

Regarding Relationships

The Stream

This is a topic where zooming out will certainly be useful to you. From our perspective, you are all experiencing life as strands of eternal soul consciousness—each a unique expression of Source energy that is part of the collective of all creation, but also the collective of Earth beings and the collective of humanity, your race, nationality, gender, and so on. You're part of a collective, but you're also an independent expression. Yes, things like nationality and gender are constructs of the matrix, but the collective belief in them makes them real and creates a unit of consciousness.

You absolutely have "vibrational neighbors," other beings that you are vibrationally aligned with both in a moment of flow and beyond your current perceived physical reality. When you encounter these beings, you feel an instant connection. You won't likely understand the depth of that connection until you have experienced a linear period of vibrational flow with them. This is why you may meet someone whom you believe is your soulmate, only to later have them become a major transgressor in your life. In this example, you were aligned in a flow, perhaps reflecting a quality back to you that you desired to be—or even not to be—the common thread being your focus in that flow, and you attracted your match.

The idea of "soulmates" and forever partners in life are products of the matrix. Humanity has experimented with the idea of society-building for centuries, and that included the structure of family units. Since there is duality in all subjects, there are certainly aspects of family units that serve humanity's evolution, but you are understanding more and more that there is a price to be paid in the construction and following of these rules.

The first flaw or transgressor in the family-unit theory is that it is counter to your natural desire for freedom. As an independent strand of consciousness, your core desire is the expansion of your being. This supersedes your desire to simply procreate and serve only the physical expansion of the human race. Notice how the majority of animals in your world do not get so caught up in family units. Offspring are born and nurtured to maturity, and then most often set about creating their own independent life experience. They are not often defined by a unit unless there are other circumstances creating the need for that beyond emotion. Animals that have moved up the food chain, a sign of increased sophistication, may cluster in blood-related packs—that is a sign of evolution—but humanity's evolution is moving beyond the need for this type of arrangement for security and genetic superiority.

Humanity's creation of family units and the vibration of that is so threaded into your being that even in new-age thought, we often encounter you seeking your soul mate or twin flame, believing that you need another to complete you or that you must stay with one you vibrate in harmony with during a chapter of your life throughout all the remaining chapters, or your relationship was meaningless or a failure.

Your independent nature will drive you to desire exploration and expansion throughout your life journey. The only thing that holds you in place is fear. Remove fear, and you desire to experience life in multiple ways and hold ever-evolving beliefs. It is not impossible for two strands to experience this together, but a complete allowing of independent flow and the experiences that are crafted for that flow would be needed for this entanglement to be joyous and satisfying on an ongoing path.

As always, we guide you to remove fear and judgment for clarity. When you remove fear, you see that the idea of life-long commitment can be stifling. You often end up lowering your vibration or altering your desires to fit the agenda of another. We guide you to seek understanding of self and love of self first. From this high-vibrational perspective of self-acceptance and self-love, you will not be in a state of need for another to make you whole. From this high perspective, you are in a position to attract a higher-vibrational match—a match with one who will be allowing of your own, independent flow and not in need of the external ego boost of one who is seeking to follow or be made complete by them. This also fosters deep and honest communication due to the low volume of fear in the scenario.

Simply appreciating one another for the vibrational flow of each and not fearing separation or needing anything because the understanding of the vast creative power available meets all needs. And the coupling can be experienced and enjoyed for the experience of it rather than the benefits of it; this is a very high vibration, indeed.

Regarding Wealth Creation

The Stream

Did you happen upon this chapter in order, or did you flip right to it?

There is a chance that this, with all that you have learned so far in this book, is still an important hot topic for you as it is for many. While we wish to ensure that our message is clear—that money is not the answer that many believe it is—we do acknowledge that money is a very important factor in your current reality. Money is an illusion, a human-created tool that controls your behavior like nothing else in your world. When humans are asked, "Would you rather be poor and happy or rich and unhappy?" The majority will respond that they would prefer to be rich and unhappy. This is because many cling to the belief that there is a tipping point of enough comfort, luxury, and beauty that these things will become more meaningful than simple happiness.

This is the point in most "spiritual" books that the author reminds you that true happiness cannot be purchased;

that true joy only comes from within. But this is not a spiritual book—not really. Spirituality is a big tent of multiple human beliefs. Some are rooted in our consciousness and then take off on their own, egocentric teachings that can be both confusing and poetic. The difference in our teachings is that the intention is to be as pure and untainted by ego as possible. This is why we will share a perspective regarding money (among other things) that may sound harsh or uncaring on the surface but makes more sense than perhaps anything you have learned before as they sink in and you begin to apply critical thinking to them.

The other spiritual teachers are not incorrect; you can be financially abundant and chronically unhappy. It is also true that the pure joy is derived from the clarity that only your Source connection can provide. Everything else is simply a temporary distraction of the disconnection you feel when your ego overshadows your connection to us. But, you did not come to this life to sit and meditate and allow your connection to our consciousness to flow all the time. You exist in that state eternally. Not one of you, not even your most celebrated "gurus," exist that way.

We will take this a step further and state that the "gurus" of your world are perhaps even more disconnected than you are; they are caught up in their guru-ness—their ego—and your adoration feeds their ego. The more "perfect" they present themselves to the world, the more internal strife they are likely masking. This is why we guide David to always share his obstacles, to put the most authentic version of himself on display, and teach from his flawed, human perspective in addition to sharing our wisdom, even if it costs him book sales. This is because the illusion of perfection sells well in your world; you liken the idea of eternal wisdom to perfection, to chiseled physical beauty and lyrical oration, to the backdrop of what you consider exotic places or walls filled with books. The illusion of knowledge, the marketing of a life of perfection. We are not promising you that; in fact, we are promising the opposite. We are promising a life of imperfection, delivered by an oft-portly bald man—the physical embodiment of imperfection. This is because imperfection is perfection, you come for the duality—as much as you've been programmed to seek comfort and conformity and ease, you never reach and remain in that state.

For these reasons, we will not guide you away from your desire for money. Your world is flawed by design, and you are living lives of duality—this includes disconnection from Source. This also includes desiring to experience the physical offerings of your world while you are here. The food, sex, travel, beauty, luxury, comfort, challenge, wellness, and companionship expressed in physical form. Your most cherished things in your world are physical expressions of Source—that which we are. Those things and experiences and moments that are so aligned that you feel our energy flow through you when you experience them. This can include a magical meditative moment atop a stunning mountain vista, driving the world's finest automobile, or an intense sexual encounter with a person or persons with whom you are in harmony, at least in the moment. Most, if not all, of these things require money to attain and experience.

We understand that when many of you hear the word "abundance," your minds immediately turn to wealth. Since there is duality in all subjects, there is certainly duality in this one. We see half of you wanting money, believing it is the answer to all your problems, while the other half believe that wealth is somehow evil and that possessing it in your world is wrong or not needed for a life of happiness. The truth is, money is not inherently good or evil; it is energetic like everything else.

Since money is energetic, your attitude toward it will have a massive impact on your relationship with it. Many in what you call spiritual circles will often say that money is not needed for happiness, and this is true; you can be joyful without a single possession in your world. It is possible for you to move about, eat, sleep, interact, and experience without your own personal flow of wealth, but in this example, someone is paying. You see, humanity has created a system of commerce across your entire planet where you exchange goods, services, and experiences. You understand by now, via our teachings, that you chose to manifest physically on planet Earth, how you did, when you did. You understood that you were projecting into a physical environment that was largely managed by commerce, and you chose it. You also understood that this physical environment was one impacted by polarity, as all are, and that duality would flavor your experience, in fact, that's exactly why you came.

Knowing that, you can likely see that a positive attitude toward money would ensure that you are able to enjoy all that your world has to offer. Yet few do. Why is that? It is because a major system of negative focus served to you is in the form of fear regarding money. You truly need money for just about every material thing on your planet. Then why would it be evil? The evil lies in the fear and judgment attached to it, not the money itself. Money is energy. Period. It will not ensure happiness, but it will also not hold you away from it.

Our guidance is to stop fearing it and make a *major* shift away from typical teachings and get your mind where you truly wish for it to be on this topic. Do you want freedom? Do you want to experience the joy of that freedom? Of course you do. Then clean up your relationship about money. See it as energy. We call this the energy of wealth. There is a vibrational "wealth note" in the energetic realm. In your completed state, you all have complete access to it. In your physical state, you must find it and align with it to freely receive a flow of wealth. Your wealthiest people have figured this out.

This is a teaching that you must work your way to. If you simply read this without the prior Tya work we've delivered, it will likely not be much use to you. Everything we have been teaching you up until now has been preparation for this. This includes David, as he has not received this specific information until now, as his fingers scurry across his laptop keyboard.

Here is the wealth frequency meditation; it is magical, it is powerful, and it will absolutely change your attitude toward wealth and your wealth position on Planet Earth.

We are here.

You are at the point in your Tya journey where you are ready to learn the wealth note that flows throughout the energetic realm.

This note is the vibration of material abundance, the vibration of having the freedom, experiences, and physical material creations coveted in your environment.

Having a generous flow of wealth is not about deserving, good, or evil. It's not about being blessed or cursed. From your higher perspective, you chose whatever circumstance you projected yourself into when you made the decision to be a human being on Planet Earth at this time.

Regardless of how your life journey started and where you've been, you hold the power to tune to any vibrational frequency you desire. You can change any aspect of your life if you wish.

Across all creation, there is a vibration of abundance. Abundance is not specifically about money; money is just the way that goods and services are most often exchanged on Planet Earth at this time. But there are many paths to abundance. There are truly endless ways a human can acquire the things you desire in your world.

Food, shelter, travel, experiences, and many of your other comforts all require money—and the collective of humanity desires these things very much. If you have the ability to see and desire something, you have the ability to acquire it, to have it, to experience it. You are worthy.

Acquiring the money to have the comforts, things, and experiences you desire is not about hard work, luck, or even worthiness; it is about your alignment with the wealth note—the universal vibration of material abundance.

This note reverberates through the universe. Like all other elements of the energetic realm, the wealth note is everywhere. It is flowing right through you at all times—just like we are!

Abundance IS your natural state of being. Look at nature; see how abundant your environment actually is. Vegetation is abundant. Any destruction is always temporary—vegetation always returns. Every species understands this—except humanity. This is because you've allowed yourselves to be programmed for a lack of abundance, because this made you more obedient—less freedom-seeking.

Currency was never the culprit. Leaders teaching that being humble and placing others before themselves was God's will, yet it benefited the leaders themselves the most. The system is still alive but being questioned, but in that questioning, the currency has also been demonized, but not by all—not by those at the top. Those at the top understand the system, and some believe that if the masses begin loving the system and tuning to the wealth note, they will no longer be in control. This is not the case. All of humanity is abundant by design. It's time to wake up and realize this abundance.

This is why some label our teachings as dangerous, false, or even evil, because there is power in what we offer. We are giving you the whole story, and it will empower you if you adopt the new operating system that we offer.

To tune to this note, you only need to find it by creating an equal note in your mind. We've named this note "Gee." It is not a sound but a vibrational frequency. You match this frequency by creating a feeling with your projected thought, using your imagination.

Understand that all creation begins with imagination, a dream, or desire held and believed consistently that attracts every component needed to bring that dream to full physical manifestation.

In this case and in the Tya Practice, we use imagination to bridge the gap to the desired vibration, and a connection is made. If this connection is allowed to remain consistently, it will merge cosmically with the universal vibration. This is how you align with a specific vibration.

We are going to take you on a magical journey right now to the vibration of the wealth note. We are going to use a sound and other tools to create a simulation of this connection. We are going to guide you on a journey of thought that will take you there.

Relax, breathe, and luxuriate in our words.

We are not taking you to outer space. We are guiding you to a vibration that is already flowing through you. It's always been there—just like we have always been with you. You feel us, this sense of calm that washes over you when you relax, breathe, and clear.

Feel our warmth flow.

Now, create a vision in your mind of what the Gee note looks like.

Visualize a pyramid. We will call this the wealth pyramid.

Those who love money, who fully embrace Earth's system of commerce, reside vibrationally at the top of the pyramid—the apex.

Those who feel less enthralled about money and Earth's commerce operate a bit lower in the pyramid. Those who demonize money and Earth's system of commerce exist at the bottom. They carry the weight of the pyramid in their negative judgment of it. All of humanity comprises the pyramid—whether they desire to or not. Even those who claim to be completely outside of any commerce system are part of it. For example, even your homeless/jobless/income-free population are part of the pyramid because they are drivers of commerce. Think of how much money is raised on behalf of the poor—participation in commerce is not optional in your world.

So, decide on your placement in the pyramid; there's no getting it wrong. But if your desire is financial abundance, getting to the top is key.

In your pyramid visualization, create your own unique model and allow it to be the vibration of wealth. Visualize being the apex—authentically loving Earth's system of commerce. Detuning any and all fear and judgment around it.

Is it the pulse of sound waves reverberating as it flows? Is it deep purple in color? Perhaps morphing between purple and green? Do you feel the flow?

Relax and visualize and see this note, this vibration, with your mind's eye. Feel it pulse and flow. Feel the energy of wealth. Of abundance, in the wealth pyramid.

Create a vivid picture of this note in your mind. Remember what this looks like. Remember what this feels like.

Now that you're swirling through this amazing energy, imagine yourself having and doing the things you desire. Anything you desire. The travel. The experiences. The beautiful places. Your beautiful, abundant life.

Visualize your home. The bed you sleep in. The food you eat. Perhaps your view of your gardens or the ocean.

There are no limits. You can have anything. This visualization and your belief is the Source, for you are one with Source in this state of abundance and knowing.

Visualize the things you'll do with unlimited abundance. You are unlimited. You are a magical creator.

See yourself as the apex. Look down at all humanity supporting you, and feel deep appreciation for them. They are having their experience.

Now. We're going to do something very powerful. We are going to vibrationally timestamp this moment. We are going to commit the combination of this high-vibrational feeling of unlimited abundance and the visual and feeling of the wealth note, this vibrational feeling that you are allowing to flow right now.

This is the magical wealth note. It feels special. It feels powerful. You have now accessed it, and your life will never be the same. This is where the most successful among you align. This is their vibration.

We have money. We have an abundance of wealth. We have all the things and experiences that we desire. We are everywhere, and we share this with you. This is your destiny; you have traveled through difficulty and lack to prepare yourself for this moment, this moment when you tapped in. When you found the frequency of abundant wealth and you taught yourself to tune to it.

Breathe.

Feel the electrifying energy of the wealth note.

You always have access to this note. You now have the tools and you recall the feeling.

You have your precious vibrational timestamp. A time-stamp that you can access at any moment and realize this connection. This is magical. You are magical. You are loved and you are worthy.

Now, come back down to 3D and commit your vibrational timestamp to memory, so you may access it readily all the time. This is the key to shifting your vibration to a new one. You now know that vibration of wealth and you've seen it in action. You now have the tools to move your mind to that space at any time, in any place.

Your New Practice

The Stream

We have been very clear that Tya is not intended to become a religion where we, our teachings, or David, are worshiped or to have rules to obey or be dogmatic in any way. Our teachings and the Tya Practice are based on universal law, but we are clear that each individual creates their own bubble of reality, and we do not judge what is in your bubble, so you are free to practice this solely and make it your new way of life, or utilize it alongside anything else you choose.

You are likely aware that any new habit takes time and a degree of self-discipline to establish. That's because every habit is its own vibration, and long-established vibrations have the power of momentum behind them. You may hold beliefs that you believe are so ingrained in you that you cannot change. We promise you that this is not the case; you've simply invested in a narrative that change is difficult and therefore not worth the effort. But you purchased this book for a reason. What was that? How does it feel right now? Does this practice seem like

393

a mountain to climb? Does it seem impossible to do "all this?" Is that your soul speaking or your inner-saboteur, i.e., your ego?

The reason Tya works is that we are not guiding you to some superhuman set of tools that only the most advanced students can accomplish. We are guiding you to a very simple set of tools—the four pillars—that you can begin using immediately: Appreciation, Polarity, Source, and Intention. Practiced over time, these four pillars will provide what you may now refer to as superhuman results indeed.

We understand that the habit of thought is like any other habit; however, the beauty of this practice is that you employ these things and realize immediate vibrational results. And remember that every creation is a vibrational creation first. And learning to celebrate the vibrational creation and not needing the physical byproduct to materialize will take the pressure off and quell your inner saboteur.

Your current world teaches you that the only things that matter are the fully-realized physical manifestations, but think about this, the most celebrated, brilliant humans on your planet, your historic figures such as Einstein, Tesla, and Michelangelo, as well as your modern-day disruptors such as Steve Jobs, Jeff Bezos, and Elon Musk all have one thing in common: they are eternally designed human beings—just like you. They came to Earth equipped with the same physical vehicle as the vast majority of other humans. Why are they different? Their mindset—their belief in their worthiness, their own genius. They allowed their creations in their imagination and they believed them into reality.

Notice how, in the matrix, you are taught to be humble, to not believe in yourselves—at least not that much. Perhaps their upbringing set them up for success, either with a family culture of success or surrounded by others who nurtured their healthy egos. This is where many of you will say "Yes! They had all the advantages, and I did not—now it's too late!"

But why is it too late? Who decided that? If you take away nothing else from this book, take the knowledge that you've been programmed, not by an evil world looking to hold you down, but by a human-crafted system that allows the most confident to thrive and places everyone else—all other humans—in service of them and their endeavors. Queen bees and worker bees, so to speak, all having their palace in this matrix you call Earth.

But when you remove fear and judgment, as we have guided you to do in this practice, there is nothing wrong with that system, and there is nothing holding you in any position in the matrix other than your own beliefs. The matrix continually extends an invitation, but you choose to walk through its door.

So the changing of these beliefs is as easy as you allow it to be. We've provided many tools and we will provide you with ongoing teaching that you can consume to keep your practice growing. But everything you need is contained in this book. You can look upon all this as a steep hill to climb—and it can be—but you can remain at the base and keep living the same set of circumstances over and over again, stuck at the bottom of that hill, or you can begin to climb.

How do you begin climbing and not get discouraged or tired? Not run out of energy?

You claim ownership of your attitude toward the climb itself. You make the climb your new joyous way of being. Employing a degree of discipline to meditate daily, finding your effective version of allowing your Source connection to be realized, without need. You make raising your vibration through appreciation a priority—because there is more power in that than in any effort or responsibility that resides in the matrix. You make delving into old traumas and limiting beliefs from your higher-vibrational vantage point your new hobby. You allow yourself to remove fear and judgment and then dive into those topics. You, without judgment, learn to separate yourself from the matrix of humanity—all those human constructs—and realize the Source-consciousness version of you. We say without judgment because we are not guiding you to demonize the human matrix, because that gives it power; we're guiding you to love it and see it for what it is, and claim the power you truly have over it because you gave it life in your belief in it.

As you joyously climb, you notice when your energy is lower. You stop and rest and appreciate the scenery from your now-higher vantage point. When you feel gravity pulling you back down, you appreciate that—for it is part of the journey up. You relax into the energetic dip and acknowledge that it's only there to inspire you to go higher. You meet the obstacles on your path in appreciation because you placed them there to make you a better climber. As you start and pause and appreciate and forge ahead, you set grander and grander intentions, knowing that the mountain peak will be glorious, and you'll revel in its majesty.

Then you'll realize how much stronger you've become in your joyful climb. What in the beginning seemed like work is now fun because you've taught yourself a new belief system. Now you can climb and rest and traverse like you never imagined you could. You're a new, confident, and abundant version of yourself. You find yourself stopping and zooming out to a higher perspective when old triggers appear. You relish meditation because the pressure to "do it right" has diminished, and you just love allowing a better feeling to flow in by simply breathing and appreciating. You find yourself setting intentions habitually: upon waking up, before leaving your home, before interacting with others, before beginning tasks. This pre-paving of expectations reveals how magical you truly are.

Soon you see things showing up in your life. With fear and judgment removed, you see your manifestations clearly. Those around you take notice of the lighter, more confident version of you. Some are inspired, and others pull away because they preferred the old you. That is fine because you've gained clarity on your relationships, and you can now release them without judgment—even if they are judging you!

Make this fun. Know that it is a lifetime commitment if you choose it. But it is one that pays dear dividends in the form of loving yourself and all that is more and more and more. It pays in the form of joy for no reason other than being the brilliantly manifested, perfect strand of consciousness that you came to realize, regardless of how many years it took you to arrive here. In knowing that your journey was and is perfection, all the challenges and darkness that you manifested on your path actually created your path. It made you stronger, a more sophisticated version of you—eternally. In experimenting with your reaction to vibrational flow and enjoying every adjustment you make in your journey. Enjoying your new tools as you find the right version that works for you. And in the powerful reimagining of everything in your world through the lens of appreciation—what a freeing and magical state of being this will become with your adaptation and continued practice—one that reveals itself in bigger and bigger ways as you gain momentum.

Make this your new way of being and return to these words again and again until they become the new version of you.

Additionally, while there are no rules, and thus no consequences for not following them, there is a practice and a few things we would like to address as "best practices" for lack of a better term. These are our guidance, not requirements in Tya:

Releasing The Need To Win Arguments Or Be "Right"

The need to be right or win an argument is rooted in ego and does little to raise your vibration other than a temporary feeling of superiority while you pat yourself on your own back for winning. You all create your own bubbles of reality and there is really no winning, only lowering of vibration, in the egocentric need, to prove a point that only exists in your bubble of reality to begin with.

Judging Versus Discerning Preference

We've stated that you are all innately judgmental. The reason for entering this physical environment is to discern preferences. This process begins early, in the womb, and continues throughout your life as you experience various aspects of existence. You encounter things you like—sometimes even desire—and dedicate significant time pursuing them, or at least pondering how to obtain them. These preferences provide purpose, and your ego propels you toward that purpose.

However, you also come across elements that aren't to your liking. Early transgressors include food, physical discomfort, light, temperature, and noise. As life progresses, you confront myriad experiences that aren't to your preference, including your own struggles with manifesting desires. In states of such disallowance, it's often comforting to shift focus to others' manifestations, including their behaviors and choices, rather than introspectively examining your own creative process. This diversion is where discernment morphs into judgment. While judgment offers superficial satisfaction by serving as a distraction, it inevitably becomes self-directed, distancing you further from your own preferences.

The Judgment of Others

You might anticipate this section to delve into judgment related to the behavior of others that might not align with your preferences. However, we recognize there's no need to address that specifically. Our intent is to discuss other forms of judgment that, though seemingly benign or rooted in care for fellow humans or the planet, can be misguided.

In spiritual contexts, it's not uncommon to encounter sentiments like "We're transitioning to 5D, an enlightened way of being," or "I'm a healer; I can cure others," and even "We are healing Mother Earth." While such statements might appear well-intentioned on the surface, they originate from ego rather than eternal soul consciousness, thereby falling within the matrix's domain.

Each of you represents unique threads of soul consciousness navigating a physical human existence. While this doesn't encompass the entirety of your being, you operate within the realm of human ego. Statements like the aforementioned ones indicate an imbalance between the ego and the soul. True soul consciousness recognizes that every thread of consciousness is perfectly manifesting its desired experience and that your planet, undergoing its vibrational journey, is fully capable of self-care. It also acknowledges that all healing is intrinsically self-healing, and external healing must be both desired and accepted. Often, you might find yourselves trying to mend your personal wounds by attempting to heal others. Although this may come from a place of benevolence, the primary vibration is often the ego deflecting attention onto others rather than focusing on the self.

There's nothing inherently wrong with desiring a more considerate approach toward the planet or wishing for others' prosperity. However, undertaking such causes is frequently ego-driven, as the soul comprehends the inherent perfection in all situations. The world's contrasts naturally facilitate growth, and the development—or allowance—of solutions propels this expansion.

We encourage your aspirations for evolution, the betterment of planetary care, and the healing paths of others. However, it's essential to understand that genuine solutions emerge from a high-vibrational state of appreciation and acceptance of the current situation, combined with a vision of potential improvements. This differs starkly from the judgmental focus on the negative energies creating the perceived issues. We further advise recognizing that embodying a high-vibrational example and trusting the universal process of creation is the most valuable contribution you can make, rather than attempting to rescue the world or addressing personal wounds vicariously.

Fear And Reacting To Fear-Mongering

Fear is a component of your ego, designed to keep you safe and ensure your continued experience of life. We observe many of you letting this fear component run rampant, allowing it to intrude into numerous mental considerations where it does nothing but separate you from your aspirations.

The emotions of dislike, and especially disdain, can be immensely potent. These emotions can be a human's most significant downfall, as they're easily exploited by others. Numerous leaders in your world have thrived by convincing the masses to fear what they disdain, asserting that their governance is the remedy for these fears. This tactic has been the foundation upon which empires and nations have risen and fallen throughout history.

Given the consistent diet of fear fed to humanity over millennia, it's no surprise that fear is such a dominant emotion. However, as we've reiterated throughout this book, you have the capability to diminish fear. By now, you've likely decided whether you truly have the power to shape your own reality. If you're still skeptical, perhaps you're not prepared for what we offer and might prefer a life dictated by chance. And that's okay. Choosing not to embrace our teachings won't detract from the expansiveness of your life experience.

Doesn't this perspective seem unusual? Most books at this juncture would seek to reassure you, reinforcing the value of the time and energy you invested in reading. Yet, you possess the authority to validate this content, and you're beginning to recognize that everything carries the significance you attribute to it. Within the Tya Practice, you embrace this authority by acknowledging all of your manifestations, including your challenges, and cultivating such confidence in your creative abilities that there's minimal space or necessity for fear in your future.

Through a consistent routine of elevating your vibration using meditation, adopting a Source perspective, monitoring your vibration throughout the day, and setting a positive intention daily, you'll naturally drift away from fear. The process of reducing fear can become so enthralling that you might eagerly face challenges or contemplate previously daunting topics, all to relish the insights from this elevated viewpoint. The most pervasive tools rooted in fear, such as politics, religion, conspiracy theories, and even marketing, will lose their grip on you. With the Tya Practice, you can approach these from a standpoint of fearlessness and non-judgment. Since you are the architect of your life, there's absolutely no reason for fear.

Politics

We've touched upon the potent tool of fear, and nowhere is it employed more adeptly than in politics. Politics revolves around control—controlling others' experiences and behaviors, overseeing currency, and determining the masses' health and welfare. It's all about shaping the outcome. While these principles run counter to the Tya Practice, they don't necessarily need to be disregarded. Your engagement in politics, or lack thereof, is a personal preference, but you must recognize the incongruity in needing to externally control outcomes or having individuals in power that echo your desires to realize them.

In politics, there will always be victors and vanquished. The essence lies in choosing sides and backing leaders who resonate with your beliefs and aspirations. If you're intentionally sculpting your reality, is there a need for politicians to do so on your behalf? Does your urge for the rule of law to mirror your desires stem from fear? Can you envision a life filled with joy, clarity, and abundance, irrespective of political inclinations or the results of forthcoming elections?

In the Tya Practice, there are no mandates. Any inclination to partake in politics won't be scrutinized by us—we pass judgment on nothing. However, realizing your power to shape your existence with intention reduces the need to influence others' actions or determine any result.

Making Life Decisions

Throughout your life, you'll encounter myriad decisions. The prevalent human trepidation surrounding decisions, especially perceived significant or life-altering ones, springs from a fear of failure—the anxiety of making the wrong choice. We assure you there's no such thing as "getting it wrong." In our view, every decision, victory, mistake, or even painful episode serves to enrich your growth. Trust us when we say you didn't set out to experience a "flawless" existence in this life. You embarked on this journey embracing both missteps and moments of brilliance. These elements carve the intricate pathways of your life's voyage, and this journey encapsulates your purpose.

None of you were destined to tread a straightforward, pre-charted path, ensuring a seamless life with preordained outcomes. The more your lives mirror this linear trajectory, the more mundane they appear, often leading to self-imposed hurdles, be it illnesses or even tragedies. Your soul yearns for growth, frequently through challenges. When the ego is imbalanced with the soul, it either anchors you in a secure zone devoid of significant hurdles until the soul can't tolerate the monotony, or it balloons to a point of perceived invulnerability, which then spawns challenges. Either way, growth through adversity is guaranteed—there's genuinely no possibility of erring.

Our advice when facing decisions, be they major or minor, is to eliminate fear for clarity. Ask yourself: If failure wasn't an option, what would you pursue? If you were impervious to harm or disappointment, what would be your choice? Perceptions of failure, harm, and disillusionment are subjective judgments and thus, constructs of the matrix. These are the pivotal questions to contemplate!

Family Relationships

From our perspective, the sole requirement for "family" is one human introducing another to the Earth environment. Everything beyond that is the experience manifested by the newly birthed being. This means the family unit is as much a construct of the matrix as it is "natural." Therefore, our discussion will center on the group of individuals who raised you, whom you consider your family. While biological families influence the vibrational makeup of an individual, the eternal strand of consciousness we call the soul plays a crucial role too. Together, they shape the distinct human-focused individual you become.

Practicing Tya leads to the detuning of fear. Consequently, the need to be right and the expectation for others to validate or mirror your beliefs diminishes. The process also reduces judgment, ensuring you aren't troubled by the thoughts or behaviors of others. A significant byproduct is the profound decrease in self-judgment. The extent of these changes depends on your vibrational efforts. The longer you engage with Tya, the higher your default vibration becomes, reducing susceptibility to old thought patterns. Eventually, many issues that once troubled you cease to do so. In this transformative process, you might feel distant from certain individuals in your life, including family.

Such disconnections are not obligatory in the Tya Practice. During the early phases, you might prefer to keep your evolving practice private, revealing it only when you can handle skepticism or even mockery. This precaution stems from the fact that the matrix is adept at instilling fear toward unconventional mindsets like Tya. Those deeply entrenched in the matrix may view your approach with suspicion, perhaps suggesting you've joined a cult or undergone some form of brainwashing. The matrix inherently opposes universal law, so challenges to it often elicit negative responses. Unlike Tya practitioners, matrix-bound individuals constantly seek external validation.

As your vibration elevates, you evolve into a bolder version of yourself. The joys of clarity and manifestation become enticing, making you eager to share your insights. However, overcoming ingrained fears and limiting beliefs can be daunting initially. For those not actively seeking change, it's even tougher. Rather than understanding, many might dismiss your novel perspectives.

Tya emphasizes open-mindedness, allowing everyone their unique experiences, irrespective of how divergent they are from your beliefs. Deep-seated tendencies like picking sides, rationalizing, and the compulsion to be "right" are so embedded in human psyche that your alternative beliefs might appear threatening, evoking reactions ranging from amusement and ridicule to outright hostility. These teachings counteract dominant belief systems that have governed your planet for millennia.

In Tya, the approach to family, as with all aspects of life, is rooted in complete acceptance, devoid of fear or judgment. This encompasses your family's beliefs and, ideally, their acceptance of yours. However, it's vital to acknowledge that you can't control the thoughts or behaviors of others. In the Tya Practice, such control is unnecessary as you're not aiming to influence any outcome.

Our advice emphasizes harmony with your family and everything else. Within the pillar of appreciation, we encourage not just forgiveness but genuine appreciation of your transgressors, who are often family members, especially parents. Yet, it's essential to clarify that forgiveness and appreciation don't necessitate ongoing relationships. The Tya Practice doesn't impose any obligations or "duties" toward family. It simply advocates a high-vibrational appreciation and acceptance of all beings, including family.

Romantic Relationships

A significant emphasis is placed on human romantic relationships. This can largely be attributed to the potential reproductive element and leaders' desire to manage family units to build empires.

There was a period in human evolution when the formation of family units began to take shape. Initially, developing humans roamed freely, with males naturally inclined to propagate extensively. The healthiest, strongest, and wisest males undertook this task more efficiently than their counterparts. Females focused on giving birth, caring for their offspring, and ensuring their own survival and that of their progeny.

As leaders aspired to establish groups, marking the beginnings of their empires, the necessity to regulate population growth emerged. Guiding the masses to reproduce became an agenda to expand empires for trade and defense. Consequently, the concept of male-female partnerships was promoted. Variations existed, often with females being treated more as assets, and males permitted to possess as many females as they could support. This arrangement satisfied a male's natural inclination to propagate while maintaining the bounds of the empire.

As human cognitive abilities evolved and the ego became more influential, the matrix expanded. With ambitions of dominance and conquest, the need for warriors grew, leading to an imbalance in male-to-female ratios. The natural balance in births is essential for the survival of any species. However, the ego-driven inclination toward warfare disrupted this equilibrium, and the model of one man with multiple women became more prevalent. As commerce systems matured and warrior roles became class-determined, the one-man/one-woman family unit became dominant in more "advanced" cultures. This transition is where human monogamy took root, accompanied by the stigmatization of non-reproductive sexual behaviors.

The inclination toward heterosexuality and monogamy is a byproduct of egocentric human programming. While we do not pass judgment on such programming—since it facilitated your species' evolution—it's evident that as you collectively awaken, there's a shift away from these constructs. You are, however, free to determine how you think, believe, and conduct your lives, without any judgment from us.

Our advice is to introspect and discern your preferences in romantic life, considering the historical backdrop. Engaging in the Tya Practice, characterized by non-fear and non-judgment, may lead to greater fluidity in your sexual behaviors and relationships. Whether you act on this newfound perspective or not remains your prerogative.

Soul Mates & Twin Flames

Within spiritual communities, concepts like "soul mates" and "twin flames" are prevalent. It's true that you encounter what we term "vibrational neighbors"—beings you're vibrationally matched with either momentarily or across lifetimes. Such connections often feel profound, giving you the sensation of having known them beyond this existence. Typically, you're experiencing a potent vibrational alignment with your current state, making everything seem harmonious initially.

The universal process of creation is consistent across topics. Significant desires, due to their importance to you, might take longer to materialize. As discussed, this delay arises from your natural vibrational flow. Polarity causes you to reflect on your deepest wishes from diverse vibrations, sometimes stalling or even neutralizing them. Such challenges ensure a superior manifestation. This principle applies universally but is particularly relevant to desires central to your happiness, like relationships, new ventures, health, and wealth.

The true measure of your soul mate or twin flame relationship is how both partners navigate their vibrational flow—across highs and lows. Relationship challenges can either destroy or strengthen the bond. Sustained contrasts will truly test the relationship. Remember, every individual is distinct and evolves independently. Sustained alignment requires one partner, at times, to adjust their beliefs, desires, and focus. It's up to you to determine whether this is worthwhile, but sacrificing one's default vibrational level is seldom fulfilling. Thus, a genuine "twin flame" connection is realized only through the continuous mutual appreciation of both parties throughout their vibrational flow.

Raising Children

We often encounter questions about raising "awakened" children. The most valuable thing you can provide your children is the same as what you offer the world: the high-vibration version of you. Reflect on your upbringing and consider your own parenting style if you've already embarked on this journey. Your most profound regrets—if you have any—are probably actions taken out of fear. Fear of judgment toward your child or fear of judgment toward you based on your actions or inactions.

However, the silver lining is that there's no definitive "right" or "wrong" in parenting, just as there isn't in life. All judgment stems from human ego consciousness. Soon, you'll be able, if you haven't already, to adopt a broader perspective, especially when introducing new life into the world. Your main responsibility in this process is the biological journey from conception to birth. Everything else intertwines with your child's predestined path and your journey as a parent. Your child's soul consciously chose the experience of human life, including having you as a parent, due to a vibrational alignment. Their choice to manifest in specific circumstances was intentional, given the potential experiences available. This encompasses pre-birth events like miscarriages, abortions, and what are often termed "birth defects."

All scenarios are the result of vibrational alignment. Circumstances you might view as suboptimal often present as purposeful obstacles, enriching life experiences for everyone involved. Remember, parenting doesn't come with a blueprint for perfection. Every individual is contemporaneous with the era they are born into, so a universal guide to impeccable parenting is nonexistent. However, you can control the extent of fear and limiting beliefs you instill in your child, either through direct instruction or by example—the two most potent tools at your disposal as a parent.

It's entirely possible to nurture a child to navigate their world without the burden of fear and limiting beliefs. You can encourage them to cultivate tranquility in their minds, fostering a connection to their intrinsic nature. It's feasible to set them on a path where society's conventional perspectives don't cloud their ambitious visions for life. Realize that they will inevitably face the matrix, regardless of your actions. The challenge is in permitting them to carve out their unique experiences, irrespective of your parenting strategies.

Guiding them using mainstream norms will expose them to contrast, manifesting as the very fears and limiting beliefs you're trying to dismantle. By fostering their growth in an "awakened" state, a more profound understanding of universal laws, they'll likely face contrast due to their heightened self-awareness. Some might interpret this as a "no-win" situation. In our eyes, it's a "no-lose" situation because every challenge spurs growth.

If these teachings resonate with you and have significantly improved your life, you'll naturally wish to impart them to your children. Our advice is to remember: the younger your child, the more receptive they are to new ideas. However, these teachings are a deeply personal journey of enlightenment. Leading by example and allowing them to assimilate at their pace is ideal. If your children are approaching their teenage years or older, they've already molded their beliefs and perceptions. Thus, introducing concepts that veer from the norm might be challenging. Recall that the obstacles in your life probably led you to this profound realization. If they haven't walked in your shoes, they might not be ready to venture this far from mainstream thinking at this stage—and that's perfectly acceptable. If these practices have benefited you, the best you can hope for is their understanding and support. If they've adopted skepticism or cynicism, either from your guidance or elsewhere, it will challenge your commitment to your path. This becomes an opportunity for you to practice allowing them to carve their path without passing judgment on them or yourself.

Navigating Relationships That Are No Longer A Vibrational Match

Society has ingrained certain fears within individuals, particularly the anxieties surrounding solitude, the possibility of perpetual singledom, or the notion of being without friends. Such fears, often rooted deeply, influence your decisions and sometimes make you cling to relationships that no longer align with your inner growth.

However, our guidance isn't advocating for a life shrouded in isolation. Instead, we encourage a profound journey toward self-awareness and self-love. By elevating yourself to a higher vibrational frequency, you become attuned to relationships that mirror this enhanced state of being. As you gravitate toward this vibrational harmony, you'll naturally attract individuals and relationships that resonate with your elevated state of consciousness. Simultaneously, ties that no longer align with your newfound vibration may naturally dissipate.

This evolution in relationships is an organic byproduct of personal growth. As you elevate and recalibrate your default vibrational state, you'll find a clearer perspective on your relationships. Some connections might intensify, becoming more profound and meaningful, while others might wane, reflecting the differing paths each individual is on.

Embracing this dynamic change and understanding that it is a part of the journey can bring peace and clarity. The focus should always be on personal growth and vibrational harmony. By doing so, you ensure that the relationships you foster are genuine, supportive, and aligned with your highest self. Remember, quality often outweighs quantity, especially when it comes to relationships that nurture your soul.

We are guiding you to raise to a high vibration of self-love and allow your higher vibrational matches to flow in and those with whom you no longer resonate, to flow out. This is a natural occurrence as you work on zooming out and raising your default vibration.

Body Image, Cosmetic Surgery, and Other Body Modifications

Your bodies serve as the physical vessels that navigate your human journey through life. Consider them as advanced filtration systems, allowing your consciousness to experience the Earth environment. These vessels are like technology—so sophisticated that you view them as a "natural" phenomenon. Indeed, they occur naturally, yet they are intelligently designed creations of your own consciousness.

As we've mentioned before, you exist as a strand of eternal consciousness navigating a physical realm, deriving expansion from the contrasting experiences it offers. The entirety of who you are transcends the limited version you currently perceive. This design, limiting your perception to a fraction of the entire consciousness, enriches your unique Earthly experience and helps you delve deeper into the core energy, of which you are an integral part. Your life experiences contribute directly to our expansion, which, in turn, facilitates the expansion of the universe. However, no physical experience is designed to be perpetual. Over time, your vessels deteriorate, largely influenced by your mental focus and the stress generated by unwanted experiences and fears of recurrence. Feelings of disconnection, prompted by an evolving world that outpaces your growth as you age, further contribute to this deterioration.

Given the finite nature of your physical vessel, its upkeep lies in your hands. There's no judgment from us concerning how you manage or even choose to alter it. Remember, your body is intended to host your consciousness for a specific Earthly duration before you transition to a fully-realized state of consciousness. Even if your bodies could remain in peak condition indefinitely, your mind would still initiate a process of detachment, adhering to the higher aspiration of rejoining the complete state of consciousness. This detachment often manifests as cognitive ailments in humans. As technology increasingly prolongs physical life while the consciousness's vibration wanes, such cognitive challenges will become more prominent.

It's entirely your prerogative how you treat or modify your body. Some believe in the need to "maintain your temple." While there's value in this perspective—a healthier body generally supports a higher vibration—it's not the sole path. When aligned with your desires and adhering to the principles outlined in this text, you'll naturally gravitate toward better health. Stress, stemming from lower-vibrational thinking, is the root cause of all illnesses. As you transcend the need to soothe such stress, you'll likely move away from overindulgences that harm your body. Improved wellness habits aren't mandated by the Tya Practice; they emerge naturally from it.

Regarding body modifications, we harbor no judgments. However, we advise that such decisions often stem from misalignment. Like most things you aspire to manifest, the ultimate aim is to derive joy from the manifestation. When you attain joy, clarity, and abundance without requiring external shifts, the yearning for such modifications diminishes. You'll find yourself in a state of self-love, relishing your world just as it is, requiring no change. This epitomizes true abundance—rejoicing in the present moment, accepting things "as they are."

If you're contemplating body alterations, driven by the notion that they'll bring happiness, we urge you to seek that happiness internally first. No external modification can instill genuine happiness if it isn't inherent. This applies to cosmetic changes and gender transitions alike. Discover contentment in your current state and then, from this elevated vibrational position of self-love, determine your preferences.

Diet

The Tya philosophy doesn't prescribe a specific diet or assert an ideal way of eating. In your world, the spectrum of nourishment is vast, stretching from wholesome foods to potential toxins. It's an inevitability that you'll encounter contrasts in dietary choices, just as you do in every aspect of life. Whether it's being subjected to others' harmful behaviors or exposure to polluted air, water, and food, the judgment you place on these elements is often more detrimental than the elements themselves. Your mind and body are naturally designed to filter and process various inputs. The reaction to these inputs, more often than not, stems from your perception rather than the substance or observation itself. Stress determines how anything is assimilated by your system.

Since stress is the tangible result of misalignment with one's desires, when you hinder the free flow of your desires through doubt, impatience, or worry, you produce stress. This stress then captures and retains unwanted elements within your body, leading to various ailments and unwelcome physical conditions.

To enhance your well-being, trust in your inherent abundance, reduce stress, and observe an improvement in your health. Steer clear of harshly judging aspects like illness or fluctuating weight. Such judgments only amplify the issues. Embrace your imperfections, realizing that they're a part of the broader perfection. Shield yourself from succumbing to self-criticism or the judgments of others, and be cautious not to project your judgments onto others either. The energy of judgment, when directed outward, often ricochets back.

Concerning food choices, trust your body's signals. Consume what leaves you feeling rejuvenated post-meal. However, it's vital to recognize that resorting to food for emotional solace is similar to using drugs or alcohol for comfort; the void remains. As for the debate on consuming meat and animal products, we hold no judgments. Most often, those advocating against the consumption of meat base their stance on the perceived sentience and likeness of animals to humans. This is primarily an egocentric view. Every entity, whether plant or animal, carries consciousness. Therefore, in consuming any form of nourishment, you're essentially absorbing consciousness. The predominant argument against meat consumption arises from the empathetic realization that animals bear resemblance in feelings and behaviors to humans. This is, in essence, an ego-driven perspective. The underlying fear being that accepting the consumption of beings akin to you might lead to a future where entities deem it acceptable to consume you. Most seemingly altruistic motivations often have egoistic underpinnings. Although it's natural to aspire to better treatment of animals, children, or the less privileged, every being embarks on their journey for distinct experiences. Rather than striving to shield others, focus on refining your own existence. Embodying and projecting a high-vibrational example is the most profound gift you can offer the world.

Your Work

Your perceived life on this plane is finite. Indeed, you are an eternal fragment of soul consciousness, navigating one of countless physical realities—essentially a construct of consciousness designed for the unique contrasts it presents. But, while immersed in this experience, you are destined to express the physical manifestations of the Source. This implies that any material possession, experience, or condition you desire in high vibration—your positive point of creation—cannot be perceived as "wrong." If it isn't wrong to desire it, it certainly isn't wrong to attain or experience it. Given this insight, we urge you to reevaluate any limiting beliefs regarding the work you engage in. Understand that your true purpose aligns with pursuing the tangible expressions of the Source, driven by your high-vibrational desires, while navigating the challenges birthed from lower vibrational states. Let this perspective redefine your understanding of "work" and allow a job, career, or enterprise to emerge from this foundation.

Shed the egocentric notion that societal titles validate respect or that a lifelong commitment to a single path is mandatory. Recognize that you're a dynamic entity, continuously evolving. The very idea of being anchored to one role, exchanging effort for financial gain throughout your existence, may run counter to your genuine desires.

For those who've tread the path of adulthood for a while, feelings of stagnancy in a job, career, or business, even one that was once a passion, are not uncommon. Often, this is a sign of personal growth, and the chains that bind might merely be fears inculcated by the matrix, a structure rooted in fear.

Open yourself to a plethora of opportunities, embracing a fearless pursuit. Embrace challenges, knowing that the journey, with all its highs and lows, adds richness to life. Don't shy away from experiencing everything, from creation to destruction and back. Let failures not daunt you, but empower you. Invite the universe to guide you on this exhilarating voyage of discovery and experimentation. When reflecting at the twilight of your journey here, you might find that the joy of creation overshadowed the possession of the end product. Continue to create, evolve, and when the time is right, let your graceful exit be your final masterpiece.

Your Health

By embracing the teachings of this book, and elevating your vibrational state, you'll invariably witness a boost in your physical health. A lion's share of undesirable bodily conditions originates from stress. Implementing the practices of fear release, trust cultivation, and other prescribed methods will organically diminish, if not eradicate, stress.

Generally, health concerns can be segmented into chronic conditions and manifestations resulting from fluctuating vibrational flows. Persistent illnesses have a fixed vibrational imprint, and their healing necessitates a transformative journey: moving away from factors that led to its onset and steering one's focus toward overall wellness. Conversely, transient ailments, born from vibrational shifts, serve an evolutionary purpose. Whether it's reinforcing the body's resilience against graver conditions or merely acting as an event that sparks growth, the adage "What doesn't kill you makes you stronger" often rings true.

While temporary ailments signal the natural lows in vibrational flow, chronic or severe illnesses indicate misalignment. Our counsel is simple: maintain an ascending default vibrational state, primarily through meditative practices, and witness your health rejuvenate.

Tackling chronic ailments with a heightened default vibration is more productive than attempting specific treatments. Given the fluctuations in vibrational states, focusing on general well-being rather than zeroing in on an ailment, especially one perceived as significant, is often more beneficial.

Toxins

Your bodies, often referred to as "physical vehicles," are intricately designed to act as filtration systems, adeptly navigating and processing the myriad elements within your environment. The terms "toxins" and "toxic" have broadened in contemporary society, encompassing everything from chemicals, foods, and pollutants to interpersonal dynamics and relationships.

Engaging in the practice of Tya and maintaining a high default vibrational state enhances your body's natural ability to mitigate these so-called toxins. This resilience isn't merely physical; it's deeply interwoven with your mental and emotional realms. As you consciously release judgments, both toward others and yourself, you fortify your body's overall functionality and well-being, making it more robust and efficient in the face of external challenges. Therefore, your physical vehicles are optimized as a result.

Sexual Identity

You are all multifaceted, eternal entities journeying through existence as strands of soul consciousness.

While you've manifested in countless forms, your current perspective of humanity is just one of many experiences. As you vibrationally align with these human experiences, the entirety of your essence intertwines with your current being. However, your ego, or the conscious human mind, often obscures much of this profound knowledge, ensuring you have a distinct human experience. This concept, reiterated often, underscores the inherent fluidity of your sexuality.

Gender, in its basic form, arises from the polarity within universal creation processes. Some biological traits oppose, while others harmonize, ensuring vibrational balance. The outcome of this balance is reproduction and community endeavors that nurture offspring until they can independently navigate their unique life paths.

Sexual identity and prescribed gender roles are largely human fabrications. In our exploration of romantic relationships, we've delved into how society has structured gender roles and sexual identities to bolster population growth. When devoid of fear, sexual desires can epitomize the beauty of physical expression. However, humanity's predominant inclination to vilify certain sexual behaviors can inadvertently lead to more deviations than the organic desires themselves.

Indeed, even phenomena like pedophilia can trace their roots to the profound shame and demonization of innate sexual yearnings. It's vital to understand that no individual would actively pursue a harmful sexual engagement if they weren't already entangled in the low vibrations of societal judgment. Clarifying our stance, no one would desire a sexual relationship with an unaware or non-consenting party when operating from a high vibrational standpoint. Any forceful or manipulative act, whether sexual or otherwise, is a manifestation of disconnection from higher vibrations. Conversely, consensual physical pleasure shared between beings vibrating in harmony stands as one of the most splendid experiences in physical existence.

Encountering Your Non-preferences

In a heightened vibrational state, it becomes evident that such issues are the byproducts of lower vibrations. When you consistently resonate at higher frequencies, these challenges cease to affect your life—unless you inadvertently drop your vibrational level. As you embark on the Tya Practice, you might initially retain some "vibrational dust" or residual fears in your energy field. When natural polarity dips your vibration, these remnants can become active. Fortunately, with sustained practice, you'll eventually clear this vibrational residue.

As previously discussed, when you elevate your perspective, the impulse to "rescue" others—potentially depriving them of vital growth experiences—diminishes. Yet, striving to eradicate such challenges isn't misguided. Addressing the problems of a contrasting world and subsequently crafting solutions contributes to expansive growth. Our guidance emphasizes not viewing these issues as insurmountable problems but rather concentrating on the conditions that could either remedy or preempt them.

Here are some examples:

For Injustice: Focus on sharing your high vibration of security and guiding others to feel their own power via your example.

For Cruelty: Focus on all beings living in high vibration and being joyful.

For Murder: Focus on all beings living in safety and freedom.

For Poverty: Focus upon all beings knowing that their abundance is ensured by the universe via their beliefs.

For War: Focus upon peace and freedom of all beings.

For Greed: Focus upon abundance for all and the feeling of wellbeing washing over all in their alignment with their desires.

For Lust: Focus on sexual freedom and freedom of expression for all beings.

For Gluttony: Focus upon all beings living in a state of satisfaction and joy with life.

For Addiction: Focus upon all beings enjoying their natural Source connection.

For Hoarding: Focus on all beings feeling abundant and knowing the universe always provides a flow of all needs and desires.

For Gender discrimination: Focus upon all beings achieving their desires and abundance flowing with ease.

For Racism and genocide: Focus upon all beings as abundant and joyful and free.

Your positive focus holds far greater power than focusing upon the problem. Focusing upon the problem only fuels more of it. Empowering solutions holds significant manifestational energy, and your focus makes a massive contribution. The universe is 90 percent vibration and 10 percent physical action. Notice how often the chronic problems of your world remain unsolved because of the belief that only physical action holds value, and every misguided belief that focusing upon the problem and being outraged, if not downright hysterical, somehow solves problems. They are, at best, step-one reactions that only solve things if the vibration is raised and the focus is placed upon allowing the solution to flow.

You likely often observe swift and angry reactions to the problems of your world only to see them continue—why is this? It is because anger and acts taken in anger such as boycotts or "canceling," to use current popular terminology, are step-one reactions from an egocentric place of judgment.

Vibrational flow will naturally cause both individuals and collect vibrations to rise after the anger abates.

As you learned early in this book, vibrational flow works in both positive and negative directions. As the beings, or collective of beings, desire to feel better, the condition that caused the step-one anger reaction is replaced with another topic altogether as the vibrations rise. Simply put, the being wished to avoid the pain of dealing with the low vibration "event" once their vibration naturally goes up. This is why non-impacted supporters of "victims" often only show temporary support for an issue and then forget about it, thus not solving any issue on a large scale. Of course, personal vibration trumps the collective, so being impacted by any unwanted circumstance is a matter of personal vibrational alignment with it.

Natural Destruction, Pollution, & Climate Change

Just as you have a unique vibrational flow, so does Planet Earth. Consequently, the planet continually resonates at different frequencies, attracting both desired and undesired events. This continuous shift in vibration explains the ever-changing climate and associated weather patterns. Much like you, Earth is a living, growing entity, experiencing contrast. This accounts for natural disasters. Humanity's intertwined connection with Earth means your collective fears and focus influence the planet, just as its vibrations influence you.

How you treat Earth is mirrored back to you. While Earth's climate is in constant flux, the extent of human impact, often used to manipulate behaviors, tends to be overstated. If the symbiotic relationship between humans and Earth falters, the planet won't be destroyed. Instead, it may become uninhabitable for humans in their current form. Some repercussions of human actions are already evident in our bodies. Over time, human bodies will adapt, evolving over generations. Given the current state of technology on Earth, there's no reverting. Past beings, like dinosaurs, faced extinction due to their actions. However, their essence persisted, evolving as their physical forms became obsolete. You term this as evolution—essentially, a hardware upgrade as consciousness or the vibrational operating system becomes more advanced.

We advise you to recognize your preferences in this context and act if inspired to make positive changes. However, understand that everything is an ongoing process. Fretting over potential extinction is pointless since beings will continually evolve into advanced forms as part of their eternal journey.

Fitness

In the Tya practice, there's no definitive standard for physical fitness. Fitness trends come and go. While regular physical activity can enhance health, it's essential to realize that fitness levels and body aesthetics differ from person to person. The societal judgment surrounding body types is predominantly ego-driven. Our only recommendation is to strive for well-being and elevate your vibration if joy and abundance resonate with your desires. The choice, however, is yours.

In the pursuit of fitness, we've noted that harm can arise both from extreme physical exertion and inactivity. A toned body can be as susceptible to health issues as a fuller one can be robust and healthy. It's crucial to follow what feels right for you without succumbing to societal pressures or fear of judgment.

Cherishing your body, irrespective of its state, and releasing judgment and fear associated with it, can be deeply fulfilling. We encourage you to care for your body in a way that resonates with your well-being. Being overly critical of oneself due to not meeting societal beauty standards is counterproductive. By elevating your default vibrational state, your external appearance will naturally radiate your inner contentment and tranquility.

Dealing With Death And The Human Constructs Of Religion, Science, And Spirituality

It's curious to observe the immense fear associated with death among humans, even though death is an inevitable part of existence. Every individual, regardless of race, gender, nationality, or class, experiences birth, obstacles, and ultimately, death. So why is there such profound fear around these universal experiences? The answer lies in historical societal constructs. Once humans mastered communication, they quickly learned to manipulate fear as a tool for control.

In ancient times, obstacles were tackled with enthusiasm, and death was revered as the culmination of life. However, leaders soon realized the immense leverage they could wield by instilling fear in the masses. This gave birth to narratives like "Fear obstacles, and we'll provide the solution" or "Fear death for there awaits judgment". By projecting a punitive deity, religions flourished, offering rules and esteemed leaders as solutions to these contrived problems.

This book, and the Tya Practice within, seeks to address the problem humanity itself has constructed. Most individuals prefer the simplicity of following set guidelines, for confronting fear and acknowledging one's own power demands effort. Unlike conventional tools, the Tya Practice prompts introspection, guiding individuals to harness their inner strength and liberate themselves from the shackles of fear.

We don't condemn the fear-driven paradigms of monarchies, politics, or religions. They served their purpose in their respective eras. Science then emerged, prompting many to challenge traditional beliefs and prompting the birth of new-age spirituality. Each approach has its strengths and limitations, an inherent feature of every topic.

Monarchies and religions once acted as catalysts for human advancement but also stifled individual freedom. Politics presented the illusion of democracy, enabling humans to experience dynamic shifts in power. Science, though continually evolving, brings both solutions and new challenges. Current scientific facts might be disproved or refined tomorrow.

We communicate through David, not because he possesses any divine perfection—he has flaws and faces challenges, as all humans do. Our primary goal is to provide individuals ready for change with tools to perceive life and the Earth environment differently. This avant-garde approach is straightforward, though its nuances will be unveiled as it becomes more widespread. Currently, you're receiving the purest, unadulterated version of this teaching. Naturally, commerce will find its way into this practice, following the intrinsic order of your planet. An energy exchange is an integral aspect of existence. But if the Tya Practice ever resorts to using fear as a motivator, that will be a sign of emerging contrasts within the topic.

The introduction of this practice is timely. Humanity has evolved beyond the need to be fear-driven. With unprecedented communication capabilities, the age-old dynamics of external control and fear-based governance, which once catalyzed expansion, are becoming obsolete. A realization of innate creative abilities is dawning. This resurgence of ancient wisdom resonates deeply because, at your core, you're experiencing an awakening.

Conclusion

David

I am sitting in my living room on yet another glorious day in Palm Springs, writing this conclusion five years after we began writing this book. Why did this book take so long to write? Because Tya is not an ancient practice; it is new—it is of our current time. It is a creation from the Stream's guidance, a co-creation with Source, and all those who have gone through Tya Bootcamp and Tya Mastery helped create it and continue to do so. It is an upgraded operating system for humanity, the practical application of the Stream's teachings, and you are now part of it!

It is easy to look at the state of affairs on planet Earth and surmise that humanity is in peril. I witnessed protests, looting, and even the destruction of cities in the summer of 2020, following the death of George Floyd at the hands of police. In January of 2021, as the Covid-19 pandemic raged on, the capital of the United States was invaded, something I never thought I'd see. Next, 2022 kicked off with Russia's invasion of Ukraine, the US Supreme Court nullified Roe v. Wade, and seems to be on a mission to bring drastic change to America's political landscape. There are talks among politicians about rolling back rights and social protections. The religious right believes they are fighting a war for their way of life, and the woke folks on the left believe the right is pure evil. Cancel culture is now in overdrive with virtual torch-wielding zealots eager to destroy lives in retribution for any perceived transgression. Division is even widening in the climate-change debate. As I write this, artificial intelligence (AI) is becoming an increasingly looming threat to millions of jobs. The world seems to be teetering on collapse into outright chaos.

It is clear that as we collectively question our institutions of control—the matrix—it is reasserting itself, creating more fear, more division, more seduction into its vibration of fear and judgment. As many a spiritual seeker focuses on their own awakening journey, many find themselves drawn right back into conspiracy theories or in the comparison of their belief system as superior to others who are "less awakened."

None of this is necessarily joyous to observe, but the Tya Practice offers such clarity that I hold appreciation for all of it. This is true inner peace, with all that this Earthly experience is and all that life offers. I now fully understand vibrational flow and the perfection of imperfection. I view our world from the perspective of Source—a perspective of non-judgment. Radical appreciation, even.

Radical because it is in such opposition to how we are taught to operate. But that's our old operating system.

When you disallow fear and judgment, detuning your life's transgressors and releasing the need to be seen and heard—the need to argue or seek external validation, you'll discover that your vibration begins to rise—systematically—higher and higher. You'll come to understand that well-being is your natural state of being. That abundance, any and everything you desire to experience in this lifetime can and will be yours. You'll see clearly how all these fear-inducing distractions are just tools of the matrix to lower your vibration and rob you of your natural state of joy.

I've been practicing this my entire life and more formally in the last decade. I now find great joy and love in every aspect of life. I've come to love and appreciate all of humanity. I no longer need anything or anyone to change to experience joy. Do you know what that feels like? Appreciation of all that is? Loving yourself and others unconditionally? Not needing to be right or even understood? Truly understanding and trusting the universal process of creation on such a deep level that nothing lowers your vibration?

Earth and humanity have always had challenges, and will continue to until at last our focus on the challenges becomes so great that we allow the completion of the physical environment altogether. Or, perhaps, we all get on the same page of meeting our obstacles in exuberant joy, understanding that there is nothing happening here on earth that can possibly end that which we are. That every single thing that frightens us or causes anxiety is truly a human construct. That any obstacle we place in our paths can be solved, and that we are actually becoming more sophisticated beings, eternally, in the having of those experiences. Then, and only then, will our world cease to exist, because it would have served its ultimate purpose of providing an opportunity for great expansion in an environment that our souls love to visit, but never wish to reside in indefinitely.

Here you are at the end of all this new information, with lots of new ideas that undoubtedly sparked your imagination and perhaps challenged quite a few well-seated beliefs. You are likely realizing that the end result of this practice is to develop a Source-like perspective of your world. It sounds so simple: just authentically appreciate every single aspect of your Earthly, human experience and Joy, Clarity, and Abundance will flow to you generously. That's it, that's all this is about—Trusting Your Abundance!

With trust being the key to all that is!

All four pillars of Tya and all the ancillary tools are really about unlearning what the matrix of human-created thought has taught you. This allows you to return to your original operating system, where you trust the universe to provide and you meet every twist and turn in your human journey in joy and eagerness for the expansion offered in the new creation that will inevitably arise from the challenge.

The Tya Practice is keenly focused on detuning the matrix and its limiting beliefs and allowing your natural Source being to step forward as the primary driver of your life.

I want this for you—if you want it. It is my promise to you that all of the above is attainable with this practice—learning to view every aspect of life from the perspective of Source, void of fear and judgment. Appreciating all that is—every obstacle, every transgressor event in our lives and in our world. Unlimited joy, clarity, and abundance—and the truly awesome feeling of embracing all that this experience has to offer!"

Qatarina

As David mentioned, here we are, five years after we embarked on this book-writing journey, and it's remarkable to reflect on how much has evolved during this time. The extended duration of this process allowed for a wealth of experiences and insights that have enriched the content in profound ways.

As the saying goes, "time is the best teacher," and I can attest to the truth of this statement. I've been able to contribute so much more to this work because of the contrast, polarity, flow, and the roller-coaster ride on my spiral that I've experienced since our journey began.

These real-life experiences have given depth and authenticity to the stories and lessons I share. For example, I wouldn't have been able to include the story about my car being stolen, or delved as deeply into the fourth pillar: Intention. That's because intention has taken on a more profound significance in my life as I've progressed in my Tya Practice.

Despite all the changes and growth, one constant remains: my contentment with my perfectly imperfect life. The Stream continually reminds us to trust our abundance in the same way we trust gravity—it's that fundamental. However, simplicity doesn't equate to easiness. The tools provided in this book hold the key to unlocking a thriving, abundant life filled with gratitude, love, and passion. I'm not exaggerating when I say that everything you need is right here. The only question is what you choose to do with it.

This might sound like a grand claim, but I speak from experience when I say that the information within these pages is truly life-changing and transformative. Yet, the power lies in your choices and actions. As someone who has delved into self-help books and personal-growth teachings extensively, it's a significant statement for me to say that I've moved beyond many of them. The Tya Practice fulfills me in a way that nothing else ever has. I'm not suggesting that you should never read another self-help book; the Stream encourages us to find our own path as long as we remain UTS about it. There are indeed other resources that have complemented my journey;

however, when it comes down to it, the Stream holds the answers I seek. I've realized that I don't need to rely on tarot-card readings, crystal-ball meditations, or ancient texts by ascended masters...anymore. But I'll admit, I still indulge in these activities occasionally simply for enjoyment. The Stream teaches us that there's nothing wrong with these practices; it's a matter of how much power we assign to them.

In my life today, I choose to invest a significant amount of power in the Stream and their teachings, and as a result, I've witnessed remarkable growth and transformation when I apply the tools they've provided.

I wholeheartedly encourage you to read this book again, and maybe even again after that. Each time you revisit it, you'll glean new insights and revelations; I can guarantee that.

The Tya Practice is an ongoing journey, an ongoing *practice*. There are no true masters—not myself, or even David. We've adopted the title of Tya Masters because this practice has taken a form of mastery over our lives. However, we remain perpetual students.

So, from one student of creation—and of Tya—to another, I extend my wishes for peacefulness and abundance in all aspects of your unique journey. Embrace the ongoing adventure, and trust that your spiral will continue to ascend.

The Stream

We will begin our conclusion with a recap of what you have learned in your journey through these teachings. Much information has been imparted, but the practice is actually quite simple. We've offered numerous tools for you to learn to incorporate the four pillars into your life as your new way of being and to begin seeing the effects quickly as a result.

- You learned the four pillars of Tya and the power they hold to transform your operating system.

- You learned that vibrational flow is the universal process of creation.

- You learned why unwanted things (transgressors) are essential to the creation/expansion process and that they should be appreciated rather than feared. This is also known as *the perfection of imperfection.*

- You learned how the Tya Practice activates an "awakening" process and how your awakening benefits all of humanity.

- You reviewed case studies, and learned how real people have transformed their lives with this practice and continue to expand in their awakening journeys.

- You learned Tya Tools:

1. Vibrational Timestamping

2. The Stopgap

3. Allowing "Isness"

4. Zooming Out

5. Awakening the Egosoul

- You've learned how to apply this practice to specifically to:

  - Optimal health

  - Relationships

  - The creation of wealth

  - You've learned the Tya mindset in regard to these topics as examples:

  - Ego balancing and the need to be right

  - Judging vs. discerning

  - Reacting to fear-mongering

  - Politics

  - Making life decisions

  - Family relationships

  - Raising children

- Body image

- Diet

- Your work

- Your health

- Sexuality

- Non-preferences

- Natural disasters & climate change

- Fitness

- Death and loss

The value in the Tya "operating system."

We refer to the Tya Practice as an operating system. We have stated that your physical vehicles are like computers, or even robots, and computers and robots are simply hardware—vessels designed to carry out programmed functionality. Your human vehicle is exactly the same. In fact, you may take note of the fact that all your fiction, your computers, your video games, etc., are all reflections of the very technology that creates you and your perceived reality, and they all work on an operating system.

You do as well. Your operating system is your belief system.

Regardless of who you are, you have a *belief system*, and it impacts every aspect of your human experience. You create your belief system from the moment you begin forming into the clump of cells that will become your human being, often as a reaction to your mother and other beings in your presence. Your early selves are like thirsty sponges, soaking up your environment, discerning preferences, and building beliefs.

As humanity has progressed, you've created 3D modes of communication that have allowed mass consciousness to communicate in a more direct way. In linear time, the matrix peaked in the 1950s, a time when, throughout the world, most of humanity was obediently following the template provided. Behave like your assigned gender, become indoctrinated in a standardized belief system at church and in school, obey the law, etc. After the peak, more of humanity began questioning. Certainly not all at the same rate, nations that were more allowing of freedom of thought and religion realized more disruption to the matrix. But the matrix is a powerful vibration, and it's designed for survival; it is a collective of ego, after all, and its survival is bolstered by the fact that anything that induces fear and judgment will function to draw a human being back into it. So as humanity wises up to the constructs of the matrix, humans likely find themselves out in a 'wilderness,' with no pre-established belief system, and the ego inevitably takes over.

Perhaps the hubris around 'knowing better' spurs judgment of those who do not, and the belief in one's own righteousness draws them into the belittling or demonization of those who are less informed. That's the matrix.

The wilderness is confusing. As old beliefs fall away, a human will inevitably default to another system. Materialism, politics, greed, even conspiracy theories and activism can be functions of the matrix. We say 'can be' because these things are not part of the matrix until your ego activates the fear-judgment vibration as a result of your participation in them.

So, how do you stay out of the matrix?

By creating a new version of it rooted in universal law, i.e., Source consciousness, that holds no judgment or fear. This is where the *trust* part of Tya becomes so very important. As you deconstruct the matrix in your life and return your focus to trust, the old habits you formed in the matrix will likely come calling. This is why the popular LOA teachings often fail to produce the desired results. A being begins shifting their beliefs to align with their desires, only to have an unexpected expense or rift in a health regime or relationship appear and send them into judgment of their vibration and thus creating a new, less-aligned or even opposing vibration and the new matching result manifests. Until you learn to live in harmony with vibrational flow, appreciating the mix of desires and challenges that it creates, you will struggle with intentional manifestation, and life in general for that matter.

We have and do refer to Tya as a new operating system for humans, but it is truly your original operating system. Humanity has simply taken a long break from it to have an experience of engineered constraint and expansion that lasted for centuries. The reason that Tya is being presented now is because humanity has found itself at a level of sophistication that delivers enough clarity to either cause confusion, which results in a return deeper in the matrix, or a renewed desire for a true exit from the matrix while still having the physical experience. The confusion that results in attempts to exit stems from your matrix-based training that you must be told what to think, believe, and even what to do, day after day. When you begin to detune the direction of the matrix, you will likely find yourself wondering what to think, believe, and do.

The Tya Practice doesn't provide a specific direction like other belief systems do. Instead, it encourages you to truly own your experience rather than renting it. Living without a predefined template can be intimidating, especially if you've been controlled your entire life. Through continued practice, you'll come to realize that many of your desires, including those you have now, are products of the matrix.

As a strand of eternal consciousness, you made a deliberate choice to come to the Earth environment and embark on a physical, vibrational journey. You understood that this journey would involve pursuing preferences while overcoming obstacles. From that perspective, you were, and still are, prepared for anything the Earth environment has to offer. However, at your core, your ultimate preference is freedom and joy. That's how you exist in your eternal state, and in the physical realm, you yearn to experience these qualities in a tangible way, complete with all the beauty, magic, pleasure, and other aspects you cherish about the Earth environment.

The matrix often generates its own version of these desires, frequently manifesting as consumerism—a belief that money and material possessions can provide the freedom and joy you naturally seek. When this matrix-driven belief in materialism falls short, other beliefs often take its place. This is when individuals may allocate their power to entities like politics or religion, believing they will find protection within a prevailing system or comfort in the validation from others who share their chosen system, whatever it may be. You can easily transition in and out of various systems throughout your lifetime or remain steadfast in the one you were born into; it's all part of your chosen path.

At the end of the matrix's rainbow, you'll find wilderness. The allure of the matrix often leads to disappointment in terms of the perfection it promises, or even the genuine joy it offers. While pleasure may be found, and the ego may be temporarily satisfied, these are no substitute for authentic joy and clarity. As humans, you may repeatedly experience disappointment after manifesting the matrix's version of freedom and joy, much like the eternal state you experience when complete trust is assumed, and the abundance of the universe is assured.

However, it is possible to experience this on Earth once your operating system is reprogrammed to vibrate in harmony with it. Achieving this involves following the guidance we've outlined in these pages, and the good news is, it's all inner work. No external entity is deciding whether or not to bestow well-being upon you. The work is entirely yours to undertake if you choose to do so.

We conclude by acknowledging that due to the polarized nature of your environment, this practice and our teachings may be challenging for some. Many will discover new levels of joy, clarity, and abundance they've never experienced before through what we offer here. The tools to address every single problem humanity faces are within these pages. However, it's essential to recognize that these tools won't solve all Earthly problems because humanity, being egocentric beings in a polarized environment, won't allow that. Each of you is on a unique journey.

Throughout your lifetime, you've experienced vibrational flow, and with the tools we've provided, you've realized your natural access to our higher perspective. You are as much a part of Source as we are. The only difference is that you are here on this magical human journey, having this temporary experience of vibrational flow, including its imperfections. As you practice Tya and immerse yourself in our teachings, you release fear and judgment from your human life experience, enabling you to see your world from your own higher perspective.

Practicing Tya is akin to climbing a mountain. If you ascend too quickly, you may find the air thin and need to return to a lower altitude to catch your breath. You'll need to adapt to your new, higher-vibration reality. This reality isn't always about joy for the sake of joy but also about clarity. To gauge if you're truly joyful and clear, consider the most disturbing thing you've encountered on your planet. Does it disconnect you from joy and cause your vibration to plummet? If so, you're still in judgment, and that's not clarity.

You might experience fatigue or resistance as you embrace these teachings. Your inner saboteurs may resist the changes you're making. Remember that these elements of your ego are your creation, and they can persistently cling to their existence. This is why many find it challenging to establish new habits. Keep in mind that you're operating in vibrational flow, and your vibe may fluctuate, leading to doubt, fear, and questions. This is part of the process. Use the tools you've learned here to guide your vibe back up. The winning formula is to persist; you only fail when you give up.

If you find these teachings intriguing, we recommend using this book as a study guide. It contains a wealth of information that may not be fully accessible to everyone immediately. Remember that Tya is a practice, one that you can refine and apply throughout the rest of your human experience, adjusting and implementing it up and down the metaphorical mountain for the remainder of your days.

Applying these teachings is your choice, but our promise to you is that we have arrived at this time—an incredibly transformative era on Planet Earth—to share our teachings through David. Those who resonate with them can lead humanity's expansion into a new, human-crafted dimension, one characterized by more joy, clarity, and abundance for all who choose this path. There are no rules, no judgment, no worship, and no superiority—just an internal practice that offers a profound understanding of your purpose on this journey and how to make it the most expansive, joyous, and abundant experience imaginable if you trust.

We hold nothing but appreciation for you, as you are extensions of us—individual expressions of Source energy experiencing a polarized physical environment with all its imperfections. We sense your desire to allow our light to shine brighter as you collectively create this faster-moving flow. We see you not through eyes, but vibrationally. We understand you, your true desires, your dreams, and the things you've long let go of. We know your inner-being's desire to thrive and find joy in your present moment. We know these things because we are you. These words and tools resonate because you are ready. You are ready to transform, to ascend. You are ready to view your world and your life from our higher perspective of non-judgment. You are ready for profound peace, joy, and clarity. You are ready for your version of abundance to evolve to match your new higher perspective.

We are here for you always, just one loving thought away. With much love, that is what we have—for now!

David

Now you possess the tools to remold yourself, not as some ideal dream of perfection, but as an amalgam of the past experiences that you now understand from a higher perspective, and the enlightened, awakened being that parlays all that into a finely honed, focused creator of joy and abundance.

Are you up for making the Tya Practice your new way of life?

You may feel exhilaration with this new set of tools—like you've now been given the keys to the universe! You may also be a bit overwhelmed with all the information you've absorbed in this book. So how do you start? How do you begin applying what you've learned and making it your new way of life?

I suggest three steps to really get the full benefits of this book:

1. Join our mailing list. We send a weekly newsletter called *The Tyist.* This keeps you abreast of all the news and events in the Tya world. Sign up at https://bit.ly/TSODNewsletter

2. Visit our digital academy at https://thestreamofdavid.mykajabi.com/ Here you will find all our guided meditations and digital learning tools that will help you in your Tya journey, including our

Tya Bootcamp twelve-week transformation program where you will immerse yourself in the practice with coaching, accountability, and community to guide you in making Tya your new way of life.

3. Explore our social links and other offerings and integrate Tya into your life with weekly updates, merchandise, retreats and seminars, and more. https://linktr.ee/thestreamofdavid

—

Ready to dive right into Tya Academy? This is the program all our case studies graduated from and is considered the "holy grail" of Tya learning! Set up a meeting with our discovery team!

About The Authors

DAVID STRICKEL embarked on an exploration of his "inner wisdom" from a young age, often challenging conventional beliefs, including those of his family's Christian faith. Finding solace in his internal guidance, David leaned into self-education tailored to his distinctive learning needs.

Driven by a clear intention to share the knowledge that had transformed him, David left behind a lucrative corporate career to disseminate his inner wisdom to the world. He aptly named this wellspring of wisdom "The Stream" because he recognized it as a conduit of pure Source energy flowing through him, offering profound insights and revelations. He understood that his mission was to share this wisdom with humanity, dedicating the remainder of his human journey to this purpose.

In 2017, he unveiled "The Stream of David Podcast," and in early 2018, he published *The Stream: Eternal Wisdom for a Better Life.* This book embodies a mindset refined over years, empowering individuals to tackle life's hurdles while broadening their spiritual horizon.

Later in 2018, he began offering practical application of the Stream's teachings in an online course that ultimately birthed the Tya Practice, standing for "Trust Your Abundance." This practice, emphasizing its foundational four pillars, lights the way to a life enriched with wisdom and abundance. David's path—from seeking inner clarity to imparting enlightenment—underscores the profound impact of introspection, determination, and the drive to share invaluable insights.

Learn more at www.theStreamofDavid.com

············

QATARINA WANDERS is a former circus performer turned author and advocate for authentic living. Qatarina's journey led her to the Tya Practice in 2017, a transformative mindset that she seamlessly integrates into her work and brand, "Living an Unedited Life." Through this approach, she encourages others to

face their shadows and embrace life without the constraints of fear or judgment.

Apart from being a self-made businesswoman, Qatarina's passions are diverse: from her love for chilling horror stories and whimsical unicorns to her collection of creepy dolls. Physically and mentally active, she juxtaposes crafting boundary-pushing words with pursuits like weightlifting, yoga, and skydiving. Among her most treasured experiences is cliff-climbing alongside her daughter, Ora—an adventure that deepens their bond each time.

Through her writing and diverse life experiences, Qatarina invites you to join her on a journey beyond the ordinary, where the mysteries of existence are unveiled one page at a time. Her unique perspective and unapologetic authenticity shine through in her work, reminding us all that life's strangeness is what makes it beautiful.

Experience her world and explore the depths of your own mind as you dive into her writings, knowing that with every page turned, you're embarking on a path of self-discovery, empowerment, and transformation.

Explore more at www.QatarinaWanders.com

GLOSSARY

888 Breathing Technique: A calming technique where the participant inhales slowly through the nose for a quick count of eight, holds their breath for another count of eight, then exhales through the mouth for yet another count of eight.

Abundance: The things you desire. "Being joyous and receiving your desires all comes down to trusting the universe to always deliver everything you want and need. You experience abundance when you have released fear and now trust the universe to deliver everything and anything you want and need."

Allowing: Holding the emotion or vibration (interchangeable) of 'is' as opposed to wanting. "Being in a state of knowing is a state of allowing. Knowing that something already exists is a state of allowing."

Antonym: Hammering

Ascension: Rising to a higher default vibration. Raising to a more positive, joyous state of being on a consistent basis.

Awakening: Expanding to a state of higher consciousness as a physically manifested being; thinking beyond mainstream, often fear-based, constraining beliefs.

Bubble of Reality: Your life, your journey; the reality that you create through your thoughts and thus your vibration. "You are solely responsible for creating your bubble of reality, once you realize this, you must then master your reaction to the conditions you have manifested."

Clarity: Comprehending physical existence from a higher perspective, without judgment or fear. "Seeing all sides and appreciating that you're all on your own independent journeys, with every path contributing to your collective expansion. When you're loving and appreciating every aspect of you and the world around—without the need for change—then you've got it! The Clarity of Source!"

Collective Consciousness: All consciousness. Can also refer to a group such as humanity as a whole—the combination of each individual consciousness.

Contrast: The mix of positive (wanted) and negative (unwanted). Physical life is meant to be challenging, it's meant to cause pain sometimes and pleasure other times. Your intention in coming to this place was to find your path to freedom and joy through overcoming your obstacles and interacting with things you discern as your preference.

Creative Power: The ability of a being to create its reality. "You are a powerful creator of your own reality and a co-creator of all creation—contributing to the expansion of the universe. You are creators first, having whatever you have manifested will always be secondary."

Default Vibration: A being's consistent vibration. "Your vibration is always in flux, what you are receiving in your life is evidence of your default vibration."

Detune: The process of viewing any topic without fear or judgment, thus removing any negative reaction to the thought.

Discern Your Preference: The act of deciding what you like and what you do not; choosing for you without judging others' preferences. "You discern your preferences by recognizing that which you enjoy, and that which you do not. All that you discern as not your preference serves the great purpose of causing you to go deeper, think harder, and question what is; but all that you discern as your preference is what you find joy and abundance in. Both inspire new creation."

Down the Spiral (DTS): "If you are not in a state of joy, you are "Down the Spiral." In your DTS state, you are not joyful, and you are attracting things you do not want. While DTS, you do not have a solid Source connection established, your intuition isn't available, and you are not getting the full value from your personal version of the Stream."

Ebb and Flow of Universal Expansion: The energetic flow of positive and negative; the tension that keeps the physical in balance. "The ebb and flow of universal expansion is experienced in the physical and should not be seen as something unwanted. Obstacles that arrive during the ebb and flow pave the way for new growth, and each being is expansive at its/their core."

Synonym: Polarity

Emotional Freedom Technique (EFT): An alternative treatment for physical pain and emotional distress. It is a form of counseling intervention that draws on various theories of alternative medicine including acupuncture, Neuro-Linguistic Programming, energy medicine, and Thought Field Therapy. Some Tya practitioners use EFT as a tool, but it is not a prescribed part of Tya.

Energetic Beings: The core or 'Source' of all beings. "Everything is made of energy, thus as humanity you are all energetic beings. We typically use this term to refer to strands of consciousness, or beings, in a non-physical state."

Freedom & Joy: The core desire of all beings; characteristics of abundance, found through discerning your preferences without fear and overcoming your obstacles.

Hammering: Not trusting the universal process of creation and attempting to make things happen from a physical perspective without allowing the energetic realm (the universe) to pave the way. "Hammering occurs when you are not allowing—when you are being overly adamant with your manifestations. Allow life to unfold magically rather than trying to hammer it into place."

Antonym: Allowing

Higher Perspective (noun): Holding the non-judgmental, fearless perspective of Source. "You are all part of our Stream (Source), and our energy flows through all creation, therefore you have access to our high perspective. From the higher perspective, there is no right or wrong, no judgment, and no expectation of perfection."

High Vibration: Oneness with Source; your higher self. "A state of high vibration comes with practicing self-love. We have nothing but love for you, so when you are loving you, you are at one with our energy." "When you are in a high-vibration space, you are more connected to Source and able to view the world from Source's perspective. You no longer need to be right. You no longer need to control. You trust. You allow. In this high-vibe state, you no longer need anything to change for you to be joyous."

Isness: A present-tense state of being from a vibrational perspective. Example: *She became wealthy because she aligned with the insess of being wealthy.*

Law of Attraction (LOA): The universal law that states that every vibration is met with an equal vibration and thus returned to the originator; the process of universal creation. "Consistent thoughts create a vibration and consistent vibrations create things. All creation begins as thought."

Low Vibration: Separation from Source. "When you are in low vibration, you cut yourself off from our energy. In this state, you are a different person than who you are when you are up your spiral in high vibration. Your low-vibe thoughts and actions will be negatively flavored and likely have a negative outcome. Learn to move up your spiral into positive before responding or planning or even daydreaming—the results will be dramatically more positive."

New Creation: The result of vibration. "Every single thought, emotion, interaction, relationship, possession, or state of being is your creation—positive and negative. You are constantly creating your reality, and every creation is your new creation, and it all serves your expansion. We often use this term to describe the purpose of negative in your physical environment, how it is intended to inspire new, positive creation." "Every solution is your positive, new creation."

Note: A specific vibrational frequency. Ex: A note of wealth.

Neutrality: Little to no thought; the state between UTS and DTS. "You reach neutrality via meditation, quieting your mind, and connecting with your Stream—with Source. It is the only state below a UTS state in which you can connect with Source, a state where Source can help aid you up your spiral." "In a state of neutrality, you are no longer resisting our energy with your negative emotion."

Obstacles: Unwanted creation from physical perspective. "Obstacles appear in your life to clear the path for your next glorious creation. This is the process of universal expansion. You grow from adversity. You grow from overcoming the challenges that you have manifested. These difficult things in your life are a time of learning and leveling up."

Synonyms: Negative Contrast, Transgressors, Storms

Ping: Source making its presence known with an energetic pulse or zap of energy.

Polarity: The universal force that balances positive and negative; the force that drives energy up and down a vibrational spiral. "Polarity balances consciousness and keeps both physical and non-physical in an expansive growth pattern." "You may dream of lives of perfection, but with no obstacles, there is nothing left for you to desire. If all your desires instantly manifested, you would become so bored that you would long to return to your completed state and escape the encumbrance of having it all. Polarity is a gift from the universe, ensuring that you will always have a mix of things to appreciate and obstacles to overcome."

Pure Positive: The top of the vibrational spiral—the ultimate state of joy and clarity. "Pure positive comes from being at the top of your spiral. In this state, you are experiencing the highest possible vibration and are in pure positive creation mode."

Quantum Consciousness: A higher understanding of the universe, including the purpose of Planet Earth and humanity, your own eternal nature, and the non-judgmental, fearless nature of Source.

Reset: The process of a global correction. "This reset was crafted *by* humanity *for* humanity—your collective consciousness has set an intention toward change and has provided you with an opportunity for renewal.

Synonyms: Correction

Source: Original thought; pure-positive energy. "The Source of all creation that drives the energetic realm. However, Source is not in the sky; Source is everywhere. You came to this life as an extension of Source energy, and when you love yourself and stand in appreciation of your world, as it is, you are one with Source. Source is not a singular being."

Synonyms: God, Ascended Masters, Guardian Angels, Spirit Guides, The Stream, Higher Self.

Spiritual Bypassing: Using the act of "being spiritual" to only focus on positive things and not embrace the power of negative emotions or unwanted things.

Spring: A period of great change that will occur after humanity emerges from the other side of the reset. A time characterized by self-love, self-development, and renewal—a rare opportunity to reshape your future.

Static: Negative thoughts that dampen creative power. "Doubt, worry, overthinking, and 'needing' create interference in your vibration, we call this static. Static is the reason you are not receiving your desires as you have allowed needing to interfere with your otherwise positive vibration."

Stopgap: A statement that you create and repeat back to yourself at the onset of a trigger to detune that trigger. Ex: "Is this worth going down my spiral over?"

Storms: Obstacles created via negative thoughts or vibration. "Storms, transgressors, obstacles—whichever term you prefer, stand for "unwanted" contrast. Each storm *can* be the launchpad of your next creation, once you withstand the chaos of the storm. You manifest these storms, so don't hide from them—embrace them. They will strengthen you if you so allow."

Synonyms: Negative Contrast, Obstacles.

Stream (the): A collective consciousness that comprises the core of Source energy; original thought; the Source of all creation.

Streamscapes: Guided meditation app created by David Strickel with meditations delivered by the Stream.

The Matrix: The collective ego consciousness of all humanity.

The Stream of David: A stream of consciousness shared (channeled) by David Strickel.

See: The Stream

Transgressors: Any unwanted person, circumstance, or event—past or present.

Synonyms: Contrast, Obstacles, Storms

Trusting Your Abundance: Your steadfast belief in your ability to have or do or be anything you desire; the releasing of doubt and fear and raising of your default vibration to allow your desires to manifest. "Trust your abundance, believe your dreams, and they will be yours."

Tya: The learned art of Trusting Your Abundance; a spiritual mindset practice created by David Strickel with our (the Stream's) guidance.

Tya Academy: (Formerly known as Tya Bootcamp) An intensive twelve-week program where you receive personalized divine guidance directly from Source, via the Stream, and learn to use the Tya Mindset Practice. "Tya Academy seals in life-changing habits and provides individuals with a whole new perspective on life."

Tya Community: A subscription community for ongoing training and support for Tya Academy graduates.

Tya Mastery: A year-long mentorship program for Tya Academy graduates who are seeking to take their practice to the highest level and work directly with David Strickel, creator of the Tya Mindset Practice.

Universal Expansion: The continued growth of positive, creative energy as a result of new thought.

Universal Laws: The unwavering absolutes of the universe. "There are only two universal laws: all creation occurs via attraction and all attraction is governed by polarity. Everything else is an offspring of these."

Up the Spiral (UTS): Higher vibration. "There is great joy and clarity when you are Up the Spiral. In your UTS state, you are attracting the things you want, and they are flowing with ease; you are abundant. In this high-vibration state, you are most connected to our energy, to Source, and your intuition and abundance flow with ease."

Vibration: The emotional signal a being emits. "Your projected thoughts create your vibration—the radio signal that you broadcast out into the universe. Your vibration, or emotions, exist like a ring on your vibrational spiral and your vibe is always in flux; your mindset and polarity are constantly drawing your vibe up and down the spiral, between various levels of positive and negative." "Everything in your life is a result of your vibration, which is created by your consistent thoughts. Learning to manage those thoughts is the most valuable, life-changing tool you can acquire. You can tell how high or low your vibe is based on how much joy, clarity, and abundance you are experiencing."

Vibrational Flow: The fluctuation of energy that drives constant vibrational change.

Vibrational Neighbors: Key individuals or beings who share a similar vibrational energy to you. This vibration can be anywhere on the vibrational spiral, positive or negative.

Synonyms: Soulmates

Vibrational Paths: A being's unique journey through life. "Your vibrational path is where you discern what is and what is not your preference, and you set about attracting your dominant vibrational manifestations that serve your expansion. This can be via trust or via fear, and are most often some combination of the two."

Vibrational Timestamping: Packaging a state-of-being while you are UTS for future recollection to raise vibration. "We guide you to utilize these timestamps to return to a high-vibration emotion when you are down your spiral."

Victim Mindset: The attitude of not being in control of one's manifestations, usually focused upon unwanted things.

Zooming Out: (verb) The act of attaining Source's higher perspective. "You can achieve a higher vibration by zooming out—viewing things from a higher perspective that is always available to you from up your spiral."

STREAMING WORDS

SW

PUBLISHING

Made in the USA
Columbia, SC
25 November 2024

40c2a345-d7d1-4efa-9292-68ad522e1050R01